BERNARD SHAW AND THE COMIC SUBLIME

Also by David J. Gordon

D. H. LAWRENCE AS A LITERARY CRITIC
LITERARY ART AND THE UNCONSCIOUS

Bernard Shaw and the Comic Sublime

DAVID J. GORDON

*Professor of English at Hunter College and
the City University of New York Graduate Center*

St. Martin's Press   New York

First published in the United States of America in 1990

Printed in Great Britain

ISBN 0–312–04067–9

Library of Congress Cataloging-in-Publication Data
Gordon, David J.
    Bernard Shaw and the comic sublime / David J. Gordon.
        p.   cm.
    Includes bibliographical references.
    ISBN 0–312–04067–9
    1. Shaw, George Bernard, 1856–1950—Criticism and interpretation.
2. Comic, The, in literature.   3. Sublime, The, in literature.
I. Title.
PR5368.C56G67   1990
822'.912—dc20   89–24157
                                                                CIP

Contents

Acknowledgements

I wish to thank those colleagues and students at Hunter College and the CUNY Graduate School, as well as those members of the New York Shaw Society, with whom I discussed the subject of this book over the course of more years than I care to think about. For valuable criticism and practical encouragement, I am grateful in particular to Porter Abbott, Harold Bloom, John Hall, Jan Heissinger, Norman Holland, Richard Horwich, Stanley Kauffmann, Alfred Kazin, Naomi Lebowitz, Rhoda Nathan, Ruth Newton, Edgar Rosenberg, Joseph H. Smith and Thomas Steiner.

Hunter College provided timely assistance by way of a Fellowship Leave and a Scholar Incentive Award.

DAVID J. GORDON

List of Abbreviations

B   *The Bodley Head Bernard Shaw: Collected Plays with their Prefaces*, ed. Dan H. Laurence, 7 vols (London: Max Reinhardt, 1970–4).

C   *The Constable Standard Edition of the Works of Bernard Shaw*, 37 vols (London: Constable, 1930–50).

CL   *Bernard Shaw: Collected Letters*, vol. i: *1874–1897*, vol. ii: *1898–1910*, vol. iii: *1911–1925*, vol. iv: *1926–50*, ed. Dan H. Laurence (vols i and ii: New York: Dodd, 1965–72; vols iii and iv: New York: Viking, 1985–8).

CP   *The Complete Prefaces of Bernard Shaw* (London: Hamlyn, 1965).

DI   *Bernard Shaw: The Diaries 1885–1897*, 2 vols, edited and annotated by Stanley Weintraub (University Park, Pa.: Pennsylvania State University Press, 1986).

LC   *Bernard Shaw's Nondramatic Literary Criticism*, ed. Stanley Weintraub, Regents Critics Series (Lincoln: University of Nebraska Press, 1972).

MDD   *My Dear Dorothea: A Practical System of Moral Education for Females Embodied in a Letter to a Young Person of That Sex*, ed. Stephen Winsten (New York: Vanguard, 1956).

NDW   *Selected Non-Dramatic Writings of Bernard Shaw*, ed. Dan H. Laurence (Cambridge, Mass.: Riverside, 1965).

OTN   *Our Theatres in the Nineties* by Bernard Shaw, 3 vols (London: Constable, 1948).

P&P   *Platform and Pulpit*, ed. Dan H. Laurence (New York: Hill, 1961).

RS   *The Religious Speeches of Bernard Shaw*, ed. Warren Sylvester Smith, Foreword by Arthur H. Nethercot (University Park, Pa.: Pennsylvania State University Press, 1963).

SM   *Shaw's Music: The Complete Musical Criticism*, ed. Dan H. Laurence, 3 vols (New York: Dodd, 1981).

moral vision a moral psychology, very much in the sense that Iris Murdoch has described her own work as moral psychology. Shaw's socialist idealism and commitment to the power of the will are at the very opposite pole from Murdoch's ascetic vision distilled from Plato and Simone Weil. But both writers are concerned, centrally, with the drama of unselfing, the transcendence of personal egotism. The difference is that Shaw would work toward this goal by expanding the will to embrace a larger, communal idea of self-interest whereas Murdoch would reach it through a process of emptying the will.

Consider the style of Shaw's logic in one of his favourite arguments, for the abolition of both rich and poor through an equal distribution of income (*CL* III 24–5 and elsewhere). He rejects the idea that this argument should be put forward on the idealistic grounds that all men are created equal, for the psychological realist knows they are not. He will not, then, come on simply as a moralist, attacking the inequality of capitalism in favour of the equality of socialism. Rather, his attack is directed at our reasons – our rationalisations really – for defending the status quo. We say that the poor do not want to change or are worthy in the sight of heaven, that the rich are more deserving because they work harder or that wealth creates opportunities for all. Such reasons are not completely wrong, but we create them primarily to blind us to the less flattering reason for our defence: we do not want to recognise the snobbish pleasure we get from feeling superior to others by having more privileges than they do. By making excuses for the capitalist status quo we protect the pleasures of a personal egotism and do not see that our true self-interest, our enlightened self-interest, would comprehend the fact that the poverty of the poor and the idleness of the rich degrade everyone. Shaw's argument tells us that rationalisations must be jolted before we can want to achieve this higher level of pleasure. His moral vision has this psychological basis. One could, of course, rebut that his psychological realism is limited in that it does not really understand the tenacity of our investment in snobbery. But within its range it is a lively propaedeutic, a psychological exercise in moral or spiritual discipline.

The Shavian moralist assumes that our consciences are educable because we are not so much selfish by nature as ignorant of how the best in us is being curbed and suppressed:

List of Abbreviations

B   *The Bodley Head Bernard Shaw: Collected Plays with their Prefaces*, ed. Dan H. Laurence, 7 vols (London: Max Reinhardt, 1970–4).

C   *The Constable Standard Edition of the Works of Bernard Shaw*, 37 vols (London: Constable, 1930–50).

CL   *Bernard Shaw: Collected Letters*, vol. I: *1874–1897*, vol. II: *1898–1910*, vol. III: *1911–1925*, vol. IV: *1926–50*, ed. Dan H. Laurence (vols I and II: New York: Dodd, 1965–72; vols III and IV: New York: Viking, 1985–8).

CP   *The Complete Prefaces of Bernard Shaw* (London: Hamlyn, 1965).

DI   *Bernard Shaw: The Diaries 1885–1897*, 2 vols, edited and annotated by Stanley Weintraub (University Park, Pa.: Pennsylvania State University Press, 1986).

LC   *Bernard Shaw's Nondramatic Literary Criticism*, ed. Stanley Weintraub, Regents Critics Series (Lincoln: University of Nebraska Press, 1972).

MDD   *My Dear Dorothea: A Practical System of Moral Education for Females Embodied in a Letter to a Young Person of That Sex*, ed. Stephen Winsten (New York: Vanguard, 1956).

NDW   *Selected Non-Dramatic Writings of Bernard Shaw*, ed. Dan H. Laurence (Cambridge, Mass.: Riverside, 1965).

OTN   *Our Theatres in the Nineties* by Bernard Shaw, 3 vols (London: Constable, 1948).

P&P   *Platform and Pulpit*, ed. Dan H. Laurence (New York: Hill, 1961).

RS   *The Religious Speeches of Bernard Shaw*, ed. Warren Sylvester Smith, Foreword by Arthur H. Nethercot (University Park, Pa.: Pennsylvania State University Press, 1963).

SM   *Shaw's Music: The Complete Musical Criticism*, ed. Dan H. Laurence, 3 vols (New York: Dodd, 1981).

SSS   *Sixteen Self Sketches by Bernard Shaw* (New York: Dodd, 1949).

ST   *Shaw on Theatre*, ed. E. J. West (New York: Hill, 1958).

ThC   *Theatrical Companion to Shaw: A Pictorial Record of the First Performances of the Plays of George Bernard Shaw*, ed. Raymond Mander and Joe Mitchenson (London: Rockliff, 1971).

UN   *An Unfinished Novel by Bernard Shaw*, ed. Stanley Weintraub (London: Constable, 1958).

Introduction

As he moved into full command of his powers during the 1890s, Shaw excitedly began to describe himself as a dramatic poet. I shall attempt in this study to justify that claim, understanding the word 'poet' in an extended but fairly definite sense.

Clearly his imagination was stimulated by political and social questions. But it would be much too limiting to describe Shaw as a topical writer committed to specific changes in the now outmoded institutional forms of his time and place. He was not really intent on the practical success of a programme such as the equal distribution of income or of a doctrine like Creative Evolution. Rather, he was interested in the adequacy of belief concerning the arrangements sanctioned by the institutions of his society. He was more eager to expose the motives underlying these beliefs than to alter behaviour as an end in itself: 'It is not that what [doctors] do they do badly – on the contrary; but their reasons for doing it – oh Lord' (*CL* II 66)! Addressing himself to the Church's claim that marriage is a sacrament, he wrote: 'So it is; but that is exactly what makes divorce a duty when the marriage has lost the inward and spiritual grace of which the marriage ceremony is the outward and visible sign' (*B* 3: 534). This counterclaim is hardly a practical argument for divorce but a witty exposure of the fact that the Church is protecting the letter and ignoring the spirit.

Although Shaw liked to describe his language as didactic and propagandistic, these epithets do little justice to the distinctive playfulness of his polemicism, the rhetorical art of his wit. If propaganda is writing intent on the achievement of particular goals through an adjustment of means, necessarily more concerned with what people do than what they feel, then Shaw did not write propaganda, though he certainly in principle valued practicability (sometimes called pragmatism or possibilism) and certainly valued willingness to act as a test of sincere conviction. Shaw was much less a political writer than an impassioned moralist, and his Shelleyan or Wagnerian passion for reforming the world has been justly described, by Lewis Turco and others, as a moral vision.

But because the psychological element is always important in Shaw's effective plays and arguments, I should prefer to call his

1

moral vision a moral psychology, very much in the sense that Iris Murdoch has described her own work as moral psychology. Shaw's socialist idealism and commitment to the power of the will are at the very opposite pole from Murdoch's ascetic vision distilled from Plato and Simone Weil. But both writers are concerned, centrally, with the drama of unselfing, the transcendence of personal egotism. The difference is that Shaw would work toward this goal by expanding the will to embrace a larger, communal idea of self-interest whereas Murdoch would reach it through a process of emptying the will.

Consider the style of Shaw's logic in one of his favourite arguments, for the abolition of both rich and poor through an equal distribution of income (*CL* III 24–5 and elsewhere). He rejects the idea that this argument should be put forward on the idealistic grounds that all men are created equal, for the psychological realist knows they are not. He will not, then, come on simply as a moralist, attacking the inequality of capitalism in favour of the equality of socialism. Rather, his attack is directed at our reasons – our rationalisations really – for defending the status quo. We say that the poor do not want to change or are worthy in the sight of heaven, that the rich are more deserving because they work harder or that wealth creates opportunities for all. Such reasons are not completely wrong, but we create them primarily to blind us to the less flattering reason for our defence: we do not want to recognise the snobbish pleasure we get from feeling superior to others by having more privileges than they do. By making excuses for the capitalist status quo we protect the pleasures of a personal egotism and do not see that our true self-interest, our enlightened self-interest, would comprehend the fact that the poverty of the poor and the idleness of the rich degrade everyone. Shaw's argument tells us that rationalisations must be jolted before we can want to achieve this higher level of pleasure. His moral vision has this psychological basis. One could, of course, rebut that his psychological realism is limited in that it does not really understand the tenacity of our investment in snobbery. But within its range it is a lively propadeutic, a psychological exercise in moral or spiritual discipline.

The Shavian moralist assumes that our consciences are educable because we are not so much selfish by nature as ignorant of how the best in us is being curbed and suppressed:

I will not ask these critics who are so indignant with my 'distorted and myopic outlook on society' what they will do with the little money their profession may enable them to save. I will tell them what they *must* do with it, and that is to follow the advice of their stockbroker as to the safest and most remunerative investment.   (*CP* 678)

The attack for all its vehemence is not a condemnation of our sinful nature. It positively appreciates our plight ('the little money their profession may enable them to save') and wittily exposes our innocence as a collective error to which we are driven by our ignorant participation in a capitalist economy. The wit consists in the sudden, unexpected liberation of a 'repressed' idea, stimulating us imaginatively to the possibility of a nobler vision.

The plays of Shaw are more deeply imaginative because they dramatise the varieties of such psychological action in symbolic form. They present characters who act out the desires and resistances of the author and, potentially, of the audience. In the major dramatic debates, according to J. L. Wisenthal (1974), 'it is not a question of Shaw versus anti-Shaw, but of one aspect of his temperament in opposition to another' (p. 41). 'His stage at its best', in the words of Thomas Whitaker (1983), 'does not set before us photographs of "real people" but invites us to participate in stylized explorations of our intellectual and emotional life' (p. 7). A self-definitional drama resonates, or is implicated in, the extroverted drama of ideas.

The phrase 'dramatic poet' evokes, for English speakers at any rate, the model of Shakespeare, and by that standard the claim of dramatic poet on Shaw's behalf can easily seem unconvincing, all the more because of his aggressive and, for the most part, unwise insistence on comparing himself to his towering predecessor. Shaw's prejudice against Shakespeare's sensuous language and tragic/elegiac tonalities will prove quite pertinent to understanding the structure of his imagination, but it is best for the moment to put the comparison with Shakespeare aside and use Ibsen instead as our model of a different but none the less authentic kind of dramatic poet.

In the problem plays of both Ibsen and Shaw, prosaic as they might be in Yeats's judgement, language, incidents and gestures are often so weighted with, or coloured by, subjectivity that the drama, for all its surface realism, enacts a kind of symbolic action.

Ibsen and Shaw have poured something of their own aspiration into their heroes and something of their own scepticism into whatever destroys, unmasks or baffles their heroes. The characters do not simply meet the requirements of the plot, as in melodrama and farce. Nor can they simply be identified with social standards unconsciously accepted by the author, as in the plays of Pinero and Jones. In Ibsen and Shaw 'a morality, a system of values, is worked out . . . as opposed to [most nineteenth-century drama] in which the morality is fixed and pre-established' (Wisenthal, 1979, p. 73). Their plays dramatise a change in a level of understanding or an opposition between differing levels of understanding. Often the protagonist possesses a portion of his or her author's sense of irony.

Ibsen's irony, to be sure, is more corrosive than Shaw's. A harsher judgement is passed against his protagonists, one that involves the radical imperfection of their nature rather than the corrigible error of their understanding. The structure of Ibsen's plots leans toward tragedy as the structure of Shaw's leans toward comedy. Because tragedy confronts human fears and limits more starkly than comedy, I can understand why some critics (for example, Keith May) find Ibsen deeper than Shaw. But Shaw's 'heights' and Ibsen's 'depths' derive from a similar intrapsychic conflict, differently resolved. The Shavian hero struggles to overcome, is engaged by, or is overcome by a certain resistance, which, like his desire, derives from the will of his creator.

Theorists of comedy sometimes stress the subversive function of the genre and sometimes the conservative function. Shaw's brand of comedy illustrates both. His protagonists possess a good deal of iconoclastic force as they attack an entrenched social morality. At the same time, their ability to effect revolutionary change is, in one way or another, mocked. But I am interested in stressing the dynamic interplay between heroic will and the resistance to it, and so would not incline to one side or the other of this antithesis.

The idea of a heightened level of consciousness resulting dynamically from the overcoming of a certain resistance has, since the days of Hume, Burke and Kant, been known in criticism as the sublime. Although the term is not inevitable – this study will sometimes use 'heroic' or 'ideal' or 'visionary' as adjectival synonyms – it is particularly suggestive because it implies, as other terms do not, an initiating casting-out of degraded meaning that enables a renovation or intensification of language at a 'higher' level. Readers will be confused by my title phrase, the comic sublime, if they take it to designate genre or a combination of genres. Still less is the sublime intended herein as a value judgement denoting something like Arnold's high seriousness, as one of my readers has supposed. The sublime and the comic are, rather, psychological concepts, signifying movements of authorial will that may or may not be effectively realised in their expression. The one is a quest for a conflict-annulling transfiguration of the commonplace, purchased inevitably at the cost of a certain repression; the other cuts across this questing by means of ridicule or contrary argument or exposure of what is necessarily incomplete in this very effort of totalisation.

Movements of the will cannot be analysed without a terminology of some sort, and the tradition of the sublime usefully provides one because of its psychological base and thereby its responsiveness to contact with Freudian psychoanalysis. This enriching contact will enable me, for example, to throw light on the antithetical – and neglected – concept of the beautiful, an important concept in Shaw despite, or because of, its negativity.

The effect of sublimity achieved by Shaw always depends on the creation of a palpable resistance, for raising consciousness to a higher level involves not mere addition to knowledge but what Nietzsche called a transvaluation of values and Freud a conversion of affect. This resistance may be roughly identified with Shaw's sense of the comic. The empathetically rendered 'hell' of reality, made to look comic because of its partiality in relation to a more comprehensive view, provides the leverage for attaining the 'heaven' of a transformed reality. This comic–ironic resistance is further used to deflate or delimit the heroic will. Learning much from Charles Dickens whose work he devoured in boyhood, Shaw demonstrated a particular gift for writing arguments on behalf of complacent defenders of the status quo who articulate, more or less seductively, the claims of self-satisfaction.

I shall in this study distinguish several (overlapping) ways in which Shaw's idealism and realism interact and thereby establish a characteristic style of thought and expression that will be called the comic or Shavian sublime. These are most clearly illustrated in the plays.

In the first version of the comic sublime, heroic will attains definition from its very rejection of the conventional or the beautiful, but what is rejected possesses a certain force because it enjoys social support and can be defended with complacent conviction. The anagnorisis in the comic plot is typically a recognition on the part of the hero of a new role that requires the casting off of 'happiness' for 'strength' or 'greatness'. Mrs Warren's defence of her profession is not only plausible hypocrisy but also an incentive to her daughter's repudiation-and-ascent. Vivie associates herself hyperbolically with the voice of Job's God in describing her conversion. And this becomes the first distinctly sublime moment in the dramatic canon. Similar moments are more maturely dramatised in the roles of Marchbanks, Dudgeon and Anderson, Juan and Ana, Barbara, Ellie Dunn and Joan.

A second version of the comic sublime, though already present in the plays of the 1890s, becomes more prominent and complex in Shaw's middle period in which the dramatic use of discussion greatly increases. Instead of a sublime moment, we have in this version an interaction of figures representing higher and lower levels of moral awareness. Bluntschli's confrontation with his Bulgarian group, Dudgeon's with Burgoyne, and Caesar's and Lady Cicely's with their unimproved societies are early instances of this more discursive presentation of the comic sublime. More mature instances include the debate in hell from *Man and Superman*, Undershaft's debate with Cusins, Keegan's with Broadbent and Doyle, Shotover's with Hector and the trial scene in *Saint Joan*.

In its developed form this version of the comic sublime is particularly complex because the heroic will itself is fragmented. Instead of one figure educating a society (which we still have, of course, in *Man and Superman* and *Major Barbara*), the distributed elements of heroic will wrestle for integration. Wisenthal (1974) observes that the very basis for discussing the middle plays is 'the idea that valuable qualities are dissociated and that their union is desirable' (p. 21).

I cite one example:

CAPTAIN SHOTOVER. What then is to be done? Are we to be kept forever in the mud by these hogs to whom the universe is nothing but a machine for greasing their bristles and filling their snouts?

HECTOR. Are Mangan's bristles worse than Randall's lovelocks?

CAPTAIN SHOTOVER. We must win powers of life and death over them both. I refuse to die until I have invented the means.

HECTOR.   Who are we that we should judge them?

CAPTAIN SHOTOVER.   What are they that they should judge us?
Yet they do, unhesitatingly. There is enmity between our seed
and their seed. They know it and act on it, strangling
our souls. They believe in themselves. When we believe in
ourselves, we shall kill them.

HECTOR.   It is the same seed . . . We are members one of
another.   (*B* 5: 100–1)

In this forceful interchange, Shotover's anger is lofty and incisive
but flawed by fanaticism whereas Hector's brand of Christian
humanism makes a contrary claim but is timid. Hector is too
embroiled in philandering to be as capable as Shotover of a holy
wrath directed at the moral purposelessness of plutocrats and
romancers. His own wrath is expressed primarily as a desire to
crush the force of enthralling women yet this voice eventually
rises, as Shotover's does not, to collective self-condemnation: 'We
are useless, dangerous, and ought to be abolished' (*B* 5: 159). If
such dialogue does not quite bring the whole soul of man into
activity, lacking the Shakespearian amplitude that Coleridge had
in mind, it none the less, like many exchanges in Shaw, throws
heart and head, passion and judgement, together into stimulating
combat.

Occasionally Shaw took the artistically dubious course of trying
to fuse power and virtue in one figure, creating an achieved
superman. The roles of Caesar, Undershaft and Magnus are
all troublesome, despite their strength, because they hint at a
satisfaction with power for its own sake, leading on to Shaw's
regrettable sympathy in his later years with Europe's all too actual
dictators.

I then distinguish a third version of the comic sublime, latent
from the beginning of Shaw's career but becoming more overt later
on. Its irony is of a darker hue along the comic spectrum. It may
be described as a visionary scepticism, in part a legacy from his
adolescent literary hero, Shelley.[1] The sublime is a totalising gesture
of mind and language that masters a threat to the ego and thereby
expands and fortifies it. In Shaw as in Shelley the desire for
inclusion is pursued with enough imaginative energy to expose its
own incompleteness, as if the poet's ultimate objective were the
impossible restoration of a lost unity. But the Shavian is unlike the
high Romantic sublime in that it does not reach for the ineffable.

The magnified ego remains clear and distinct on the heights, testifying to its origin in the comic mode.

The hero – or typically the heroine – learns through the very intensity of her desire the radical incompleteness of the self. We see this in the vatic Mrs George whose heart must break in silence; in Ellie Dunn who realises that, despite her disillusioned and thus fortified will, life never does come to a point (although the ending of *Heartbreak House* gives her ambiguous hope of an apocalypse); in Lilith who understands in conclusion that hope and disappointment are forever joined in the endless process of becoming; in Joan's final insight that the world will never be ready to receive its saints; and in the cyclonic Millionairess who is unable to find on earth a mate fit to stand with her upon the heights.

Shaw always idealises self-sufficiency, so intensely that we must suspect an underlying anxiety about ego boundaries, and yet candidly enough to show that this self is edged with loneliness. Alternatively, he idealised otherness in the form of a strong woman who is both feared and adored. She is severe in judgement, impossible to please, yet, in so far as her own self-sufficiency is presented, also lonely. The idealisation of either self or other, then, leads to the knowledge of incompleteness, suggesting the subsistent presence of some desire, older than any distinction between self and other, that cannot be either suppressed or satisfied.

W. B. Yeats hoped that some day Shelley and Dickens would be united in one artist (Albright, 1984, p. 32). I cannot resist the suggestion that this unlikely hybrid materialised before Yeats's very eyes but went unrecognised.

Shelley and Dickens are, of course, not Shaw's only significant predecessors, but in general I am more impressed by the influences upon him of poets, novelists and dramatists than of philosophers. Shaw was indebted to Schopenhauer for an explicit view of a pre-rational will, to Hegel for a notion of historical dialectic used notably in *The Perfect Wagnerite* and tentatively in *Caesar and Cleopatra*, and to Nietzsche and Bergson for a few striking, confirmative phrases. But the more important lessons involved the learning of modes of sublimity and comedy – strategies, procedures, techniques – and should be associated with the names of Bunyan, Dickens, Shelley, Blake, Butler, Wagner and Ibsen. To the latter list should be added Marx, who influenced Shaw not so much through his doctrine as through his rhetorical presence or stance.

And in such a roundup of precursors, one should not neglect to mention as well those Victorian essayists – especially Carlyle, Mill, Ruskin and Morris – whose moral approach to political and economic questions simply permeated the intellectual atmosphere of Shaw's formative years.

Some of what has been said so far may imply that I intend to read Shaw autobiographically. In a sense I do, but that special sense must be clarified.

Although Shaw could write very attractively in an outrightly autobiographical mode – illustrated generously in the two volumes of his autobiographical writing selected by Stanley Weintraub (1969–70) – and although his criticism is studded with self-dramatising gestures, his novelistic and dramatic fictions only occasionally reflect or refer to the specific circumstances of his individual history. In addition to the personal aspect of *The Philanderer*, *Fanny's First Play* and *The Apple Cart*, one remembers the facetious use of his own name in *The Doctor's Dilemma* and *Misalliance* and only glancing self-references elsewhere. For a nineteenth- or twentieth-century imaginative writer, this is restrained use of personal history and hardly encourages us to think of Shaw's fictions as autobiographical.

But, as Shaw himself wrote, 'if a man is a deep writer all his works are confessions' (*SSS* 19). That is, in many narratives valued by the literary community we sense the projection and distribution of aspects of authorial identity despite the absence of specific personal reference. Such works are autobiographical in a special, perhaps even abstract, sense for, instead of reflecting a particular *him*self or *her*self, they express *the* self understood as a symbolic nexus or conceptual field. Indeed, to bring a biographic history closely to bear upon this kind of self-expression would seem to us reductive. The plays of Shaw are 'autobiographical' in the same way that many great novels are – *The Scarlet Letter*, *The Brothers Karamazov*, *Ulysses*. But I go a step farther and attempt to organise the self-invested conflicts of his dramas and arguments according to a certain structure of character, at once individual and typical. I want to show how the character of an author is implicated in a body of imaginative work and creates thereby a mythology of self.

It is easy enough to intuit the investment of self in the work of someone like Shaw but not so easy to explain in conceptual terms how one assesses and measures symbolic self-writing. Keeping to Shaw in order to avoid opening up a larger issue than I can handle, we can specify several demonstrable bases for our intuition. For one thing, certain figures are idealised or equally admired as de-idealisers, as if strong feeling is complex and must be distributed. For another, we notice that these figures line up with certain favoured qualities and recurrent antithesis: practicality vs. saintliness, power vs. wisdom, and so on. Thirdly, we notice the special intensity invested in certain words. Some, like efficiency and romance, are actively ambivalent in that the honorific and pejorative connotations always seem to be jostling for supremacy. Others, like honour and virtue and even passion, are ambiguous in a more definite way, an honorific connotation wrested from and set over against a pejorative one. What I mean by the sublime in Shaw is in fact inseparable from his strenuous renovations of the connotations of ethically charged words.

These indicators point to an investiture of authorial being in the text, but in order to organise our understanding of the character of the poet – so that we can follow, for example, characteristic conflicts as they run on from one work to the next – I have made use in this study of a suggestive psychological model, the model of narcissistic character structure and narcissistic conflict as drawn from Freudian and post-Freudian psychoanalysis. But my commentary is not to be construed as an example of applied psychoanalysis. I have learned to be wary of importing into criticism the terminology of another field because it commits us, whether we like it or not, to a system of thought governed by different assumptions and aims. The meaning of words slide when they pass from one field of inquiry to another. Therefore the few recognisable tags that I cannot avoid – repression, sublimation, narcissism – will be to some extent redefined and clarified for my purposes. Especially after the conceptually organised first chapter, this study will have only a psychoanalytic 'feel' to it rather than attempting to be systematic in its approach.

Along with some recent practitioners of a psychoanalytically orientated literary criticism, then, I conceive of an author as a field of force organising literary structures characteristically. This requires us to assume that he is also a person who has had a childhood and a determining personal history but does not require us to interpret his work biographically.[2] I shall occasionally make use of biographic fact and psychobiographic inference, my own and that of others,[3] but the spirit of criticism will prevail throughout. That is, the focus of my concern will always be the objectification of the subjective in Shaw and not the other way around.

In principle there is no reason to fear reductiveness in this approach. There are always knots in highly imaginative works of some length that seem to loosen best when the critic steps behind the objectifying author to the imperfect person who bears the same name:

> Outside the play, Shaw is against Candida. Inside it, he is both for and against her, but he is for her effectually and against her ineffectually, because the direct impression is favorable, while it is only by throwing logic back into the story when it is over that you can reach an unfavorable judgment. This means, I should think, that, though Shaw's intellect is against Candida, his emotions are for her.   (Bentley, 1960, p. xxii)

Eric Bentley's keen analysis distinguishes author as artist (the implications of the text itself) from author as person (Shaw's external comments about the play) but does so for the sake of clarifying the discrepancy between authorial judgement and predilection within the text. Maintaining a flexible relation between author and person is, I think, advantageous to the critic, though it is not consistent with the doctrine of either New Criticism or Deconstruction. In practice, skilful critics shuttle from one to the other easily and unreductively to gain insight into the difficulties of a challenging text.

The imputation of a certain character structure to a writer should by no means be understood as a way of separating him from ourselves. On the contrary, it is intended to establish a connection between him and us at a more profound level. The mind has been compared by one psychoanalytic critic to 'a branching tree, with its roots in the original fantasy and constantly branching derivatives all the way up, all still existing simultaneously' (Skura, 1981, p. 83). Psychological criticism would degenerate into symptomology if it were not based on the assumption that – despite many differences in individual development, some branches growing, others withering – nothing human and especially nothing infantile is foreign to any of us.

Of course, any critical approach highlights some aspects of

literature at the expense of others. I have already implied that my inclination to see Shaw's plays as successive responses to conflict tends to look *through* genre distinctions, although genre distinctions are definitive for some critics. Concepts like farce, melodrama, tragedy and comedy are meaningful to me but meaningful primarily as providing opportunities for, or imposing constraints upon, self-expression. My central concern is with a characteristic style of thought and expression which I call imagination and understand as a faculty of mind that seeks ever new formal means of self-representation. Beyond the theoretical first chapter, this study will trace the history of a particular literary imagination. The Shavian *oeuvre* will unfold as a drama of inner development, a symbolic drama in that it is overtly a representation of conflicts in a social world. My approach will be justified not by startling conclusions but by convincingly conveying the impression that Shaw is a deeper writer than he is widely thought to be, a writer capable, for example (as Bentley perceived), of dramatising a modern sense of desolation beneath the prevailing optimism.

My somewhat unusual way of reading Shaw may freshen some of the questions often raised or implied in the commentaries. Why does *Candida* seem both a stronger and a weaker play than its predecessors? What is equivocal about the motivation of Dick Dudgeon's *beau geste*? Why does *Man and Superman* remain so central to the canon despite its formal and even ideational eccentricity? How do we explain the fact that the pessimistic *John Bull's Other Island* and the optimistic *Major Barbara* were written at nearly the same time? Why does *Pygmalion* continue to be valued as one of Shaw's most important plays despite its seeming lack of weight? Is there a connection between the authentic depth of *Misalliance* and of *Heartbreak House* and the difficulty of bringing them clearly into focus? Why does *Saint Joan* look so much like a summing up?

Questions concerning Shaw's thought in general as well as dramatic art in particular may also be clarified. What is the connection between capitalism and sensuality that runs in a curious, covert fashion through his work? How do we reconcile his forceful libertarianism with his equally forceful emphasis on control and direction? How do we reconcile his anathematisation of romance with his irrepressible attraction to romance? How should we understand his obsession with sex in view of his decided preference for intellect and spirit? What significance should be attached to the fact that the important word 'will' in Shaw means both a preconscious, Schopenhauerean *Wille* or Freudian libido and also a progressive, essentially moral Life Force? And why is Shaw's seriousness and eloquence most effective when his comic and ironic talents are most active? Does that conjunction help to explain why wit, paradox and dialectical vivacity are the chief features or his critical as well as dramatic prose?

Beyond the first chapter, which is devoted to the concept of the comic or Shavian sublime, I shall discuss particularly and rather concisely a score of plays that illustrate best the three overlapping versions of this idea that I have distinguished. But I shall establish a contextual field for the major instances by briefly discussing some other works as well and by providing a little transitional and biographic matter where it seems useful. It ought to become apparent that the concept of the comic sublime can organise our view of the entire career.

Probably I could not have written this study if I did not somehow believe that I was getting at the truth of my subject. But when I stand back, I can see clearly enough that there can be no definitive critical truth, particularly about a writer so many-faceted as Shaw, and at best my book will have to take its place among others. At the same time, it necessarily codes another kind of truth, for criticism is also a mode of self-writing, like drama, fiction and poetry. But this truth can only be communicated by being mediated through a discourse about another, a discourse that is judged differently. To write about himself at all (and would he write if he couldn't?), the critic must convince some others of his insight into their common subject.

Part One

1

The Comic Sublime

At the outset of his first major work, *The Quintessence of Ibsenism*, Shaw salutes the 'pioneers of the march to the plains of heaven' (C 19: 15). The combination in this figure of 'pioneers' and 'plains of heaven', of a word evoking the progress of society and a phrase evoking the progress of self into new moral territory, this fusion of social Darwinism and Bunyanesque Christianity, describes the most characteristic thrust of his imagination. Both his dramatic and discursive writing carry forward, under the banner of Socialism, a vision of perfectibility at once collective and individual. The imperative of general progress is at the same time a psychological imperative, for Shaw's work typically dramatises conflict between the egoism of the commonplace social self and the higher egoism of moral passion.

The Shavian pioneers come as liberators of what is potentially noble in us but suppressed because of our reluctance to surrender a permitted pleasure or burden our already guilty consciences with a forbidden one. *The Quintessence* thus recognises two kinds of pioneers: an 'abstinence preacher' who 'declares that it is wrong to do something that no one has hitherto seen any harm in' (for example, 'to kill animals and eat them'); and an 'indulgence preacher' who 'declares that it is right to do something hitherto regarded as infamous' (for example, 'to take your sister as your wife'). Both the new enforcer and the new licenser have attained higher moral levels than those prevailing in their community. The one rises above a common form of gratification (complicity in slaughtering) that we are too lazy to recognise as cruel. The other challenges a taboo that Shaw supposes (more confidently in this early work than later on) to be rooted in artificial convention rather than vital instinct. The argument sharpens to the point of paradox: the enforcer is given testimonials but hated like the devil; the licenser is grudged his bread and water but secretly adored (C 19: 15–16).

It is important to understand in this lively scenario that pioneer and community refer not only to exceptional and ordinary persons

17

but also to higher and lower emotions within each mind. The goals of social- and of self-improvement interlock, although for polemical purposes one may be stressed at the expense of the other. Curing one's conscience privately is impossible, as is shown in *Major Barbara* and elsewhere: 'we must reform society before we can reform ourselves' (*B* 4: 93; *CL* III 473). On the other hand, there is no other way to Shaw's version of the Socialist ideal – a 'Democracy of Supermen' (*B* 2: 755), a 'communion of saints' (*B* 2: 801) – than through self-improvement. It is true that *Heartbreak House* questions whether individual conscience can remain untwisted in a twisted society, but I would, on balance, agree with Julian Kaye (1958) that, like social critics who wrote without benefit of Marx (Carlyle, Mill, Ruskin), Shaw 'believed that individual reform must precede social reform' (p. 18). In any case the prime obstacle to these interrelated goals – that which makes us cling to the status quo without and within – is private property and its psychological complement, jealousy: 'Catholicity is the stamp of the higher love, as jealousy is of the lower' (*SM* 2: 833).

Since others did not usually take so comprehensive a view, Shaw often had to remind them that, for example, war should not be distinguished from the inclination to war, that the jingoistic Englishman was tarred with the same brush as the aggressive Hun. Despite his readiness to give practical (though highminded) advice to politicians, Shaw's interest lay, as he knew, in 'the psychological side of war' (*CL* III 315). He vigorously corrected a fellow Socialist's indignation because it was not catholic enough: 'If Rockefeller *deserves* hanging (an expression which belongs to your moral system) so does every man who would do the same as Rockefeller if he got the chance' (*CL* II 161). Sharing Karl Marx's scorn of capitalism, Shaw did not intend to forget Marx's idealism as well, in its psychological as well as political dimension.

His preoccupation with conduct was inseparable from a concern with motive. Right thinking was as important as right doing. Although he sometimes stressed the pragmatic line – 'conduct must justify itself by its effects upon life and not by its conformity to any rule of ideal' (*C* 19: 133–4) – he did not at all approve, as *The Doctor's Dilemma* demonstrates, of doing the right deed for the wrong reason. (Of course, doing so could be relished as comic irony, as in the short story 'The Miraculous Revenge' or the short play 'Overruled'.) He protested a congratulation from his well-meaning friend Sidney Webb In 1916: 'I have not had my way, because I wanted the Asquith–Grey regime to be overthrown by us for the right reasons; and it has been overthrown by the Northcliffe press for the wrong ones' (*CL* iii 443). He argued repeatedly against corporal punishment, vivisection, imprisonment and hunting, not merely because these were in themselves cruel actions but also, and crucially, because they degraded the souls of the perpetrators.

I would not deny that Shaw's vision is political, even essentially so, and it is always earnest enough to be concerned with the efficient means of realising a nobly motivated goal. But it is not political in the usual sense of seeking support for a practical result whatever the feelings of those being persuaded. Shaw's socialism, in short, is much less a programme than a Utopian desire, and it is opposed much less by external circumstance than by what is unpurged and common in our feelings. Thus his polemic is typically not simply instrumental to a political purpose like most propaganda. It is dramatic, resourceful, a mode of action whose interest is fundamentally literary. H. G. Wells (1934) appreciated this quality, somewhat ironically, when he compared unfavourably Shaw's basic imaginativeness to his own 'facty' mentality (p. 457).

Here is a page from 'The Economic Basis of Socialism':

Thus is Man mocked by Earth his step-mother, and never knows as he tugs at her closed hand whether it contains diamonds or flints, good red wheat or a few clayey and blighted cabbages. Thus too he becomes a gambler, and scoffs at the theorists who prate of industry and honesty and equality. Yet against this fate he eternally rebels. For since in gambling the many must lose in order that the few may win; since honesty is mere shadowgrasping where everyone is dishonest; and since inequality is bitter to all except the highest, and miserably lonely for him, men come greatly to desire that these capricious gifts of Nature might be intercepted by some agency having the power and the goodwill to distribute them justly according to the labor done by each in the collective search for them. This desire is Socialism; and, as a means to its fulfilment, Socialists have devised communes, kingdoms, principalities, churches, manors, and finally, when all these had succumbed to the old gambling spirit, the Social Democratic State, which yet remains to be tried. As against Socialism, the gambling spirit urges man to allow no rival to come between his private individual powers and Stepmother

Earth, but rather to secure some acres of her and take his chance
of getting diamonds instead of cabbages. This is Private Property
or Unsocialism. Our own choice is shewn by our continual
aspiration to possess property, our common hailing of it as
sacred, our setting apart of the word Respectable for those who
have attained it, our ascription of pre-eminent religiousness to
commandments forbidding its violation, and our identification
of law and order among men with its protection. Therefore is it
vital to a living knowledge of our society that Private Property
should be known in every step of its progress from its source in
cupidity to its end in confusion.   (C 30: 3–4)

The combination of vivid concreteness and brilliant generalisation
(who else but Shaw could have succeeded in making Socialism
look like a perennial human desire rather than a nineteenth-century
movement?), the rapidity and force of the style with its dazzling
appositions and its disdain for the pause of paragraphing, the
punning and near-punning, the tonal swings between scorn and
rhapsody mediated somehow by logical forms of transition – such
highly dramatic writing gives pleasure in itself. It rouses us, but
not to sign a petition or write a letter to a member of parliament.
It mimes a certain psychological action, showing us what we really
want by exposing the shoddiness of what we think we want,
indicting our ignorance rather than our nature so that our uncorrupt
but lazy will is shamed and inspired to ennoble itself. And this is
all the more remarkable in 1989 (the passage was written in 1889)
when Socialism has lost its romantic aura, to say the least.

Such writing makes us realise that propaganda is not necessarily
incompatible with art. It may be a form of religious exercise, one
that stresses experience over doctrine. I am reminded of T. S.
Eliot's famous statement: 'the poet never persuades us to believe
anything. . . . What we learn from . . . religious poetry is what it
feels like to believe that religion' (Drew, 1949, p. 140).

It is therefore too simple to say that Shaw's language is 'instrumental' as Samuel Hynes (1972) would have it (p. 20).[1] It does not
work toward the solution of practical problems but delights in the
exposure of suppressed motives and in the incongruities between
conduct and belief. The readiest way to underrate Shaw's literary
strength is to be misled by his didactic tone into distilling his
doctrine or evaluating its efficacy on purely political grounds. His

strength lies in making ideas collide with energy and wit.

Commentaries on Shaw tend, in spite of their awareness of this strength, to aim at a sort of doctrinal end-product of the ideas he dramatically opposes to one another. We hear of his effort to integrate knowledge and purpose, virtue and power, principle and pragmatism, good and the means of good. This is accurate enough and probably inevitable: I myself have not been able to avoid such description. But it emphasises Shaw's 'thought' at the expense of his 'art'. It slights the activity of his language. Antithesis in Shaw is not just a matter of opposed values held judiciously in balance (what is commonly called ambivalence) but also of a restless, underlying attraction to certain concepts – most obviously 'love', 'dream', 'romance', 'happiness', 'marriage' – that are at the same time strenuously repudiated (the psychoanalytic meaning of ambivalence). We can gain some insight into the energy of his thinking by tracking this cluster of words in samples of his more spontaneous writing.

In his illuminating letters to Ellen Terry, written as he was wrestling with the question of whether or not to marry (in a sense, as the very late sketch, 'Why She Would Not', indicates, he never stopped wrestling with it), an overemphatic scorn of love is clearly mixed with a surfacing longing. The boasts about self-sufficiency are complaints as well. Shaw declares: 'Love is only diversion and recreation to me' who 'require whole populations and historical epochs to engage my interests' – then goes on to admit he is in truth merely 'a writing machine' or 'a sprite' (according to the 'remarkably shrewd' Mrs Webb), with whom 'you cannot fall in love' (*CL* I 801). He boasts in one letter of 'that most blessed of all things – unsatisfied desire' (*CL* I 702) – but tells her in another, '*I* shall never have a home. But do not be alarmed: Beethoven never had one either' (*CL* I 695). He describes himself as 'a sublime monster', and asks if she knows 'anyone who will buy for twopence a body' of no use to 'a poet' (*CL* I 591). In an especially candid letter he describes his childhood: 'the fact that nobody cared for me particularly gave me a frightful self-sufficiency, or rather a power of starving on imaginary feasts, that may have delayed my development a good deal, and leaves me to this hour a treacherous brute in matters of pure affection' (*CL* I 692–3). A few months later this boils down to: 'a devil of a childhood, Ellen, rich only in dreams, frightful & loveless in realities' (*CL* I 773).

A remarkable letter to Janet Achurch of the same period (1896)

illuminates the dynamic generating the 'plains of heaven' image.
Shaw writes of his 'growing certainty' that he can be 'a dramatic
poet' and tells her that 'ability does not become genius until it has
risen to the point at which its keenest states of perception touch
on . . . ecstasy'. He then works out the favoured image:

> The step up to the plains of heaven was made on your bosom.
> . . . But he who mounts does not take the stairs with him, even
> though he may dream for the moment that each stair, as he
> touches it, is a plank on which he will float to the end of his
> journey. I know that the floating plank image is false and the
> stair image true; for I have left the lower stairs behind me and
> must in turn leave you unless you too mount along with
> me.   (*CL* I 625)

The plains of heaven symbolise imaginative ecstasy, attained
necessarily by sexual means though the means must be finally
rejected. The old idea of Shaw as constitutionally incapable of
passion, pilloried in *Fanny's First Play*, must go down as a prime
example of psychological naïveté. He was if anything preoccupied
by sex though always uneasy about it. In the passage above, the
excitement of having achieved an exalted self-sufficiency is hedged
by two strong if covert fears: the fear of emptiness if desire for the
other is denied and of merging if it is not denied – in either case a
loss of identity, of self.

The descriptive statement that Shaw was really romantic as well
as anti-romantic, though not inaccurate, misses the dynamic aspect
of his checked yearning for romance, and it is this aspect of the
matter that has most literary bearing because it changes the
meaning of his words. Almost every stressed word in his vocabulary
is equivocal, connoting at once a common and an improved
significance. A striking illustration was provided inadvertently by
Stewart Headlam, who described his friend as 'a genuine artist,
an *idealist* with romantic notions of conduct and evidently most
sincerely impressed with an awful sense of *duty*' (*P&P* xv). One
can hardly think of any four words more vehemently scorned by
Shaw than artist, idealist, romance and duty. Yet Headlam describes him justly. The important point, not usually made with
precision, is that Shaw wrests an improved meaning of such
charged words from a degraded meaning. One meaning springs
from the other. The relation between the two will require

explanation by means of a sufficiently dynamic psychology, for it instigates Shaw's army of paradoxes.

The heroic pioneers of the march to heaven, who are explicitly modelled on Shelley, appear to the communal consciousness as deniers of pleasure and sufferers of guilt but are neither ascetic nor masochistic by their own lights. The pioneers of the one group do not deny themselves, for by means of an improvement in sensual enjoyment (to use Blake's phrase), their natural passions have become moral ones. The defying consciences of the other group are robust enough to rise above a socially derived guilt. Shaw's thought here is nearer to Blake's and Shelley's than to Rousseau's. Depravity is not innate,[2] but natural goodness is equated not with a pristine, subsisting core but with the capacity for self-improvement, the instinct for perfectibility. To equate virtue with self-denial like the conventional moralist is for Shaw to perpetuate rather than resolve a sense of inner division. The better alternative is a human being improved to the extent that he or she truly desires the common good or even achieves the state of experiencing a will to the common good as entirely natural and pleasurable. As Alfred Turco (1976) comments, Shaw was original in translating ethical imperatives 'from the language of self-sacrifice into that of self-realization' (p. 127). Ultimately, Shaw like Blake identified human with divine will: it is 'a horrible blasphemy' to say poverty and illness are the will of God 'because *you* are the will of God' (*P&P* 82).

Working out a dramatic aesthetic through his weekly notices of other dramatists whose conventional morality he found unsatisfactory, Shaw attacked their bad faith or, as he called it, their 'lies'. In plays like Pinero's *The Second Mrs Tanqueray* and *The Notorious Mrs Ebbsmith*, the supposedly serious interest in the problem of a woman with a past is betrayed by our hidden interest in her immorality and our hidden satisfaction in the knowledge that the social and economic status quo is not being threatened (*OTN* I 45–7, 59–65). Shaw imagined a more original and exciting drama. It would consist of making hypocrisy not only conscious but also plausible and forceful so that it would spur the emergence of a higher point of view. This is what Sheridan should have done in *The School for Scandal*: make Joseph Surface into a 'sincere moralist' so that morality itself could be challenged (*OTN* II 168.) This is what Shaw himself actually did in *Mrs Warren's Profession*: grant his prostitute so strong an argument that her daughter's repudiation of its underlying conventionality is dramatically conveyed as an heroic achievement. Sheridan and Fielding allow their heroes to adhere to a commercial morality, but he would emulate Ibsen and force a dilemma on the spectator. Perhaps he would go further than Ibsenite tragi-comedy and question whether the protagonist's error, based (he believed) on false intellectual positions and therefore corrigible, should acquire the force of destiny.[3]

The numerous dramatisations in Shaw of a reactive springing from the hell of things as they are toward a heavenly reaching for things as they may be or 'really' are, the masterings of threatening opposition, are authentic realisations of what literary critics have long called the sublime. This is not to be confused with transcendence if that term implies a metaphysical belief rather than the literary representation of experiencing a sudden access of power and magnitude. Shaw can over-generalise but he seldom pursues a philosophic abstraction, and he is not (in my view) successful when he does – for example, when he offers Dick Dudgeon's motive as an instance of the Hegelian racial will. It will be helpful to trace the literary history of the sublime with an eye toward the particular modern use he makes of it.

Although it originates with Longinus in ancient times, the concept of the sublime entered modern criticism during the eight-eenth century, as theology was giving way to psychology and as a new self-consciousness was absorbing a waning but still active experience of divinity. According to one student of the subject, 'The sublime proved fascinating to an age that had lost the forms of traditional piety and had diffused the religious experience – the sense of the numinous – over the natural world and over the processes of feeling as well' (Price, 1969, p. 195). Another comments that the sublime 'provided a language for urgent and apparently novel experiences of anxiety and excitement that were in need of legitimation' (Weiskel, 1976, p. 4). And another suggests that its characterising metaphor of check-and-release 'draws much of its power from the literature of religious conversion' (Hertz, 1985, p. 47).

The leading eighteenth-century theories of the sublime – those of Hume (1739), Burke (1756) and Kant (1790) – are alike in suggesting that the experience of an influx of power results from the overcoming of a resistance, from the mastery of a threatening impulse. The sublime is understood as essentially reactive, like an athlete's spring from a trampoline. Hume (1966) observed that 'opposition, if it is not too strong, invigorates and elevates the soul' (vol. 2, p. 143). Burke (1968) wrote that 'whatever is in any sort terrible . . . is a source of the sublime: that is, it is productive of the strongest emotions which the mind is capable of feeling' (p. 39). And according to Kant (1982), 'provided our own position is secure', the aspect of such phenomena as thunderclouds, hurricanes and boundless ocean rising with rebellious force 'is all the more attractive for its fearfulness; and we readily call these objects sublime, because they raise the forces of the soul above the height of vulgar commonplace, and discover within us a power of resistance of quite another kind, which gives us courage to be able to measure ourselves against the seeming omnipotence of nature' (para. 28).[4]

The beautiful, in these theories, is an antithetical concept: perfected and finite rather than obscure and boundless, objective rather than subjective (Kant said: 'For the beautiful in nature we must seek a ground external to ourselves, but for the sublime one merely in ourselves' – para. 23), associated with tender rather than strong feeling. After Kant and Hegel the antithesis is formulated more ideologically. The sublime is preferred to the beautiful. When Coleridge wrote, 'I meet, I *find* the Beautiful – but I give, contribute, or rather attribute the Sublime' (Twitchell, 1983, p. 90n), he is not only echoing Kant but also favouring the latter term by associating it with the value of Imagination. Schiller (1965) in his *On the Aesthetic Education of Man* (letter 16) distinguished a melting from an energising beauty without clear preference, but was prompted thereafter to write an essay on the sublime that downgrades the one ('beauty alone could never teach us that our destination is to act as pure intelligence' – p. 199) and implicitly upgrades the other. This ideological bias extends into our own day and is apparent in Shaw.

Later in the nineteenth century and on into the twentieth, the antithetical force of the distinction dissipated. My surmise is that beauty came to be understood as an aspect of erotics and therefore something of an embarrassment to aesthetics. The sublime, on the other hand, has in recent decades been independently revived. Ronald Paulson (1985), reviewing the work in a recent volume of *New Literary History* devoted to 'The Sublime and the Beautiful', understandably has little to say about beauty but comments interestingly that critical study of the sublime has changed from the Monk and Hipple mode of enumerating qualities in the sublime object or in the mind of the spectator to the agonistic and structuralist emphasis of such critics as Bloom and Weiskel (p. 427).

In the same volume Gary Shapiro (1985) attributes a comic sublime to Karl Marx on the basis of *The Eighteenth Brumaire of Louis Napoléon*. The idea that men can make their own history is presumably sublime, although it is comic – or grotesque – that they must shape their future from the irrational nightmare of the past. Shapiro finds the closest modern equivalent to this 'comic sublime' in Mikhail Bakhtin's idea of 'carnival' (p. 227), but this connection is misleading. Bakhtin (1984) specifically detaches the grotesque from the sublime and attaches it to the carnival spirit in literature ('the carnival-grotesque') whose function is 'to permit the combination of a variety of different elements, to liberate from the prevailing point of view of this world, from conventions and established truths, from clichés, from all that is humdrum and universally accepted' (pp. 34–5). Paulson (1985) correctly observed that Bakhtin did not want the grotesque romanticised into the sublime (p. 433), even if critics could not otherwise imagine how it could be made compatible with art.

I make a point of this because the grotesque is sometimes said to be the inevitable mode in our day of religious questing in literature. One thinks of such writers as Nathanael West, Flannery O'Connor and Samuel Beckett. Shaw himself was not drawn to the grotesque. He was too bound by both Enlightenment rationalism and nineteenth-century progressivism for that turn of sensibility. Yet irony is inseparable from his strongest effects, and it should be interesting to see how he uses it to forge a distinctive comic sublime.

The primary form of the sublime in Shaw is illustrated in the plays by a sudden (though dramatically prepared) leap from lower to higher moral ground: Vivie Warren's reactive response to her mother, 'my work is not your work, and my way not your way' (*B* 1: 353); Eugene Marchbanks rousing himself in the face of Candida's comforting with the words, 'Out, then, into the night with me! . . . I am impatient to do what must be done' (*B* 1: 593); Don Juan's leap to Heaven (and Ana's follow-up), spurred by a sustained debate in Hell. This accession of energy is of course happening in Shaw's language and theatre, whatever we may suppose to be the equivalent occurrence in his mind. Neil Hertz (1985) finely points out that the sublime turn in literature transfers power 'from the threatening forces to the poetic activity itself' and that therefore hyperbole is the figure that makes us most aware of it (p. 16). The hyperbolic words and gestures of Vivie, Marchbanks and Juan allude to vast powers and a new dimension of experience.

We also typically find in Shaw another mode of sublimity illustrated by such characters as Caesar, Peter Keegan, Lavinia, the Ancients and Joan. These do not significantly change. From an accomplished height they oppose others in discussion. Although they are subject to pressure, dramatic surprise is generated more by the clarification of motive than by the outcome of plot. Following a suggestion of Martin Price (1969), I shall call this 'the perspectivist sublime'. 'It belongs', writes Price, 'to a more assured sense of the transcendental. For the ascent lies behind it. It becomes a radical kind of vision' (p. 213).

These two forms may shade into one another. Don Juan in his debate also illustrates the perspectivist sublime, and Joan in the first three scenes of her play also illustrates the dynamic or saltatory type. The second act of *The Devil's Disciple* works up to the sublime moments of Anderson's sudden turn and then Dudgeon's; but the first act dramatises a clash of perspectives between Dick Dudgeon and others, mixing Dickensian farce and Blakean intellectual satire; and the third act features the high irony of the exchanges among Dic, Burgoyne and Judith, carried out over the heads of farcically conceived characters. After *Man and Superman*, in fact, we regularly find mixtures of action and discussion, making the Shavian sublime a complex phenomenon. The march *to* the plains of heaven yields in part to dubious battle *on* the plains of heaven, as different aspects of heroic consciousness (in, for example, Keegan and Broadbent or Shotover and Hector) wrestle together.

These forms of the sublime in Shaw imply an initiating act of transformative repudiation, either immediately dramatised or assumed to have taken place, the psychological nature of which is indicated by eighteenth-century theories of the sublime but which needs now to be brought into contact with a Freudian view of mind and specifically with the concept of repression.

We have seen that the Shavian imagination repeatedly rejects a threatening idea by reattaching its energy to a purified form of the idea resonant with moral power. The etymology of the word sublime (*sub limine*, below the threshold) seems to allude to the repression that makes possible, paradoxically, this sudden release and expansion of energy. But the term repression is misleading here if it implies a psychological process beyond the range of preconscious, artistic direction. Repression in the Freudian sense causes a distortion and deformation of an idea rather than a Nietzschean transvaluation of values. Complex works of art embody the 'derivates' of instinctual conflict (Stamm, 1965, p. 254), and are not easily discussed in terms of fundamental inhibitions.

That seems to open a way for the word sublimation. But this term, ambiguous enough even within a psychoanalytic framework (Laplanche and Pontalis, 1973, pp. 431–3), is also misleading. If it means, as Freud usually said it did, a desexualisation of the aim of infantile sexual impulses, typified *par excellence* by artistic achievement, then we are again concerned with a process too fundamental in the development of mind to be of specifically literary interest. That is, if all art is *a fortiori* a case of sublimation, then we cannot use the concept to distinguish one kind of art from another. Unless it is somehow combined with repression, the word does not suggest the intensification of language and gesture that we find in the Shavian sublime. But we can hardly describe those who write effectively at all, much less writers of genius, as extensively repressed, no matter how peculiar their sexual lives may be. Most people have not salvaged enough energy from childhood for any but the most modest creative achievements. Surely when we talk of intrapsychic conflict in regard to such persons as Bernard Shaw, we are taking for granted a freedom from the more limiting inhibitions.

The two terms in combination, however, suggestively describe the enactment in Shaw of the double process of pressing down and lifting up, the subjection of the cruder components of pleasurable ideas in order to exalt an ego-ideal. If we cannot strictly use Freudian terms with reference to very high levels of mental functioning, we may profitably modify them for our purposes.

Harold Bloom (1976) has pointedly rejected sublimation in favour of repression as a conceptual tool for criticism (p. 25). My disagreement with him on this point is by no means fundamental. What chiefly turns Bloom away from the concept of sublimation is its link with the idea of substitution, implying that art is a secondary world, and I too feel that criticism needs to make an adjustment here. Although he modifies Freud for literary use by knocking out what might be thought the corner-stone of psychoanalytic theory – childhood – and considering only adult and highly sophisticated filiations, he yet preserves the spirit of Freud's dynamic psychology in analysing the deformations of poetic influence.

To appreciate this, we might contrast his use of the term repression with other redefinitions of repression that have influenced criticism, particularly those of Lacan and Derrida. For Lacan 'repression . . . is the tax exacted by the use of language' (Wright, 1984, p. 109). That is, the desire of a subject inscribed in language is always as well the desire of the other and so is basically an illusion, *a méconnaissance.* Derrida's deconstruction 'is simply the examination of what is repressed in order to sustain the distinctions that are crucial to all writing. That writing requires an act of suppression [sic] in order to come into being is the main tenet of deconstructive thought' (Scholes, 1982, p. 107). These concepts of repression have prompted a good many critics to discover repeatedly the illusoriness of subjective identity and of textual meaning. But it is not usually admitted that something is lost in the process. The shift of attention from psychology to logic, and thus from conflict to contradiction, loses the affective quality of Freud's concept of repression. Conflict involves the idea of palpable resistance whereas contradiction leads only to logical play with the idea of negation. It is this dynamic aspect of Freud's thought that Bloom has retained and that the French theorists, by making critical difficulties into categorical impossibilities, have lost.

The passage in Freud that seems to me most pertinent to the view of the Shavian sublime being presented here concerns 'the peculiar narcissistic character of pride.' Its importance must override the fact of an awkward translation:

> Whereas instinctual renunciation, when it is for external reasons, is only unpleasurable, when it is for internal reasons, in obedience to the super-ego, it has a different economic effect. In addition to the inevitable unpleasurable consequences, it also brings the ego a yield of pleasure – a substitutive satisfaction, as it were. The ego feels elevated; it is proud of the instinctual renunciation, as though it were a valuable achievement. (Freud, 1957, vol. xxxiii, pp. 116–17)

The internalisation of external authority (that is, the superego), Freud goes on to say, has in this case become a portion of the ego. Disappointments thus strengthen rather than weaken one's self-esteem. Shaw himself, in non-analytic language, captured Freud's sense of the matter when he wrote to Ellen Terry after learning that she would not play a part he had written for her: 'I have pitched so many dreams out the window that one more or less makes little difference – in fact, by this time I take a certain Satanic delight in doing it and noting how little it hurts me' (*CL* II 148).

One wishes that Freud had not used a phrase like 'substitutive satisfaction' to indicate what could be a 'valuable achievement' for the culture at large as well as the individual, although one understands that, from the genetic perspective he regularly adopted, it made sense to do so. Fortunately, the critic does not need to impose his own modification of the term superego. It has evolved within psychoanalytic literature itself. As attention has shifted from the Oedipus complex to a pregenital model of conflict, Freud's superego has to some extent been replaced by the more flexible concept of the 'ego-ideal', a term that Freud himself once referred to as the heir of primary narcissism. In the words of Christopher Lasch (1984), summarising the development of the ego-ideal within psychoanalytic literature:

> the concept is indispensable [because] it calls attention to the links between the highest and the lowest forms of mental life, between the most exalted aspirations for spiritual transcendence and the earliest illusions of omnipotence and self-sufficiency. It shows how the impulse to restore those illusions expresses itself in regressive fantasies of a magical symbiosis with the world or of absolute self-sufficiency but also in a loving exploration of the world through art, playful scientific curiosity, and the activities of nurture and cultivation.   (p. 179)

With Shaw in mind, we should add that the complementary regressive fantasies of magical symbiosis and absolute self-sufficiency do not in his work receive quite equal emphasis. The dream of merging is irrepressible but is mostly fought off; the image of the strong, mothering woman, on the other hand, looms large, while the threat of her devouring force is deflected by a stress on her own self-sufficiency. And this imbalance has more than personal significance when we consider the relation between the sublime and the beautiful in a Freudian age.

Hume, Burke and Kant were concerned with the perception of magnitude and force in natural bodies and only to a lesser extent in works of art. Kant (1982), in fact, tried to exclude art from the sublime because it was bounded, while having to admit parenthetically that art was only 'restricted by the conditions of an agreement with nature' (para. 23). I infer from this hedging that he sensed an association between natural and human bodies, and tried to keep sexual feeling out of consideration by bounding beauty and keeping the sublime impersonal. One may then say that a return of the repressed has sexualised the meanings of both words – beauty first and more obviously but also the sublime, characterised by a mixture of excitement and anxiety. At the same time, we have learned in a post-Freudian age not to be so alarmed by these affective associations, and it should be possible now to restore the antithesis for critical use. My attempt to do so via Shaw will be reminiscent of Schiller's melting–energising relation before it was moralised and also of the dynamic emphasis in eighteenth-century criticism but with a psychoanalytic slant.

The word beauty (often in association with such other words as romance, love and marriage) connoted for Shaw the relaxed or dissolving will. Dissolution of the will threatened the firmness of ego boundaries and brought into play a heightened assertion of resolution and independence. The idea of beauty stirred in him a profound desire for the ideal symbiosis of infancy and, with it, a fear of being swallowed up or lost as a separate self. Whether the lure is Shakespearean word-music or the charms of Stella Campbell (in a few of his letters, notably *CL* III 95, these particular lures are virtually fused), he is terrified of an enchantment that leaves him 'nothing to seize, nothing to refuse, nothing to resist'. This is 'to have a woman's love on the same terms as a child's . . . everything for nothing' (*CL* III 155).

Shaw often invoked names like Bunyan, Blake and Handel, not so much to make a critical point as to fire up his own will.[5] Similarly, he liked to belittle Shakespeare and Dickens (though he read them 'without shame or stint' – *B* 2: 520), not only to make a defensible point about the dangers of cultism or the historical march of intellect but also to express an objection to their implicit acceptance of human limitation, separateness, incompleteness. His impatience was aroused to the boil by the gorgeous plangencies of Cleopatra or Macbeth or Othello, seductive word-music in the service of tragic resignation. By his very eloquence, Shakespeare glorified and idealised the dissolving will and thereby an accommodation to defeat and death. These grand resignations eroded ego boundaries rather than enlarging and extending them.

I am proposing a distinction, then, between the sublime of the resolving will (illustrated by Bunyan's 'Yet I do not repent me',

Blake's 'I shall not cease from mental fight', and Handel's choralised 'Unto us a Son is born') and a sublime of the dissolving will, which may take several forms. It may be resonantly tragic like the final speeches of Cleopatra and Macbeth. It may be grandly nostalgic like Pater's La Gioconda and Yeats's Celtic Twilight. Or it may be a form of mystical ascesis like the Wordsworth studied by Weiskel and called by him the romantic sublime or like this single line by Hart Crane (1958, p. 62) – 'O Answerer of all, – Anemone – ' – in which selfhood, lying infinitely open to vowel and vortex, is delicately refined out of existence. Tragic, nostalgic and ascetic art are alike here in evoking an ultimate immobility, harmony and peace. I suggest that these qualities of a will-dissolving or melting sublime are what may validly be meant today by the beautiful in art.

Freud's disciple Hanns Sachs (1942), considering the quality of sadness associated with the beautiful in art, observed that most people do not in fact look in art for beauty but for excitement, for what he called 'interest and action'. Beautiful works (Sachs instances the Venus of Milo) tend toward 'the annihilation of all Id drives' by 'striving after permanence, stability, immobility'. They elicit the idea of peace and ultimately of death. 'The sadness of beauty . . . is more than ordinary mortals are able to face in their everyday lives' (pp. 168, 173, 236, 240).

Shaw's artistic sensibilities were, of course, highly developed and ought not to be confused with those of the majority alluded to by Sachs. But in the light of this speculation, his resilient contempt for beauty is remarkable, especially when it is considered along with his extraordinary intolerance of the idea of death, an intolerance that underlies his insistent doctrine of Creative Evolution as well as such notorious idiosyncracies of behaviour as jesting on the occasions of the deaths of his mother, wife and friends. It was congenial for him to identify with a greater power like a Life Force but not to yield his will to such a power.

One may reasonably suppose that Shaw's fear of yielding control in mourning or sexual merging checked a desire to do so, a desire that must have derived from his admitted idealisation of his mother in childhood and that must have been intensified by the presence of two older sisters and a feckless father. Shaw boasted that his mother's 'almost complete neglect of me had the advantage that I could idolize her to the utmost pitch of my imagination and had no sordid or disillusioning contacts with her' (C 33: xv), but the boast sounds rather hollow in the light of his admitting to Ellen Terry the 'frightful self-sufficiency' generated by his 'devil of a childhood'. When he came to write *Pygmalion* he recognized that a son's attachment to an admired mother could cause an arrest of sexual affection, though he explained it as a rational admiration for a real superiority. He was still more candid when he admitted in 1930 that such idealisation can 'sterilize us by giving us imaginary amours on the plains of heaven so magical that they spoil us for real women and real men' (*SSS* 177).

For me the most poignant of Shaw's unconscious self-revelations is a letter he wrote as a young man of twenty-nine to Mrs Pakenham Beatty: 'So like [your infant] brightly and rationally. But dont love him – that will smother him. A woman's love is too much for a child: besides there is always something fierce and selfish in it' (*CL* I 142). Shaw is trying to erase by reversal his own devilish childhood, playing the parent to this mother much the way he played the parent to his own mother and surviving older sister in the coolly advisory letters he wrote to them. But he is advising Mrs Beatty to perpetuate the horror of his own mother's neglect, as if what he really suffered from was too much love, not too little. There is, of course, an indirect truth here. Like D. H. Lawrence, he suffered from an excessive attachment to his mother, aroused no doubt by her coldness. She really does seem to have been impossible to please. Astoundingly she wrote to Archibald Henderson (1932) in 1908, when her ferociously hard-working son had achieved so much fame that a biography of him was being planned, that she looked forward to his book 'with impatience, but I much fear it will be sorely tried if its publication depends on G.B.S.'s preface. He is a dreadful procrastinator' (p. 182).

Shaw's work is filled with images of powerful women. The heroines of the first two plays, Blanche and Julia, like some of the women in the novels, possess force in excess of the dramatic requirements. Yet we sense that these overcharged heroines carry a potentiality of significance, that they represent what the play is trying to become but is not ready to become because of the strength of its author's ambivalence toward the strong woman.[6] As his art refined, Shaw learned to handle this force more subtly, but Raina and Judith Anderson are somewhat overchecked by their men while Candida and Lady Cicely are still too strong for theirs. Gradually Shaw learned to balance his superpersons (*Man and Superman* is the most notable instance) or to allow the woman to evolve into a sort of demon-goddess, like Mrs George in *Getting Married*, Lina in *Misalliance*, Hesione in *Heartbreak House*, the judging female Ancients in *Back to Methuselah* and Epifania Ognisanti di Parerga in *The Millionairess*. Margery Morgan (1972) suggests that Epifania, the ultimate producer, incarnates the spirit of capitalism (p. 327). She is also the ultimate consumer or devourer, who can find no man strong enough to stand with her upon the heights. But Shaw had the imaginative courage to allow his superpersons, from Caesar to Eppy, to feel their loneliness. Although he cherished the idea of being continent or tranquil on the heights, there is really no way in his Eden to be at ease. Within a week of writing to his future wife about tranquillity and self-possession, he is commending to Ellen Terry the blessedness of unsatisfied desire.

This ultimate aspect of the Shavian sublime will be taken up again later, but we need first to show how the process of subliming (that is, of repressing/sublimating) functions concretely. The most specific evidence is provided by Shaw's manipulation of synonyms, his love of polarising associated meanings so as to renovate one at the expense of the other. A famous example is Don Juan's tirade:

> They [the Devil's friends] are not beautiful: they are only decorated. . . . They are not religious: they are only pewrenters. They are not moral: they are only conventional. They are not virtuous: they are only cowardly. They are not even vicious: they are only 'frail'.   (B 2: 681)

And so on to much greater length.

In this passage rhetorical energy seems to derive from an act of verbal polarisation. An improved or sublimated meaning springs from the very repression of a grosser meaning. Similar examples abound, and may be introduced casually: the mirror-less and upholstery-less Egyptian palace of *Caesar and Cleopatra* is '*handsome, wholesome, simple and cool, or, as a rich English manufacturer would express it, poor, bare, ridiculous and unhomely*' (B 2: 195).

The earnestness of this wit is perhaps more evident when we observe Shaw subjecting a particular word or phrase to the very process of transvaluation. He writes: 'Pragmatism means making the best of people as they are; and what they are depends on what they believe' (*EPWW* 232). The first half of this statement seems to submit to a common meaning of the term, but the second half improves on it to show what pragmatism should mean or really means. Again, notice his manipulation of a phrase like 'natural historian'. Shaw was fond of claiming that label for himself, but we see that he manages not to separate 'natural' from 'moral':

> You are an economic revolutionary on a medieval moral basis of pure chivalry – Bayard educated by Marx. I am a moral revolutionary interested, not in the class war, but in the struggle between human vitality, and the artificial system of morality, and distinguishing not between capitalist & proletarian, but between moralist and natural historian.   (*CL* II 163)

Observe in this important letter to a fellow Socialist that the word moral does double duty: 'moralist' is tarred by association with romantic chivalry and an artificial system while 'moral revolutionary' is logically linked with 'natural historian'.

Notice again what happens to the phrase 'genuinely scientific natural history' in the following often-quoted declaration:

> The tragedy and comedy of life lie in the consequences, sometimes terrible, sometimes ludicrous, of our persistent attempts to found our institutions on the ideals suggested to our imaginations by our half-satisfied passions, instead of on a genuinely scientific natural history'.   (*C* 8: xix)

The phrase is made to mean not what is actually the case but, in a Platonic sense, what is really the case, that is, what ought to be. This is but a version of the dialectical strategy that pervades *The Quintessence of Ibsenism* whereby the ideal and the real are identified respectively with 'is' and 'ought', reversing our common sense of that antithesis.

Often Shaw will use a 'respectable' word, like gentleman, with irony:

> MENDOZA [*posing loftily*].   I am a brigand. I live by robbing the rich.
> TANNER [*promptly*].   I am a gentleman. I live by robbing the poor.   (*B* 2: 621)

But if possible he will try to reclaim it, as when he selected as a topic of debate with G. K. Chesterton the resolution 'I assert that a Democrat who is not also a Socialist is no gentleman' (*CL* III 53).

One might call it a harrowing of the vocabulary of hell. Certainly 'passion' is one of those words that he was unwilling to surrender to the devil. 'Is the devil to have all the passions as well as all the good tunes?' cries out an exasperated John Tanner (B 2: 571). After all, 'intellect is a passion' (ST 185) and 'moral passion is the only real passion' (B 2: 571). In the preface to *Major Barbara* Shaw spiritedly attacks conventional playgoers for whom 'Passion, the life of drama, means nothing . . . but primitive sexual excitement' (B 3: 34). This word he wrests away from the tribe with particular energy, perceiving perhaps the strength of the conventional usage.

The word 'art' also required a working over, for it was associated, on the one hand, with dignity and refinement, on the other, with idleness and luxury. Like his novelistic protagonist Trefusis, Shaw was roused by the fact that one word – art – was used to describe both one of the most exalted and one of the most dishonest of human activities. What is called art often panders to and flatters the status quo (NDW 364). Yet 'fine art is the subtlest, the most seductive, the most effective instrument of moral propaganda in the world' (B 1: 236). The fact that 'art for art's sake' was a phrase that excited his scorn can hardly be taken as proof that Shaw did not also revere art. More than a few passages celebrate the word with a fierce eloquence that suggests a release from constraint (B 1: 25, 236; B 4: 121, 315; CL I 385, 398, 461, 589; P&P 20; OTN II 96). One such passage nicely captures the very process of transvaluation:

> For it must not be supposed that the poets and artists are the romantic people, and their readers and audiences the matter-of-fact people. On the contrary, it is the poets and artists who spend their lives in trying to make the unreal real; whereas the ordinary man's struggle is to escape from reality, to avoid all avoidable facts and deceive himself as to the real nature of those which he cannot avoid.   (SM 3: 98)

The phrase 'on the contrary' serves as a pivot, turning a truism into a misconception and revealing a surprising, paradoxical truth. In dramatic forms, this truth may be more extended and less overt: Octavius in *Man and Superman* is a seeming artist, sweet and ineffectual, whereas Tanner, though a self-styled revolutionary, proves by his energetic use of language to be a true artist on the robust, Shavian model.

It is not surprising that the strain of effecting these transvalu-
ations, of remaking the language of the tribe, should occasionally
become too great. For it may involve repressing what one also
really loves, since Shaw at his best is wrestling with his own
feelings, not simply scolding other people. The most striking
instance of breakdown (of a return of the repressed) in Shaw's
vocabulary is the word 'romance'. Usually it is scorned: 'Don't talk
to me of romances: I was sent into the world expressly to dance
on them with thick boots, to shatter, stab and murder them' (*CL*
I 163). Sometimes it will peep around the corner after a strenuous
suppression, as when the super-prosaic Bluntschli is finally exposed
as a romantic. But occasionally it will be indulged. Especially under
the potent influence of his middle-aged infatuation with Stella
Campbell, Shaw let his vocabulary riot. His letters to her are laced
with the rhetoric of a third-rate Rossetti. The anti-romantic now
cherishes 'romantic glamor', 'delightful dreams', 'a thousand beau-
ties', 'a figure from the dreams of my boyhood – all romance',
'wild happiness' vs. 'loathsome conscience'. He tells her: 'I want
my Virgin Mother enthroned in heaven. . . . my dark lady . . . my
Freia with her apples. . . . my day's wage, my night's dream, my
darling and my star' (*CL* III 96, 136, 150–1, 153, 185).

We must allow Shaw his portion of ordinary human foolishness,
and can at least grant him in the Campbell correspondence a
measure of insight into the infantile origin of his infatuation,
illustrated for example, by the nicely placed comma in the sentence:
'I should like to spend an hour every day with you, in the nursery'
(Dent, 1952, p. 75).[7] In fact, it contains not unrelated insight into
his art as well: 'My plays must be acted, and acted hard. They need
a sort of bustle and crepitation of life which requires extraordinary
energy and vitality, and gives only glimpses and movements of
the poetry beneath. The lascivious monotony of beauty . . . is
hideous in my plays' (ibid., pp. 23–4). This is shrewd and directori-
ally useful self-evaluation. He knows that. Dreaminess is not a
congenial atmosphere for plays whose actors should, he knew,
'exaggerate the contrasts' (*CL* IV 15).

Yet the claims of romance must be heard before they are denied
or Shaw's wit and eloquence do not work. More than any other,
the subject of marriage considered in its sexual aspect seemed to
stupefy his rhetoric: 'Every thoughtful and observant minister of
religion is troubled by [the fact that] the known libertines of his
parish are visibly suffering much less from sexual intemperance

than many of the married people who stigmatize them as monsters of vice' (*B* 3: 461). This facile statement has the form of many of Shaw's best thrusts: X (an acknowledged evil like war or prison or in this case libertinism) is not nearly so bad as Y (a seemingly innocent condition like poverty or school or, in this case, marriage). But the wit is weak. Shaw needs to stand back from the subject of sex and marriage just enough to let his ambivalence find expression, as when Dick Dudgeon, about to repudiate Mrs Anderson, finds the hearth-and-home atmosphere she epitomises distasteful but 'almost holy' (*B* 2: 94). Or as when he reported, in the wake of repeated physical mishaps: 'My objection to my own marriage had ceased with my objection to my own death' (*CL* II 51).

Literary strength and emotional limitation are closely allied here, for the subject of sex or marriage, if not sex *in* marriage, is the crux of his most recurrent polarisation, the forcing apart of happiness and greatness. Happiness, associated with marriage, is 'despised' as far back as 1883 in a 'love letter' to Alice Lockett (*CL* I 68). In the plays it becomes a spur, not merely a sour taste. Marchbanks is the first of Shaw's dramatic figures to make explicit this particular *gran rifiuto*, claiming 'I no longer desire happiness: life is nobler than that' (*B* 1: 594). Thereafter it recurs in half a dozen plays, most memorably in *Man and Superman* in which the protagonist, after extending masculine diffidence to unprecedented lengths, makes a final speech defining his forthcoming marriage as a renunciation of happiness for strength (*B* 2: 732); and in *Heartbreak House* where the end of romantic hope provides the heroine with an accession of what Shotover, who himself dreads happiness, enthusiastically calls strength and genius (*B* 5: 148–9). *Caesar and Cleopatra* is interesting in this regard because the pertinent speech ('Now . . . I do what must be done and have no time to attend to myself. That is not happiness; but it is greatness' – *B* 2: 256) is given to Caesar's tutee Cleopatra who will soon practice revenge and thus show herself an imperfect student of her teacher.

The secret underlying the strength of this sort of hyperbole in Shaw is the energy he invested in resisting the vibrant questing for the heights. Such resistance is essential to his art, and in its various forms may be subsumed under the heading of the comic spirit. Learning how to interrelate the comic and the sublime is in a sense the whole story of Shaw's imagination, but we can get some sharply focused insight into his technique by noticing how he modified, or absorbed the influence of, two of his principal masters, Ibsen and Dickens.

From Ibsen he learned an important stratagem for developing comic irony in the heroic mode, the separation of sin and sinner, of questionable conduct and good intention. With his comprehensive Socialist vision as background support, Shaw would extend the tonal range of Ibsenite tragi-comedy in two directions, toward the sublime by imagining heroes capable of transvaluing the ideals of their societies, and toward farce by imagining the absurdities involved in heroism whose field of action is a society dominated by a bourgeoisie. In working out the farcical aspect of his comedy, on the other hand, Shaw was greatly indebted to Dickens, who taught him how to relish, not merely articulate, the egotism of all-too-human souls. A character like Lickcheese in his first play is Ibsenite in that his complacent self-justification reflects false social ideals, and Dickensian in that the style of his self-justification is so broadly ironical that it mocks the speaker and draws us toward an opposite conclusion. Each of these major influences requires fuller comment.

In Ibsen, Shaw was fascinated above all by the technique of exposing as villains certain figures who meant well – Torvald Helmer in *A Doll's House*, Pastor Manders in *Ghosts* (via Mrs Alving, who lets herself be influenced by him), Gregers Werle in *The Wild Duck*, and Rosmer of *Rosmersholm*. Principles and conduct which an audience was accustomed to think of as virtuous and even noble were shown here to have destructive consequences. These figures seemed to exemplify a new possibility for serious drama. Since their ignorance was encouraged by the social ideals they upheld, much of the responsibility for the harm they did fell on their society at large.

But if the two dramatists agreed that the community idealised its own morality in order to think well of itself, Shaw departs from Ibsen in implying that it does so in order to prevent itself from recognising its own potential heroism. He was right to say that Ibsen wounds our complacency, unlike the popular English dramatists whom Shaw reviewed in the 1890s, but Ibsen was not so sanguine as his disciple about the educative and self-transforming powers of his heroes and, more often, heroines. He was more suspicious of greatness, though no lover of community.

Nora Helmer's future is sufficiently open-ended that several writers composed sequels to her story, including the youthful Shaw who not very credibly brought her back to educate Krogstad in the vital truth that men no less than women must escape the doll's house of respectability.[8] But the sombreness of her departure is underlined by the parallel between her future circumstances and the past ones of her hard pressed acquaintance, Mrs Linde (Northam, 1965, p. 106). Mrs Alving doubted whether Manders's advice to stay with her licentious husband was sound, but was too weak to act accordingly, and cannot now prevent the catastrophe. Significantly, Shaw paraphrased the plot of *Ghosts* so as to imply that Mrs Alving is presented as an active protagonist rather than a passive witness to the consequences of prior events (Turco, 1976, p. 48). Rebecca West followed her desire so far as to drive her lover's wife to her death, but suffers from a guilty conscience and comes to a tragic end. The challenge for Shaw, with his Shelleyan and Wagnerian passion for reforming the world, was to work out in his own dramatisations an alternative mode of unmasking, one that kept the problem in the drama open to the possibility of a hopeful future.

He soon learned to accelerate the education of morally naïve characters, showing that it was not too late to escape the influence of the past. Vivie Warren learns first to acknowledge the claims of her mother's deliberate complicity with an unjust society but finally to rise above even that general guilt and ascend, bare but buoyant, into her own heaven. Raina Petkoff has discovered through Bluntschli the artificiality of her romantic attitude toward love and war, and is ready by the end of the last act to put even him in his place. For such a change to be credible within the span of a play, the false idea must be shown as not too deeply rooted. It must seem an aspect of a more educable social neurosis and not at the same time, as with Ibsen, a less educable individual neurosis. Such plays as *Mrs Warren's Profession* and *Arms and the Man* dramatise Marx's version of self-deception rather than anticipating Freud's. Toward that end Shaw abandoned (after his early 'unpleasant plays') Ibsen's retrospective method, and exploited the resources of farce, accelerating and exaggerating the action.

It should be made clear that Shavian farce usually stops short of a commitment to the farcical mode, which, in Margery Morgan's (1972) definition, 'concentrates on the mechanistic process of violent action and plays down or disregards its emotional content' (p. 199). It is closer to the tradition of comedy than of farce, Stanley

Kauffmann (1986) reminds us, because it tends both to render character and 'to aim toward amendment and change' (p. 36). Shaw liked to call himself a dramatic realist, by which he meant that he was careful to preserve psychological truth despite the exaggerations of dialogue and incident. 'Absurdity is the one thing that does not matter on the stage', he wrote, adding, 'as long as it is not psychological absurdity' (*OTN* iii 18). His riposte, 'A Dramatic Realist to His Critics', makes a point of explaining that the sudden collapse of Raina's romantic attachment to Sergius in the face of Bluntschli's scepticism – a charge objected to by his critics – was both credible and honourable in spite of the farcical surface (*B* 1: 509). Shaw at his best is able to make farce suggest the gaiety of mind implicit, as he wrote Florence Farr, in 'all genuinely intellectual work' (*CL* i 332).

He expressed distaste for artificial comedy, even for such elegant artifice as Restoration and Wildean comedy, because the laughter-generating surprises did not arise from a deep enough reality to disturb our self-satisfaction. They did not challenge a conventional attitude with a subversively vital one. 'The Importance of Being Earnest . . . amused me, of course; but unless comedy touches me as well as amuses me, it leaves me with a sense of having wasted my evening. I go to the theatre to be moved to laughter, not to be tickled or bustled into it' (*OTN* i 42; cf. *C* 29: 302 and *CL* iv 871). One could and should consider this opinion illustrative of one limit of Shaw's sensibility – his refusal to recognise Wilde's profound subversion of the Victorian ideals of work and progress. He did after all make use of Wilde: the figure of Lady Bracknell certainly lies behind such successful Shavian creations as Lady Britomart and Ariadne Utterword, and probably the figure of Wilde himself is encoded in Don Juan's Devil. But it is true that Wilde does not use farcical situations to imbed symbolic truth, does nothing comparable, for example, to Shaw's use of Cusins's casuistic account of his foundling status as a hint that he is in spirit the true son of Andrew Undershaft. Morgan (1972) comments that Shaw often flaunts the arbitrariness of incident because he 'is not dramatizing a story with a moral, but creating a dramatic image of his conflicting emotions and ideas' (p. 149). I would further suggest that farce, like paradoxical wit, is congenial to the sublime mode because accelerated and exaggerated physical actions may imply corresponding psychological ones. The lyric and the novel seem better able to convey the inwardness of the sublime experience,

but the confrontational aspect of drama can highlight the dynamics
of sudden emergence and rapid inflation, as well as the perspectival
clash of higher and lower levels of consciousness. For much the
same reason, perhaps, Shaw liked, as Bentley (1967) observed, the
manners if not the ethic of melodrama (p. 212).

Shaw's farce, then, is not to be confused with burlesque, even
though the later work is often marred by facile reversals of
expectation. Especially in the early plays, before the prevalence
of discussion itself slows down the action, the physical and
circumstantial unmasking typical of farce serves the end of psychological and moral revelation.

In *The Quintessence*, written just before the launching of his major
career as a playwright, an unmasking process, an education in
hygienic disillusionment, is imagined as proceeding from a solitary
'realist' directed against a large group of 'idealists', who are intent
on preserving those Victorian ideals, the Womanly Woman and
the Angel in the House, and a still larger group of so-called
Philistines, who are innocent bystanders in regard to the marriage
question, finding the arguments theoretic and of little force when
it comes to budging their attachment to available, conventional
pleasures.

The scheme has a whimsical, shrewd wit, but its application to
the plays, despite admirable efforts by Nethercot, Wisenthal and
others, is not in my view quite successful. There is too much
movement and even mixing among these types. Ann Whitefield is
no mere Philistine since her heroic energy is parallel to Tanner's.
The Devil is no mere Idealist since the cogency of his arguments is
comparable to those of Don Juan. Undershaft cannot quite be
called a Realist since his function is, like Wotan's, to yield finally
to a more truly heroic vision that he has helped to create. And the
scheme seems even less pertinent to plays like *John Bull's Other
Island* and *Heartbreak House* in which the theme is the fragmentation
of heroic consciousness itself.

Nor, I think, does it fit even the plays of the 1890s very well.
The realist–unmasker is hardly unscathed. Charteris, Bluntschli
and Dudgeon are mocked to a degree; the higher ground gained
by Vivie and Caesar is paid for by a measure of loneliness; and it
appears at the end of *Candida* that realist and idealist have in some
fashion changed places. More important, those who are unmasked
make telling arguments, up to a point, against the urge for
perfection. They provide a resistance to the sublime that gives it

an ironical edge and rhetorical tension. Without Mrs Warren's articulate and convincing endorsement of a lower realism, Vivie's leap to a higher realism would lose its dramatic power. Without the temptation of domestic peace embodied in Judith Anderson, Dick Dudgeon's noble deed would have more theoretic than dramatic interest. Without the efforts of ordinary mortals to understand Caesar, his superiority would not sufficiently engage the human situation. Actually what makes the scheme of *The Quintessence* most misleading is that the 'Philistines' therein described are upgraded in the plays and merged with the idealists as resisters of a higher consciousness. They are made articulate and blandly self-possessed, like the superservants in *Arms and the Man*, the waiter of *You Never Can Tell* and Burgoyne in *The Devil's Disciple*.

It is this empathetic appreciation of a lower realism, manifestly learned from Dickens, that I wish to stress here, for it becomes in Shaw an essential component of the comic sublime.

Shaw described himself to Chesterton as 'a supersaturated Dickensite' (*CL* II 646), and the Dan Laurence and Martin Quinn edition called *Shaw on Dickens*, along with the bibliographical researches of Edgar Rosenberg, certainly supports his own hunch that his work contains more references and allusions to Dickens than to any other writers. What he chiefly learned from the novelist was how to render the idiom of another's egotism, the style of another's self-justification, while the character is unwittingly satirising himself. P. N. Furbank (1968), introducing *Martin Chuzzlewit*, attacks the idea that Dickens created fixed little caricatures from the outside, and describes what in fact he did do in a way that provides a fine insight into Shaw's comic genius as well:

> In creating [characters like Pecksniff and Gamp] he uses his talent for comic invention in a curious way – he doesn't so much employ it to depict them, as lend it to them for their own use. And that is why one comes away from the novel sensing a complicity between Dickens and his hypocrites. Both Pecksniff and Mrs Gamp have a wild and daring imagination and the most exquisite command of phrase. (p. xxvi)[9]

From Mrs Warren and Mrs Dudgeon (the latter specifically modelled on Mrs Gargery and Mrs Clenham) down to the Mussolini figure Bombardone in *Geneva* we see this Dickensian talent on display.

Northrop Frye (1970) commented that, 'Like Blake, like every writer with any genuine radicalism in him, Dickens finds the really dangerous social evils in those which have achieved some acceptance by being rationalized' (p. 270). Shaw certainly belongs in this group. Consistently he attacks respectability rather than crime: 'I came not to call sinners but the righteous to repentance' (*B* 5: 478). Although Dickens and Shaw usually made these rational-isations funny, theirs was a serious kind of joking and did not obscure their moral indignation. The fun of Dickens, Shaw observed, would end in 'mere tomfoolery' without his 'capacity for taking pains': 'The high privilege of joking in public should never be granted except to people who know thoroughly what they are joking about – that is, to exceptionally serious and laborious people' (*SM* 2: 892–3). Although their comedy in a sense distances us from evils, it also, by virtue of its irony, implicates us in them.

The radicalism of the Dickensian vision is somewhat restricted in that it is bound up with the ethic of melodrama, with the conception of a society that will finally mete out appropriate justice to inherently good and bad people. Shaw does not share this vision of society, but his radicalism is also limited by the fact that his world contains no outright villains, only persons whose understanding is compromised by ignorance and by the kind of egoism that finds its necessary support in social proprieties. As Chesterton (1956) pointed out, his attacks, though lethal, are directed at 'certain ideals', not at 'particular men' (p. 27). He attacks the unconscious assumption while finding the rationalisation itself beguiling. 'Has there ever been a satirist', Gilbert Murray (1951) wondered 'so free of personal malice' (p. 8)? That is why his hypocrites (for example, Ann Whitefield and Alfred Doolittle) can be enchanting, his prigs and dolts (for example, Stephen Undershaft and Charles Lomax) endearing. Only occasionally – and always disastrously – does he truly jeer at one of his characters: Burgess in *Candida*, the journalist in *The Doctor's Dilemma*, Spintho in *Androcles and the Lion*, De Stogumber in *Saint Joan*.

It is difficult, therefore, to describe Shaw as a satirist, even in the complex sense that Dickens was a satirist, for the Shelleyan or visionary strain is compounded with the satirical in his sensibility. The two elements are most intricately mixed in the major plays.

John Tanner is not simply mocked for a parting moment like Bluntschli but is both teacher and learner throughout the comedy and is transformed in the dream sequence into a vehicle for an outrightly visionary point of view. Barbara Undershaft, though stripped of her faith, renews it at a higher level, while her unmasking father is finally not so much unmasked by her and Cusins as dissolved in them, finally more of a dialectical principle than a character. Peter Keegan is a vehicle of vision and his rival Broadbent of satire on soulless efficiency, but Keegan's despairing powerlessness is also emphasised and so is Broadbent's praiseworthy pragmatism. Captain Shotover and Hector Hushabye are hostile to the society they know yet exemplify its inadequacy. It is pleasant to think that the most complete dramatic image of Shaw's desire is that of the ex-wrestler turned salvationist (Todger Fairmile in *Major Barbara*) enforcing the conversion of a prostrate Bill Walker by a combination of prayer and muscle power, of good and the means of good. But of course, the very drollery of the image indicates the unsatisfactoriness of a simple description.

Shaw asserted, 'I have never written a satire in my life' (*B* 4: 820), and one can see what he means. The term implies criticalness without idealism. 'I never burlesque anything; on the contrary, it is my business to find some order and meaning in the apparently insane farce' (*B* 3: 188). 'Great humor', he insisted, 'is serious' (*SM* III 582). That is why some such phrase as visionary satire – reminiscent of the kind of satire to be found in Blake or Carlyle or Kierkegaard – seems useful to describe the distinctive quality of his art and thought. The cutting edge is typically pointed at the normal and good – what decent people do – for the sake of the supernormal or better. He could, of course, turn the edge the other way, against the egotism of the hero, and show the normal in a sympathetic light, which he does so impressively in *Pygmalion*. But he had little interest in, or tolerance for, the subnormal, the pathological or the criminal. Shaw's moral vision is made psychologically interesting by his appreciation of the role of fear in the formation of attitudes. ('There is only one universal passion: fear', according to his Napoleon in *The Man of Destiny* – *B* 1: 630.) But it is not after all a tragic vision, seeking out the darkest and coarsest in human nature.

It should be understood that Shaw's resistance to the elements of tragedy was principled: 'I do not want there to be any more pity in the world because I do not want there to be anything to pity;

and I want there to be no more terror because I do not want people
to have anything to fear' (*ST* 197). Fired by such conviction, tragedy
becomes, as Bloom (1985) said it became for Shelley, 'the falling
away from imaginative conduct on the part of a heroically minded
individual' (p. 17).

But however committed to the mode of comedy, a Shavian attack
disconcerts as it strikes home by showing us that we are better
than we are rather than worse. The aggressivity of scorn strips off
the repression of a latent moral energy. We read of 'the man of
business who goes on Sunday to the church with the regularity of
the village blacksmith, there to renounce and abjure before his
God the line of conduct which he intends to pursue with all his
might during the following week' (*C* 30: 7). The hypocrisy involved
here is so familiar as to seem beyond our responsibility; it is part
of what we lazily learn to think of as the human condition. But
the comic abruptness of the contrast is peculiarly incisive. Under
cover of laughing at human absurdity, Shaw's rhetoric forces an
underlying cynicism to the surface, seeks to make us ashamed of
our acceptance of things as they are and to rouse our receptivity
to a more honourable point of view. A similarly serious wit char-
acterises many Shavian jibes that seem on the surface to be merely
flat insults: 'When any person objects to an Ibsen play because
it does not hold the mirror up to his own mind, I can only remind
him that a horse might make the same objection' (*OTN* iii 30).
Since we are not horses, this apparent insult is telling us that
we are capable of finer artistic responses than we think we are.

The force of Shavian assertion should not conceal from the critic
the subtlety of its irony: 'Mrs Warren's defence of herself is not
only bold and specious, but valid and unanswerable. But it is no
defence at all of the vice which she organizes' (*B* 1: 255). The 'not
only' construction prompts us to expect a logic of succeeding
degree rather than of contradiction. But Shaw is mounting a
dialectic that turns contradiction into something like succeeding
degree. After the first 'but' exposes the element of truth in
falsehood, the second indicates the partiality of that truth from a
more comprehensive point of view. A deceptively casual style may
obscure a complex irony: 'As a matter of fact, I am overrated as an
author: most great men are' (*P&P* 37). Self-deflation in the first
statement is itself undermined by the unexpectedly vain second,
yet the two together constitute another, more interesting kind of
self-criticism.

Shaw's rhetoric is active, insinuating, maieutic. In a sense it is therefore didactic and polemical. But it is not doctrinaire. We cannot reduce any of his dramas of ideas to a social or political issue, as Raymond Williams (1969) does: 'Shaw is able to tell us, by naming a problem, what each play is about – slum landlordism, doctrinaire free love, prostitution, militarism, marriage – and the phrase is always an adequate explanation' (pp. 246–7). Nor does any of the plays really preach (with the possible exception of *Blanco Posnet*), though they are full enough of preachers. Shaw's art lived up to the claim that 'your great dramatic poet is never a socialist, nor an individualist, nor a positivist, nor a materialist, nor any other sort of "ist," though he comprehends all the "isms," and is generally quoted by all sections as an adherent' (*ST* 62). He was, I believe, justified in telling Virginia Woolf, who queried him about Roger Fry and economics, 'I am an artist to my finger tips' (*CL* IV 556).

Part of the critical difficulty is that didactic tends to be confused with doctrinaire. And Shaw complicates the task of a critic who would try to rescue his didactic art, for he uses the adjective aggressively. But it should be easy enough to see that he uses it either disingenuously and impishly (as when he described *Pygmalion* as 'intensely and deliberately didactic' on the grounds that it dramatises the 'dry' subject of phonetics – *B* 4: 663) or else provocatively as a dialectical manoeuvre to discredit genteel and sentimental art in favour of a robust realism, in favour precisely of the kind of play that dares to put on the stage a slum landlord and a prostitute.[10] This provocative spirit governs the quotation Williams alludes to and governs also the flaunting subtitle used for *Widowers' Houses* in its first performance: 'An Original Realistic Didactic Play' (*ThC* 21).

The prefaces, of course, sometimes resemble tracts, but consider carefully this tract-like sample:

Mrs Warren's Profession was written in 1894 to draw attention to the truth that prostitution is caused, not by female depravity and male licentiousness, but simply by underpaying, undervaluing, and overworking women so shamefully that the poorest of them are forced to resort to prostitution to keep body and soul together. . . . Also I desired to expose the fact that prostitution is carried on without organization by individual enterprise . . .

but organized and exploited as a big international commerce.
(*B*1: 231)

He would 'draw attention to the truth' and 'expose the fact', but,
in the play, the presumptive cause of prostitution is an argument
put forward by one of the characters and has dramatic force much
less because of its insight into a social problem than because it is
surprising yet credible that Mrs Warren would believe and defend
it. One little manuscript change nicely indicates how careful Shaw
was to avoid imposing on his characters a critical judgement that
was his rather than theirs. He had originally written for Vivie,
when she confronts her mother in act 2, 'I don't believe in
circumstances – at least not after a certain point' (British Library
MS 50598). The phrase following the dash is the voice of a social
critic, judiciously balancing the importance of circumstance and
character in assessing motivation. Shaw wisely omitted these
words in revision, making Vivie's challenge more passionate and
individual, the voice of a temperament rather of authorial scruple.

This is not at all to say that Shaw wrote without bias. As Gilbert
Murray (1951) aptly remarked, 'he never wrote as a judge, always
as an accuser or an advocate' (p. 8). Indeed, he erected frank and
open bias into a critical principle. 'In taking your side, don't trouble
about its being the right side . . . but be sure that it is really yours,
and then back it for all you are worth' (*CL* i 722). 'Never in my life
have I penned an impartial criticism; and I hope I never may. . . .
One must, of course, know the facts, and that is where the critic's
skill comes in; but a moral has to be drawn from the facts, and
that is where his bias comes out' (*SM* 2: 666). Passionately he
warned Archibald Henderson against the dangers of judiciousness
even in writing a biography of G. B. S.: 'Be as accurate as you can;
but as to being just, who are you that you should be just? That is
mere American childishness. Write boldly according to your bent:
say what you WANT to say and not what you think you ought to
say or what is right or just or any such arid nonsense' (*CL* ii 516).

These are not excuses for self-indulgence. They are vigorous
advocacies of a precept that since Shaw's time has gained ground
even within the academy, though more in theory than in practice:
namely, that critical judgement cannot repose upon stable ground,
that the critic's subjectivity is necessarily involved in interpretation
and therefore should not be left out of account. Shaw was more
interested in the psychological than the philosophical aspect of

this argument. He sensed that a coolly reasoned attack was often the more offensive because it tended to veil personal dislike. His own unselfconscious style of attack proved in fact remarkably inoffensive, perhaps disarming. (Frank Swinnerton (1950) jibed that Shaw wooed the English 'with all the blandishments of insult' (p. 47) and might have added that the wooing was successful.) There is a good deal of psychological truth as well as personal pride in the rationale of his technique: 'When, as a critic or debater, I *have* to inflict pain I do it like a dentist, with great reluctance, and with all the anaesthesia I can produce. But note that as nothing is so maladroit as any show of sparing the victim's feelings I always hit out as exultantly as I can. . . . I like my man to feel that he has had a good fight and been worthy of my steel, and not that I have been showing off my good taste at his expense' (*CL* IV 169).

This unselfconscious openness enabled Shaw to hit out with exceptional impunity. It also energised his style by impassioning his conviction. 'Effectiveness of assertion is the Alpha and Omega of Style' (*B2*: 527). The passionate style is the core, the assertion itself only the shell. Shaw quoted with approval Nietzsche's dictum: 'Convictions are prisons' (*OTN* II 93). Yet convictions were useful because, fuelled by inevitably ambivalent passion, they were likely to clash with contrary convictions and generate a dramatic rhetoric.

When it came to practising the specific art of drama, Shaw knew the importance of subduing belief to temperament. Although he wrote dramas of ideas, 'there is only one way to dramatise an idea; and that is by putting on stage a human being possessed by that idea, yet none the less a human being with all the human impulses which make him akin and therefore interesting to us' (*SM* 3: 444). Usually his dialogue is faithful to this precept and to a related one as well, set forth finely in a youthful letter explaining that in 'good dialogue, such as you will find in great perfection in Shakespeare and Molière . . . each speech provokes the one which follows, so that instead of a series of statements, or a mere catechism, you have the play of one person's mind on another's, expressing a state of feeling sprung, coaxed or startled into existence by the other' (*CL* I 52). Here, in an early play, is an exchange between two people in a concrete situation who are feeling each other out:

VIVIE.   . . . *Now* you know the sort of perfectly splendid modern young lady I am. How do you think I shall get on with my mother?

PRAED [*startled*].   Well, I hope – er –

VIVIE.   It's not so much what you hope as what you believe, that I want to know.

PRAED.   Well, frankly, I am afraid your mother will be a little disappointed. Not from any shortcoming on your part, you know: I dont mean that. But you are so different from her ideal.

VIVIE.   Her what?!

PRAED.   Her ideal.

VIVIE.   Do you mean her ideal of ME?

PRAED.   Yes.

VIVIE.   What on earth is it like?

PRAED.   Well, you must have observed, Miss Warren, that people who are dissatisfied with their own bringing up generally think that the world would be all right if everybody were to be brought up quite differently. Now your mother's life has been – er – I suppose you know –

VIVIE.   Dont suppose anything, Mr Praed. I hardly know my mother.   (*B* 1: 278–9)

Vivie's anxious boldness and Praed's kindly timidity are so credibly done that it would be crude to affix such labels on them as New Woman and Idealist, although a conflict along these lines is being developed. Shaw really did make good on his claim that 'People's ideas . . . are not the true stuff of drama, which is always the naïve feeling underlying the ideas' (*OTN* II 192). The figure of the menacing Crofts in the same play further justifies his related claim that every character must 'have fair play & be taken from their own point of view' (British Library MS 50643; *CL* II 882).

But it is, of course, true that Shaw's characters are unlike Shakespeare's in being associated with positions regarding the morality of conduct which they are ready to defend. The characters in Shavian comedy are not merely in situations but in defensible positions, according to his precept that people in false positions are not interesting. Shaw objected that Shakespeare's heroes were motivated by passions rather than principles. These passions were grand enough to exempt the poet from any charge of self-pity and prove his bitterness to be no mere grievance but an 'outrageous gaiety' (*C* 29: 124). But the heroes of these plays were not auton-omous agents, animated like Bunyan's Christian by faith, hope and courage: 'Only one man in them all . . . believes in life, enjoys life, thinks life worth living, and has a sincere, unrhetorical tear dropped on his deathbed; and that man – Falstaff' (*OTN* III 1). It is quite a trick to transform Shakespeare's most famous coward into his only true hero.

Still, there is a point in this extravagant attack, even if it is not surely made. (It is brought forward more ably in the Epistle Dedicatory to *Man and Superman.*) Bunyan's allegorical art aside, how could the capaciousness of the Shakespearian world view – which hardly recognises the existence, let alone the oppressiveness, of conventional morality – be fitted to the bourgeois world that confronted Shaw at the end of the nineteenth century? Heroic energy would have to find expression in an attack on the constraints of established institutions. Shaw proudly accepted the challenge on behalf of his contemporaries but sometimes admitted as well the inevitable limitation: 'A Doll's House will be as flat as ditchwater when A Midsummer Night's Dream will still be as fresh as paint; but it will have done more work in the world; and that is enough' (*ST* 63).

Extravagant as Shaw is when he exalts his own kind of art at the expense of Shakespeare's, he is very perceptive and enlightening when he does so at the expense of Pinero, Jones and Grundy:

> Consider that the one overwhelming characteristic of my plays is the friction between people on different planes of thought, of character, of civilization & of class prejudice (the overwhelming characteristic of the ordinary Pinero–Jones–Grundy plays being that all the characters are on exactly the same planes in these respects, and the friction is purely external & artificial) . . . (*CL* II 303)

To this list may certainly be added W. S. Gilbert who, in contrast to Samuel Butler, turns familiar sentiments inside out simply for the fun of it, to get a laugh, rather than to challenge the morality of his audience (*C* 29: 68–9). Even Meredith, who shows some awareness in his 'Essay on Comedy' that the common sense he wishes to protect is fragile, will not imagine a validly subversive comedy that ridicules self-satisfied, unconscious assumptions and 'produces a positive enjoyment of disillusionment' (*OTN* III 84f.).

In contrast, Shaw accords some empathy to characters who maintain existing social attitudes yet, at the same time, he creates others who take up a revolutionary stance beyond them. The conflict dramatised will, then, not simply be manufactured out of social circumstances while the playwright stays comfortably within a set of audience-shared assumptions. Instead, one moral system will be pitted against another, and the work will be resonant with inner debate, a society's as well as an individual's. Shaw wrote to Pinero: 'You have done everything except the one final thing: you have not given yourself away' (*CL* II 833). We should understand that, by 'giving oneself away', Shaw did not mean simply replacing one morality with another. 'In Shaw's plays, as in Ibsen's, current morality is challenged, but it is not replaced by any ready-made substitute.' For them, Wisenthal (1979) goes on to say, 'morality must be relative to circumstances', and 'this moral relativism . . . is probably the most important of the many links between [them]' (p. 73). If Shaw does not belong with Shakespeare, he does belong with an authentic dramatic poet of his own period like Ibsen.[11]

I have rebutted at some length the charge against Shaw of doctrinaire didacticism, but my conscience is not entirely easy. Perhaps I can point most quickly to the remaining problem by citing his own defence, in a remark to Hesketh Pearson, against the charge often heard, and answered with unusual vehemence in a letter to Archer (*CL* II 417–18), that his characters were all puppets or self-portraits: 'All my characters are Shaws, but to say that they are all self-portraits is silly. You must not let yourself be overwhelmed by my style' (Pearson, 1950, p. 38). Shaw makes a point. It is after all true that even Shakespeare's characters, praised for their variety, speak in a style that betrays a common root. But precisely style can be said to be the focus of our lingering dissatisfaction. It is sometimes difficult not to be overwhelmed by it. The combination of swiftness and compactness – the tumbling balances, the crisp colons – tends to be coercive. As St John Ervine (1956) puts it, Shaw's style is 'swift and tightly packed, almost too swift, too tightly packed' (p. 73). Like the character Bohun in *You Never Can Tell*, it is sometimes a 'regular overwhelmer' (*B* 1: 782).

In his study of this style, Richard Ohmann (1962) demonstrates Shaw's readiness to perceive likeness between unlike things (gentleman and thief, English patriotism and German, and so on) and comments that 'this stylistic emphasis on equivalence' not only accounts for those 'dazzling condensations' that surprise and delight us but also 'coincide[s] with a stern, disciplinary attitude toward experience' and with such characteristic defects as 'inflexibility and exaggeration' (pp. 22, 39). That is to say, the style is both exceptionally spontaneous and exceptionally coercive, and this combination may be the source of our difficulty in separating out in Shaw the libertarian and authoritarian tendencies of this thought. Ohmann comments further that 'the stylistic search for order has some recognizable parallels in the most central of his explicit beliefs', mentioning Shaw's aversion to chance (p. 26). I would add that his explicit beliefs themselves are sometimes shot through with the same ambivalence. Consider the concept of will, a cardinal one for Shaw, as for his predecessors Carlyle and Nietzsche.

On the one hand he uses the term 'will' as a synonym for Schopenhauer's *Wille*, a pre-rational motive power not unlike Freud's instinct. Shaw repeatedly denounces Rationalism, choosing to root his moral vision in a deeper or perhaps more mystical psychology (for example, *CL* I 316, II 760–2; *C* 19: 92–3, 316, 323–34; *PPR* 88; *SSS* 122; *NDW* 335–6, 412; *ST* 184). Indeed he goes so far as to say, in the 'Maxims for Revolutionists', that 'the unconscious self is the real genius' (*B* 2: 791). With equal insistence he claimed to have composed the plots of his plays spontaneously rather than deliberately (*B* 1: 40; *B* 5: 685; *B* 7: 308; *CL* I 461–2; *PPR* 22–3; *ST* 116, 268; *NDW* 235; *C* 19: 92–3; *C* 33: 306; *LC* 235; etc.).[12] But he did not follow Schopenhauer so far as to imagine that the will must cause suffering unless one ceased to strive. However unconscious in some sense the will may be, Shaw understood it also as purposive and even providential. Although he wanted it understood as an impersonal Life Force, something like Undershaft's 'will of which I am a part' (*B* 3: 169), Shaw speaks for it with so much authority that we cannot conceive of it as quite unconscious and impersonal. His defences of pre-rational spontaneity are suspiciously vehement. And the logical confusion is compounded by his inclination to oppose the will both to necessity and chance, yoking together as the common enemy deterministic rationalism and Darwinian natural selection: 'I am before all things a believer in the power of Will. . . . I believe that all evolution has been produced by Will. . . . I have the most unspeakable contempt for Determinism, Rationalism, and Darwinian natural selection as explanations of the Universe. They destroy all human courage & human character' (*CL* II 670). This pretty much turns the will into a wholly rational power. The crucial evolutionary change that occurs in *Back to Methuselah* only seems to surrender the idea that mind governs matter, for the two characters whose life expectancies are first extended had exhibited distinct signs of repudiating, not wholly involuntarily, the moral conditions of their lives. Similarly, despite Shaw's attachment to the idea of Becoming and Change, his dramatic criticism regularly and, as it were, instinctively, evaluates characterisation in terms of a fixed standard of truth to nature – an Enlightenment legacy that looks curiously conservative in the midst of his commitment to the idea of evolution.

Perhaps Arland Ussher (1953) put the contradictoriness of Shaw's thinking on this subject most neatly when he wrote: 'by instinct he remained a rationalist, even though with his reason he became a vitalist' (p. 26).

It is probably our critical sense of this instinctive rationalism that lies behind the commonly heard objection that Shaw's writing lacks feeling and heart. Stephen Spender (1953), not unsympathetically, remarked on Shaw's 'very deep repression of feeling and also a reliance on the force of one's own separate life which arises from a lack of confidence in affection' (p. 237). Shaw himself admitted to Ellen Terry that his loveless childhood left him 'a treacherous brute . . . in matters of affection' (*CL* I 692) and to Stella Campbell that he was 'a mass of imagination with no heart' (*CL* III 126). But he does not flout sentiment unfeelingly. 'Very deep repression of feeling' does not seem satisfactory as a phrase to describe his impassioned, highly charged arguments and dramatic situations. As Eric Bentley has pointed out, early and late, there is plenty of feeling in Shaw but it is often not the kind we expect. Shaw himself explained the 'odiousness' of his work in the eyes of some as 'produced by the fact that my heart is never in the right – meaning the expected – place' (*CL* IV 176).

One stylistic result of this degree of remoteness from mundane emotion is a tendency toward generalisation. But this is not necessarily a literary vice. Shaw often generalises brilliantly, even though he sometimes overgeneralises. Toward abstract language he maintained a healthy disrespect, recognising that, despite the breadth of his thinking, he was not a philosopher. 'There is no such thing as Man in the world: what we have to deal with is a multitude of men' (*SM* 3: 473). 'You expect me to prate about the Absolute, about Reality, about The First Cause, and to answer the universal Why. When I see these words in print the book goes into the basket. Good morning' (*SSS* 91).

When he thought in terms of classes of men, he was likely to imagine concrete representatives and to dramatise their situation. Ohmann (1962) aptly observed that 'his thought is always animated by a vivid awareness of specific people in specific predicaments' (p. 145). Here is a typical Shavian volley, a response to the question, 'Does married life make a difference in your views':

> What do you call married life? Real married life is the life of the youth and the maiden who pluck a flower and bring down an avalanche on their shoulders. Thirty years of the work of Atlas; and then rest as pater and mater-familias. What can childless people with independent incomes, marrying at forty as I did, tell you about marriage? I know nothing about it except as a looker-on.   (*SSS* 89)

Note the prompt imagining of married life in terms of youth and maiden whose situation is dramatised by extreme oppositions – pluck a flower vs. bring down an avalanche, work of Atlas vs. rest as pater- and materfamilias, youth and maiden vs. the same and vs. also the late-marrying and childless man.

The passage is also humanly attractive in its recognition of personal limitation. But 'the impression of want of humanity in the high comedist' (*CL* II 215) remains. In his thirst for the ideal, Shaw can be too impatient with common feeling, too ready to disown it. The work suffers when such feeling is not given enough verbal and dramatic play before judgement is passed.

Issues of sexual morality, especially in connection with improving the human race, elicited a dubious kind of hypothetical thinking from Shaw, concrete enough in diction but too remote from social and psychological realities. One of his favourite ideas of this sort, extensively argued in *The Intelligent Woman's Guide to Socialism and Capitalism*, was that incomes must be equalised so that sexual selection can be broadened across class lines and the breed improved. Another was that women naturally prefer polygamy because their maternal instinct leads them to prefer a share in a first-rate man to the whole of a third-rate man. In later years he became fond of what he called anthropometry, but the anthropometrist in Shaw resembles Jonathan Swift's projector in 'A Modest Proposal': he is a rationalistic madman.

An intolerance for disorder and uncertainty too often led him into facile paradox or into an impatient earnestness that stifles wit. Shaw is no exception to the rule that, when a man discusses what he calls his religion, he loses his sense of humour:

> To me the sole hope of human salvation lies in teaching Man to
> regard himself as an experiment in the realization of God. . . .
> Shakespeare's 'As flies to wanton boys so we are to the gods'
> [*sic*] . . . is the most frightful blasphemy ever uttered, and the
> one from which it is my mission to deliver the world. (*CL*
> II 858–9)

> The history of modern thought now teaches us that when we
> are forced to give up the creeds by their childishness and their
> conflicts with science we must either embrace Creative Evolution
> or fall into the bottomless pit of an utterly discouraging pessi-
> mism. (*B* 5: 702)

Such passages fail to convince or to inspire because their author is
so anxiously trying to convince himself, to whip his devils into
submission. Shaw's surest path to authentic eloquence is to stand
back from belief just enough to allow a clashing perspective and a
consequent wit to emerge.

Jesting in Shaw occasionally indicates a manic denial of the fear
of death (for example, his jesting response to his mother's death
and his wife's – *CL* III 153; Ervine, 1956, p. 453; Pearson, 1942,
p. 418; *SSS* 204), and this may be considered the pathological
aspect of his narcissism. As Dervin (1975) put it, 'he could not
mourn' (p. 50). But he understood the pain of separateness. His
comic sense both acknowledges a gulf between fantasy and reality
and denies some of the accompanying anxiety. Freud (1957)
observed that the grandeur in humour 'clearly lies in the triumph
of narcissism, the victorious assertion of the ego's invulnerability'
(vol. XXI, p. 162). But the more ironic the comic sense in question,
the more it does register feelings of vulnerability and the pain of
separateness. Shaw's definitions of comedy are accordingly of two
different kinds: one emphasises the capacity of comedy to unite,
to 'affirm good fellowship' (*OTN* I vi), the other is 'destructive,
derisory, critical, [and] negative' aspect (*B* 5: 335). And Shavian
comedy in practice is correspondingly complex, buoyancy and
disillusion both being pervasive. At best their interaction produces
the comic sublime.

The Shavian imagination here delineated can be labelled in the
light of contemporary psychoanalytic theory as narcissistic. The

label is suggestive, I think, if it is used to explain tendency rather than pathology in a highly creative writer, and it is easier to think of the concept of narcissism in this way after the various studies of 'borderline conditions'.

We may say that the source of Shaw's vision is the ideal state of self, in line with his description of himself as 'always on the heroic plane imaginatively' (C 2: xvi). This state may be thought of as an original, symbiotic fusion of self and other, self and mother, undifferentiated and limitlessly nurturing. But differentiation and separation inevitably and irreversibly occur, making this state forever unrecoverable. An heroic imagination may then try to restore the ideal in either of two ways. One is by idealising the self, incorporating the other into it and denying thereby the pain of separation. The alternative is to idealise the other, identifying with it as a powerful, engendering force, denying the reality of one's separate, incomplete identity. But these denials are impossible to maintain indefinitely. The fears are strong, fears of losing either the other or the self. In so far as the self is idealised, it must confront the doom of its ultimate loneliness. In so far as the other is in turn idealised, the self must confront the fear of merging, expressed perhaps by an anxiously intense assertion of its self-sufficiency. So heaven is imagined as a place of lonely though joyous battle or of feared bliss. I may seem to be subsuming Shaw's imagination under the broad topos of a lost paradise, but the imagery of this drama is very strong in his work.

The basis in psychoanalytic theory for this putative ground of vision is admirably summarised by Margaret Mahler (1974):

One could regard the entire life cycle as constituting a more or less successful process of distancing and introjection of the lost symbiotic mother, an eternal longing for the actual or fantasied 'ideal state of self,' with the latter standing for a symbiotic fusion with the 'all-good' mother, who was at one time part of the self in a blissful state of well-being. (p. 305)

Mahler's wording encourages us to link the child and the adult in our consideration of Shaw, but, of course, given the level of generality, it is hardly able to hint at the intensity of a writer's use of language in the service of either regressive or progressive fantasy.

In a recently published letter written to Gilbert Murray in 1911,

Shaw describes, startlingly, a dream about his mother who was also his wife: 'what surprised me when I awoke was that the notion of incest had not entered into the dream: I had taken it as a matter of course that the maternal function included the wifely one; and so did she. What is more, the sexual relation acquired all the innocence of the filial one, and the filial one all the completeness of the sexual one' (*CL* III 17). This is a regressive fantasy that lends support to Mahler's notion of an ideal state of self. Significantly, the preceding portion of the letter is an exuberant burlesque of *Oedipus Rex*, then newly translated by Murray.

But the progressive aspect of the self-other idealisation is an even more important underpinning of Shaw's work. Freud (1957) outlined the dynamics of such fantasying very clearly in *Beyond the Pleasure Principle*, although the concept he called 'repression', tied in for him with the Oedipus complex rather than with a pre-Oedipal, narcissistic conflict, would receive valuable modification in this context from later theorists:

> What appears in a minority of human individuals as an untiring impulsion towards further perfection can easily be understood as a result of the instinctual repression upon which is based all that is most precious in human civilization. The repressed instinct never ceases to strive for complete satisfaction, which would consist in the repetition of a primary experience of satisfaction. No substitutive or reactive formations and no sublimations will suffice to remove the repressed instinct's persisting tension; and it is the difference in amount between the pleasure of satisfaction which is demanded and that which is actually achieved that provides the driving factor which will permit of no halting at any position attained, but, in the poet's words, '*ungebändigt immer vorwärts dringt* [presses ever forward unsubdued]'.   (vol. XVIII, p. 42)

Christopher Lasch (1984) quotes a passage from the psychoanalyst Samuel Novey that reformulates this account in terms of the ego-ideal and primary narcissism – primary narcissism having to do with ego boundaries and the illusion of omnipotence as distinguished from secondary narcissism or the return of libido to the ego from an object. The passage illuminates sharply the portrait of the artist as Bernard Shaw that is being developed here:

The ego-ideal spans an orbit that extends from primary narcissism to the 'categorical imperative,' from the most primitive form of psychic life to the highest level of man's achievements. Whatever these achievements might be, they emerge from the paradox of never attaining the sought-after fulfillment or satisfaction, on the one hand, and of their never-ceasing pursuit, on the other. This search extends into the limitless future that blends into eternity. Thus, the fright of the finity of time, of death itself, is rendered non-existent, as it once had been in the state of primary narcissism. (p. 180)

The notion of Shaw as a narcissistic writer is, of course, not unrelated to his well-known exhibitionism, his obsessive self-regard. He loved to be photographed; his *feuilleton* criticism is dotted with self-dramatising references; hardly a letter in his later years fails to mention his exact age. From a strictly literary point of view, I suppose, the self-references must be justified by the quality of the wit that usually laces them and guides them to point, but what interests me now, in trying to apply a concept of narcissism deeper and less judgemental than the common idea of conceitedness, is the assumption of invulnerability that seems to underlie many of these remarks:

I do not mind confessing that I do not know half as much as you would suppose from my articles [about music]; but in the kingdom of the deaf the one-eared is king. (*SM* 2: 808)

Although I habitually stretch goodnature to the verge of weakness in extenuating and hushing up all manner of avoidable deficiencies in the performance I criticize, yet I find myself held up as a ruthless and malignant savage. (*SM* 2: 441)

I do not rank bumptiousness high as an artistic quality: perhaps because I am myself singularly free of it. (*C* 33: 314)

In the first of these remarks, self-deprecation serves as a foil for self-praise, without a touch of defensiveness and with more than a touch of aggressiveness. In the second, the idea of being unjustly maligned is mere pretence that licenses playfully exaggerated self-praise. And in the third, an obvious fault of the writer is denied with a breezy brazenness. Nothing can touch him. Yet this use of self makes us uneasy, especially when the wit is less sure, as in the second and third instances. We sense, I think, in Béla Grunberger's words, that the 'narcissistic person is one who loves himself well, but also one who loves himself poorly or not at all' (Lasch, 1984, p. 284).

There is remarkably scanty residue of Oedipal conflict in Shaw's writings and a correspondingly prominent residue of pre-Oedipal conflicts. We shall see how incipient Oedipal situations keep dissolving into something else. The closest thing to an Oedipal period in Shaw's life was around 1895 when he wrote *Candida* (in which a young man sets himself up as a rival to an older man for the love of his wife) and when he fought for Ellen Terry against Henry Irving. But one could reasonably argue in both instances that Shaw was more interested in protecting the image of the mother–wife than in defeating the rival (Dervin, 1975, pp. 130, 141). Tentative soundings of the incest motif are accompanied in Shaw by very little sense of guilt. We will encounter some less than convincing rationalisations for the incest taboo, but the fear that is presumably not being confronted seems to have little or nothing to do with castration.

On the other hand, imagery reflecting the fantasies and especially the defensive systems of pre-Oedipal sexuality, both oral and anal, are conspicuous in Shaw. The whole modality of consuming and producing, taking in and spitting out, pervades his thinking. (Consuming and producing were, of course, major themes in the Victorians essayists who influenced Shaw, but he invested them with a distinctive intensity.) His favourite mode of giving out was the activity of speech, practiced compulsively, either in the direct form of public speaking or the indirect form of writing dialogue to be spoken, over an adult lifetime of more than seventy years. As Dervin (1975) has shown, cannibalistic imagery abounds in his work (pp. 44, 51, 83), and we can hardly doubt that his assertive vegetarianism and teetotalism serve, as one of their purposes, to defend against fantasies of oral incorporation. The evidence for Shaw's continuing imaginative interest in the anal phase of infantile development is chiefly his evident fascination with quantities of money (millions, billions), his proclaimed hatred of waste and disorder, and his pride in tidiness. We hardly think of tidiness as an heroic virtue, but the hero of his first novel, a nobody named Smith, astonishes an MP by the feat of tidying up his very messy desk, and more sophisticated versions of a similar feat are performed by dramatic heroes from Bluntschli to Eppy.

Psychological insight into the origin of Shaw's all-important comic sense is harder to gain because we should have to probe the intellectual development belonging to later childhood. Shaw himself traced his penchant for anti-climax to his father's influence (*C* 1: xxiii), and he does seem to have identified with his father in some curiously negative way ('I work as my father drank' – *C* 1: xxxvii). And in a curiously positive way (mainly by adopting eccentric personal habits) the child seems to have identified with the other male adult of his household, his mother's voice teacher Vandeleur Lee.[13] Doubtless the Irish Protestant background was also very important in forming what Ohmann (1962) calls 'the posture of opposition' (p. 73) and Holland (1985) the need 'to find or to be a purposeful and fulfilling opposite' (p. 57). Dan Laurence aptly quotes Harry Slochower's comment that Shaw's Irish heritage 'contained the tradition of Catholic communality and that of political dissidence' (*CL* ivV 458).

Accepting Shaw's own definition of comedy – 'the fine art of disillusion' (*OTN* iii 85) – we may draw forth from the previous discussion three principal strategies of relation between the comic and the sublime.

One is the unmasking of a compromised form of moral awareness, an act that spurs a movement or turn toward a purer form. It is an attack not on the deviations from a norm of good sense, as in traditional satire, but on the half-conscious assumptions that support what passes for good sense and is often called morality. At bottom it is an attack on the idea that the status quo is sanctioned by natural rather than conventional law. And its full effect depends on the simultaneous expression of two kinds of self-possession, one broadly supported by a society and one the product of individual, 'visionary' conviction.

A second strategy focuses on the nature of heroic will itself, as it is expressed beyond the understanding of lesser, farcically conceived figures. Without impugning the heroic will fundamentally, Shaw in this version of the sublime exposes a flaw – impracticality, powerlessness, fanaticism – in those who dream of perfected men in a perfected society. The dramatic effect in this case is typically attained by an extended clash of differing perspectives instead of by a single movement of conversion or change.

The third strategy of relation is the most profound or the least conscious. It is an implicit recognition of what Lacan (1977) called 'the dialectic of desire' (p. 292) and Bloom (1985) 'visionary skepticism' (pp. 7–8). The quest for omnipotent self-sufficiency discovers, through its very intensity, an inevitable disappointment. For the self can never be finally idealised, being involved from the beginning with an other. Separateness, even in the optimistic Shaw, is eventually revealed to be an inescapable part of the human condition. This aspect of his imagination verges most closely on the tragic, but it is usually muted by the impetuousness of his idealism, 'press[ing] ever forward, unsubdued'. None the less, many of his heroic figures, from Caesar to Joan, are touched by an ultimate loneliness.

Dervin (1975) comments that 'Solitude was as nearly absent from his life as the soliloquy from his stage' (p. 98), but I think this overstates the case. Although he can cite remarks that illustrate Shaw's refusal to mourn and admit separateness, the sense of solitude keeps emerging, perhaps most evidently in the letters to favoured women. To Alice Lockett he spoke of 'the enormous solitude which I carry about with me' (*CL* I 95), and there are similar confessions to Terry, Campbell and others. Of all the commentators, Bentley (1960) comes closest to capturing this aspect of Shaw in defining the distinctive mood of his drama as that of 'desolation' (p. xxv; also (1986) p. 12). Fortunately the narcissistic sense of invulnerability is not perfect in Shaw. He did not like to acknowledge his need for love and for a responsive other, but his work does acknowledge it, both mimetically in the form of interacting characters and reflexively in the fact that he continued to write for, and be very alert to, an audience. He lived not only to write (often speaking of himself as a 'writing-machine') but to be written, saying, for example, 'It is only when I am being used that I can feel my own existence' (*CL* I 676). There is actually more poignancy in Shaw than we might suppose – more, certainly, than I at first supposed. But there is little resignation. Frustration is likely to be expressed instead with anger or bitterness. But the need for response is there, and it helps to humanise his work.

I stress the pervasiveness of conflict in the mind and imaginative world of Shaw. He would deny the need for love, he would be his own parent if necessary,[14] but, since he could not stop longing for the complement and hence from realising his own incompleteness, he would pass judgement upon that need: 'The heart knoweth his own bitterness' (Proverbs 14 : 10) was his favourite biblical quotation. As I see it, Shaw never really decided whether he was damned or saved, whether he was an outsider or an insider, whether he was 'mad' or 'too sane'. To put it another way, these alternatives were, in his judgement, a question of either/or but, in his imagination, a question of both/and.

A schematic overview like the one presented in this chapter has, I trust, certain advantages. But it has the disadvantage of implying that an effective literary imagination springs into life full grown. In fact, the discovery of appropriate forms, the integration of different facets of feeling and the adjustment of feeling to form were, in Shaw's case, a gradual and constantly changing process. The history of this process will be the subject of the following chapters.

Part Two

2
Emergence of the Comic Sublime

George B. Shaw made his literary début at the age of eighteen with a letter in a Dublin journal about the visit of two American evangelists (*NDW* 447). Although neither witty nor eloquent, it anticipates very remarkably not only the mature writer's preoccupation with questions of conduct and belief but also the way in which, as a Bunyanesque Protestant, he searched for authenticity.

The letter does not so much denigrate Messrs Moody and Sankey as fraudulent purveyors. Rather, it examines the unreligious motives (curiosity, free entrance to an expensive building) of those who flocked to hear them, and guesses that the effect even on revivalist enthusiasts will be merely superficial, involving no change of moral nature. Already Shaw puts aside an easy opportunity for *ad hominem* attack and focuses on the quality of response to an action. Already he is sceptical about what passes for religion, not, as he later implied, because he had been as a youth credulous about science instead (*B* 6: 747) but because he is seeking a deeper basis for belief. Whether he succeeded in his boyhood ambition of founding a new religion (Ervine, 1956, p. 49) may certainly be doubted, but his particular fusion of moral idealism and psychological realism constituted an authentic kind of religious vision.

Shaw's penchant for undermining in order to deepen the religion of the tribe is already well illustrated by the most ambitious dramatic effort of his youth, a piece of serious if not distinguished blank verse called *Passion Play* in which the subversive figure of Judas delivers an eloquent sermon on atheism. (A late sketch from the preface to *On the Rocks* opposes Jesus's genuine moral vision, cleared of its appearance of insanity, to Pilate's Roman practicality. Despite the shift from Judas to Jesus, Shaw is still identifying with the subversive speaker who seeks a living creed beneath the dead crust of officialdom, though the stress in the early piece is on self-government and in the late on the governing of others.) The work is little known, but thanks to Dan Laurence it is now accessible, and the heart of it deserves quotation here:

> How selfish are all creeds! The atheist only,
> Thirsting for truth and knowledge, sternly waives
> All paradise for himself. Of all mankind
> He is the only man who dares to die:
> The rest must bolster up their wormy lives
> With flattering lies and heavens specially made
> For their delight.
>
>   . . .
>
> A solitary watcher of the world,
> A man whose sympathies are so enlarged
> That he is lost above the vulgar crowd,
> Who straight cry 'Joyless cynic.' 'Atheist!'
> In parrot fashion. But the man, unmoved,
> Feeling the stream of happiness steadily rising
> Though but an inch gained midst a hundred ebbs,
> Exultingly foresees the distant age
> When man shall conquer pain, and on the brow
> Of Death place an imperishable wreath.
> And what more rosy vision can'st thou conjure
> With thy o'ershadowing slave-suggested God
> Than this that I have of a time to come
> When Man, impenetrable, calm, and knowing,
> Shall carry life so loftily, that pleasure
> Will almost lose its meaning.   (*B* 7: 506–8)

The Shelleyan idea of these passages remained dear to Shaw, even if its youthful optimism underwent modification. The man who can conquer the fear of death that renders us unconscious slaves of custom can lead the way to the spiritual state of perfected men – calm, lofty, almost beyond pleasure. Atheism was, of course, to be a means not an end, as is shown by the fact that the passage goes on to identify this reasoning of Judas with a dream of Jesus. But a Shelleyan style did not suit Shaw's talent, which sought engagement with particular social attitudes and situations.

In the same year (1878) he wrote a 31-page fictionalised letter, published posthumously as *My Dear Dorothea*, in which the idea of rebellion is fitted to the framework of family relations. It reads much like the real letters the young Shaw wrote to his mother and older sister (matter-of-fact, advisory, superior) and suggests a fantasy reversal of an unhappy childhood. This, however, is to neglect its wit and charm, as the budding author cuts it loose from the person in the background.

This suppositious recipient is a five-year-old girl being instructed by an older man, who combines the 'affection of a parent' (which is scarcely evident) and 'the rational interest of an experimental philosopher' (*MDD* 52) in the technique of dealing with her mother so as to preserve her independence and not be an idolator. Duty, for example, should not express the mere deference of a child placed in a weak and therefore false position. But she can be dutiful, however hypocritical, if being so helps her get what she wants. 'It is a very excellent thing to be properly hypocritical' (35). Selfishness, then, is only a vice if one is greedy or cruel, which is not socially practical in any case, so 'let your rule of conduct always be to do whatever is best for yourself. Be as selfish as you can' (25). That this will be principled conduct is made clear by the statement that 'the most important [of qualities to strive for] is called Self-control' (44).

In *My Dear Dorothea*, more clearly than in the journal letter, Shaw attacks a moral standard for the sake of improving it, and he establishes a dramatic situation that permits the irony in the situation to be perceived. A mere child can outwit her parent at her own game, and do so honourably – at least, if honour is understood as a matter of individual conscience rather than social appearance. To be sure, he almost ignores the childishness of the child, as if Dorothea could play the hypocritical role as effectively as Ann Whitefield. But there are a few playful touches – for example, the tenderly ironic advice that she read such books as *Pilgrim's Progress*, *Tales from Shakespeare* and *The Arabian Nights*, not on the grounds that they are fit for children but that they are not fit for adults: 'Some books are not fit for grownup people; but all books are fit for you' (22). She is reminded too that holy men are sometimes unhappy: 'Jesus Christ was so melancholy that he never smiled, or took any amusement, except some boating occasionally' (30–2). In maturity, Shaw would learn both to make the rebel more plausible and to surrender the protected vantage of avuncularity; 'remember', he wrote in 1900, 'that all the advice given by grown up people to young people has interested motives' (*CL* II 135).

The five painstaking novels written over the next decade, during the writer's twenties, are generally viewed as a false start to a dramatist's career. And certainly, with the possible exception of the rather charming *Cashel Byron's Profession*, they are no joy to read, as Shaw himself, a pretty good critic of his own work, readily admitted. They are overearnest, stiff in diction and syntax, and curiously choked in feeling. Their central concern is 'the irrational knot' of marriage, but the basis of the protagonists' antagonism to marriage, and hence of their grimly strenuous efforts to find it tolerable on pain of exclusion from the human scene, is not made very clear. The reader is given instead a great deal of insistence on the importance of an unsentimental self-sufficiency. But both conceptually and stylistically, we can find in the novels some evidences of an emerging comic sublime.

'The business of a novelist', wrote the Shelleyan Shaw in an essay about his own novels, 'is largely to provide working models of improved types of humanity' (*NDW* 311). It would be hard to say what his novelistic protagonists are improvements upon, for they tend to oppose weakly agreeable young women whom the reader is inclined to pity for the pounding they take. But a certain energetic wilfulness is evident enough in these protagonists, and seems only to lack a substantial target. Shaw will gradually solve this difficulty by learning to oppose moral positions themselves, which will involve a modification of novelistic realism in scene and dialogue. We can trace in the novels, then, a gradual movement toward dramatic form that makes the latter ones less successful as novels though more interesting as anticipations of a rival genre. This subversion from within is scarcely evident in the first two novels, tentative in the third, attained by a pleasant side-step into romance in the fourth, and most evident in the fifth, *An Unsocial Socialist*, which is, as a result, an artistic mess.

The protagonist of *Immaturity*, quasi-anonymously named Smith, is first attracted to Harriet Russell but his romantic feeling is quickly deflected into a fascination with her 'hard-as-nails' strength. In cool friendship he watches her adventures, observing a wastrel who covets her, a preacher who becomes crazed with infatuation for her (and preaches on that favourite Shavian text, 'the heart knoweth his own bitterness'), and an artist heroic enough to admire Rembrandt and Michelangelo (like the young Shaw) who actually marries her. The marriage is not successful – he is cold, she philistine – but is accepted by Harriet as satisfactory.

Smith becomes more energetic midway through the narrative,

offering help not only to Harriet but also to the handsome, immature daughter of his employer, with whom he flirts somewhat priggishly, more interested in teaching her self-respect than in winning her affection, even after his rival's unworthiness is exposed. Toward the end, Harriet's artist-husband, speaks for Smith too when he cries, 'What is there to live for but work? . . . Everything else ends in disappointment' (C 1: 229). Harriet also is finally checked, being described as 'the idealization of matter-of-fact, the sepulchre of emotion' (266). There is a good deal of careful characterisation and plotting in *Immaturity* but, at the same time, a tendency to stifle any development that might express sentiment.

In *The Irrational Knot* Shaw intensifies the qualities of his primary figures and sets up clearer confrontations among them. Especially he emphasises the hyperrationality of Ned Conolly, to the point that, as he later commented, 'long before I got to the writing of the last chapter I could hardly stand him myself' (*NDW* 312).

Conolly's personal force, unlike Smith's, is connected to specific abilities. He has invented an electro-motor and sings well: he is both scientist and artist. The point of the story, Shaw suggested, was that a paragon of reasonableness ('everything that a thoroughly nice woman could desire and deserve') will turn out to be hopelessly incompatible with a paragon of conventional virtue – with someone who has been taught to be ladylike rather than beautiful, to like fashion rather than taste, to have small talk rather than conversation (*NDW* 312).

The blame, in other words, is to fall on her education. But since Shaw 'took no end of trouble to make Marian nice' (*NDW* 311), the reader is likely to resist Conolly's attacks on her for being ordinary and sentimental, and to find his very bluntness on other subjects (for example, his attack on the Church for not being more like a theatre) a kind of reverse snobbery. Marian seems justified in her feeling that Conolly treats her like a doll, commenting a bit wryly that she married a working man in order to feel real but only feels ghostly. She understands well enough the coolness of his courteous contempt for her imperfections, and the reader is not convinced that her education is the principal cause of their separation; her subsequent liaison with a man of her own class is immediately disastrous. The exposure of marriage as an irrational knot is more convincing through the direct jibes of their novelist friend who is herself disinclined to marriage on grounds of temperament.

In a secondary story, Conolly's forceful sister is said to remain morally independent even though her career as a stage singer and as a mistress drives her to drink and to a dismal end in New York City. The stories of brother and sister are better related than those of Smith and Harriet. Although he is a trier-on of budding Shavian opinions (parenting is a form of egotism, happiness depends only on work, and so on), the brother is complexly and directly judged by the sister ('a man in a thousand – though Lord forbid we should have many of his sort about' – C 2: 179). And her view is echoed by Marian herself in a studied final exchange.

Love Among the Artists is more ungainly than its predecessors, probably because, as R. F. Dietrich (1969) suggests, Shaw is beginning here to fight against the very conventions of narrative fiction (p. 48). He considered this novel original because it 'exalts the wilful characters to the utter disparagement of the reasonable ones' (*NDW* 312). The contrasts are not actually so sharp but they are trying to be, and the novel as novel suffers because of it.

Mary Sutherland's romance with genteel, artistic Adrian Herbert is over-strained; later they become comfortable with each other as friends. Then Mary is subjected to the Beethovenish Owen Jack, a morose and brooding man, forceful rather than handsome, who is given to such utterances as 'Do as you are bid . . . you hussy' and 'I am an artist, sir . . . and I will not permit a young and beautiful woman to be tyrannized over in my presence' (C 3: 43, 48). He barges in and out of bourgeois families as a teacher of music and elocution, attractive and puzzling to women in part because of their fathers' opposition (though the Oedipal motif is not pursued) and because of his quixotic scorn for money. Yet Mary's rejection of him is supported by various lookers-on who remind us that 'quixoticism is tainted with spiritual vainglory' (187–8), that 'heroes are ill adapted to domestic purposes' (245), or that Jack is 'always unanswerable' (193), the same fault imputed to Conolly who makes a reappearance and whose experience is cited as proof that people like Jack, of stubborn and narrow self-sufficiency, should not marry. Jack, on the other hand, is allowed to have some personal influence as well as simply Genius. He draws forth the artistic strength in Madge Brailsford and, training her in voice production as Vandeleur Lee trained Shaw's mother or as Higgins trained Eliza, transforms her from a lady in finery into an independent actress.

Adrian has meanwhile met another musical genius, a Polish

pianist, and become enslaved by her. But nothing could be less convincing than their interest in one another, and she soon admits that her passion for music makes her indifferent to romantic love. Shaw will continue to wrestle with her type, demonic but admirable; in this early work she is scarcely contained by the fictional form though her presence seems urgently desired by the author.

The tenuous story line coils among these partnerings toward a marriage between Mary, twice burned, and a certain philistine fellow, a marriage that is neither romantic nor heroic but tolerable and workable. One senses a humane intention on Shaw's part, weakened by lack of conviction. Tentatively, however, the geniuses in the novel begin to understand that their exclusion from marriage is not simply a poignant fact but a repudiative choice on their part that sublimates erotic energy. Jack tells Madge: 'It is marriage that kills the heart and keeps it dead. Better starve the heart than overfeed it' (342). And his feminine counterpart admits that 'I can feel [love] in the music . . . but in real life – it is impossible' (327).

Cashel Byron's Profession is distinguished from the preceding novels by its crisper phrasing, more parodic tone and sharper ironies. Largely for these reasons it is the most readable of the group, the first to find publication (C 4: x), and the only one that Shaw (using blank verse!) troubled to recast into dramatic form, under the title of *The Admirable Bashville*. As the adaptation recognises, the novel's best passage is an ironic as well as dramatic courtroom scene in which a defence attorney for Cashel so skilfully perverts the truth about a scuffle leading to an arrest that he elicits from his client an admiring remark to the effect that brute boxers have to fight fairer than *that* (239). Building a plot around the revelation that the hero and aspirer to the hand of a rich, intellectual lady is only a prizefighter – an outlawed profession at the time but one conducted by rules – allows for a running light irony at the expense of a respectable profession like the law.

The ironies are gentle enough not to disguise the fact that the novel is frankly a romance. The overeducated and excessively self-possessed heroine (William Morris called her a 'prig-ess' – *NDW* 311) encounters in a forest glade a glorious vision of manly beauty, Cashel Byron, who has left a bossy schoolmaster and a neglectful actress-mother to become a prizefighter. Having been warned by her protective father against polite society as 'a temple for the worship of riches and a market for the sale of virgins' (C 4: 27), and to 'beware of men who have read more than they have worked' (31), she is ready to combine her intellectual charms with Cashel's physical ones. Shaw has a eugenic experiment in mind, but it will turn out ironically, as a similar experiment does in the much later *Simpleton of the Unexpected Isles*. His real interest is combining Lydia Carew's theoretic virtue with Byron's ability to enforce it, the latter being called 'executive power', a subject upon which Cashel delivers an implausibly eloquent speech of some length.

In this work Shaw has for the first time brought into confrontation two figures of comparably great force, but the balance is not kept. Despite his self-effacements, Cashel turns out to be considerably more talkative and even theoretic than Lydia herself. The novel starts from her point of view, then shifts over to his. Perhaps Shaw's ironic climax – the girls turn out to be like their father, the boys like their mother – acknowledges lightheartedly his own failure in narrative integration.

The last of the completed novels, *An Unsocial Socialist*, marks both a regression and, in a less apparent sense, an advance. Sidney Trefusis, a rich man disguised as a labourer named Smilash (he lashes the bourgeoisie with a smile[1]) hops absurdly about, getting involved with young women for the sake chiefly of ridiculing their tendency to regard personal relations personally rather than socialistically. (Shaw had just swallowed, but not yet digested, Marx.) He deserts his wife, whose eventual suicide goes unmourned, remarking: 'We have found that we love each other too much – that our intercourse hinders our usefulness – and so we must part' (C 5: 82). Such hollow cleverness is used also for the sake of coaxing an alliance: 'I am trying to offend you in order to save myself from falling in love with you, but I have not the heart to let myself succeed' (112).

There is far too much bumptious jesting and nervous self-regard: 'With my egotism, my charlatanry, my tongue, and my habit of having my own way, I am fit for no calling but that of saviour of mankind' (110). Again, 'He had no conscientious scruples in his love-making because he was unaccustomed to consider himself as likely to inspire love in women' (248). At his best, however, Trefusis is not shallowly mocking but seeking out the fault in the conditions that prompt our moral judgements. Why he should have been so attracted to his wife at first and so repelled afterwards 'is one of those devil's riddles which will not be answered until we have traced all the yet unsuspected reactions of our inveterate dishonesty' (108). Trefusis can even remind us of Shaw's later millionaire socialist, John Tanner, as when he turns upon a young woman who speaks of herself as unprotected: 'Unprotected! Why, you are fenced round and barred in with conventions, laws, and lies that would frighten the truth from the lips of any man' (198). In a similarly ironic vein he notifies the author himself in an 'Appendix' of his 'regret that you can find no better employment for your talent than the writing of novels' (269–70).

Excited by his discovery of Marx, Shaw was eager to create an original hero who not only 'violates every canon of propriety, like Tom Jones or Des Grieux, but every canon of sentiment as well' (*NDW* 313). But the formal means of suiting this idea were yet to be worked out. The trouble with *An Unsocial Socialist* is that these violations do not meet with enough resistance and seem bumptious and silly. Unlike *Man and Superman*, the novel scarcely probes the dialectical possibilities of a millionaire socialist. Although Trefusis admires in passing the courage of his rich father and the 'sublime selfishness' of some artists in doing what they want to do (78), the main effect created by his assaults on propriety and sentiment is self-congratulation.

Shaw himself admitted that people who will read *An Unsocial Socialist* 'will read anything' (*C* 4: xii). But in a chapter studying the growth of an imagination we ought to mention two more of its features. First, in the lively Agatha Wylie, Shaw has created, more successfully than with Lydia Carew or any earlier figure, a woman who combines force with charm. She is a step in the direction of Raina and Ann Whitefield. Secondly, it has a sort of reckless gaiety that is but a step away from the dialectical vivacity of the work for which Shaw is remembered. We see this, for example, in its attacks on the dishonesty of fiction from within a fiction, both in the narrative proper and again in the witty appendix. Shaw did not go on to abandon fiction for propaganda. He learned instead to sophisticate his imaginative forms, folding back in his dissatisfaction with the indirectness of literary action.

A subsequent, unfinished novel, though of little more than symptomatic interest, is worth a brief comment in view of the narcissistic model of textual being that I have set up in Part One. It establishes a patently Oedipal fantasy (a young doctor arouses the sexual interest of the wife of an older doctor whom he has come to the provinces to assist and whom he finds dishonest and incompetent) and then veers off into what is clearly of more interest

to the author: a contest between the flirtatiousness of the wife and
the resistance of the young doctor:

> 'Do you believe in love at first sight?'
> 'Love is the one subject that bores me . . . . intolerably. . . .'
> 'I wish you would discuss it with me,' she said
> mischievously.   (*UN* 91–2)

Shaw has not learned very well at this point how to idealise either
the sexualised other or the resistant self, and the result is coyness,
a besetting sin in his work. One can see that the conflict he most
wanted to dramatise was between the desire to be captured by the
woman and the fear of being so captured. The way it emerges in
this text helps us see that it derives from a pre-Oedipal fantasy.

Shaw served his long apprenticeship by writing not only 'the
five long novels and the bushels of articles that were refused' (*CL*
1 800) but also numerous reviews (mostly about music) and articles,
not to mention a great many speeches and tracts on behalf of the
Fabians. Surveying the reviews and articles, one can see the
stiffness and self-consciousness gradually disappear from the
writer's voice. The highlights of his earliest criticism are moments
of impudent, rather contrived wit:

> The better to convey the foppishness of the character, [X] adopted
> the unaccountable expedient of moving about as though his
> ankles were tied together.   (*SM* 1: 65)

> If it is retorted on us that generous and enlightened criticism
> should rather dwell on his merits, we reply that we have not
> yet discovered what his merits are.   (*SM* 1: 139)

By the mid 1880s he was capable of phrasing perceptions that are
worth independent quotation a century later:

> The moral of all this is that our Festival committees are mistaken
> in their policy of looking for sacred oratories. They seem to
> believe – on the unsound principle that what has been done
> once may be done again – that another Handel may turn up
> some day with another Messiah. But he will not. If Handel were
> alive today, his messiah would wear another guise, which would
> probably not be recognizable by the Birmingham committee as

a sacred one, and which would certainly not be explicitly religious.   (*SM* 1: 348)

Shaw was accurate enough in describing himself in 1890 as the kind of genius who is 'immature at thirty' (*CL* ɪ 332). But it is too simple to attribute this immaturity to the fact of having made a false start in an uncongenial form. As a Diary note of 1885 informs us, he aspired to write a new *Pilgrim's Progress*, not an easy task to accomplish either in dramatic or novelistic form (*DI* 101).

He liked to call himself a realist, in fiction or drama, but he meant, as usual, to distinguish one connotation of the word from another. Notes prepared in 1888 for a debate on the resolution That Realism Is the Goal of Fiction distinguish a visionary sense of the term exemplified in Bunyan, Dante and Shelley from a worldly sense exemplified in Zola, Thackeray and George Eliot.[2] Zola's naturalism could be admired as a necessary clearing of the ground, though it did not lead us on. Thackeray and Eliot could be admired for their marvellous powers of observation, though they did not question the social and economic system that governed and limited the thinking of their characters. But Shaw did not want to write allegory. He relished the varieties of individual temperament, especially if, in Dickensian fashion, appreciation and satire could be fused. What he sought was the means to forge a hero who stands over against the given social system yet retains in his consequent isolation an essential self-possession. And this he discovered in Karl Marx.

Later, Shaw claimed that reading Marx made a man of him (Henderson, 1956, p. 33). His enthusiasm is to be explained less by the discovery of a doctrine as such than of a prophetic style. In 1889 he had rhapsodised:

The impression [Marx] makes depends not on the soundness of his views but on their magnificent scope and on his own impenetrable conviction of their validity. . . . [He] feels not one moment of ruth for the present system of privileges, whatever can be said in its favor . . . and writes of the nineteenth century as if it were a cloud passing in the wind. He never condescends to cast a glance of useless longing at the past: his cry to the present is always 'Pass by, we are waiting for the future.' Nor is the future at all mysterious, uncertain or dreadful to him. There is not a word of hope or fear, no appeal to chance or providence,

nor vain remonstrance with nature, nor optimism, nor enthusiasm, nor pessimism, cynicism, nor any other familiar sign of the
giddiness which seizes on men when they climb to heights
which command a view of the past, present and future of human
society. Marx keeps his head like a god. He has discovered the
law of social development, and knows what must come. The
thread of history is in his hand.[3]

It is as if a burden of self-doubt has been lifted. Now Shaw need
no longer feel like a man with a grievance, worried that his moral
indignation was only a product of personal envy. Now he need
no longer feel in a false position caused by a conviction of superior
power without a clear idea, beyond self-interest, to which to attach
that conviction. He could believe now 'in the greatness of [his]
own age & time & inheritance', and thus save himself from 'the
most horrible confusion of mind and contrariety of spirit' (*CL* I
655–66).

The first effective application of this new vision was his extensive
and brilliant contribution to *Fabian Essays in Socialism* (1889) in
which Shaw analysed the capitalistic ethic with a remarkable
mixture of passion and imperturbability, of indignation at present
wrongs and confidence in the future – as in the peroration which
begins with a distinctively Shavian brand of irony: 'Let me, in
conclusion, disavow all admiration for this inevitable, but sordid,
slow, reluctant, cowardly path to justice' (*C* 30: 62). With the help
of Marx, Shaw learned to stand both in the midst of his age and
apart from it.[4] This double perspective would help him develop
an original form of dramatic comedy.

I am not really questioning the view that Shaw's natural bent
was for drama rather than fiction. Margery Morgan (1972) puts it
well: 'The external approach of setting attitude against attitude
rather than working within the first to modify and humanize it is
less suitable for the realistic novel than for the stage' (p. 17).
Certainly, the dramatic form encourages sudden and stylised
confrontations, tilting language toward gesture and speech at the
expense of reflection and description, although the plays retain
the latter to a notable degree in their prefaces and novelistic stage
directions. Many speeches in the novels seem to be asking for
more dramatic treatment, for still crisper articulation and the chance
to acquire wit by spinning off another speech: for example, 'I was
born into the world: I have lived all my life in it: I have never seen

or known a person or thing that did not belong to it. How can I be anything else than worldly?' (*C* 3: 84–5).

But this penchant for the drama does not quite explain how Shaw, with his first plays, could leap clear of Gilbert, Pinero, Jones and Grundy, and find his natural rival in Ibsen. It helps to remember that, during his apprenticeship, Shaw was schooling himself (beyond his youthful indoctrination in Dickens, Bunyan and Shelley) in Marx, Butler and Schopenhauer, and was constantly testing what he liked to call his original morality or original psychology by means of debate and speechmaking. It helps to remember, too, that the phrase 'first plays' is not quite accurate, although it is customary. Dan Laurence has assembled the evidence to show that, from adolescence, Shaw was a kind of closet dramatist, making fairly serious efforts not only in *Passion Play*, earlier quoted, and in the first (1885) version of *Widowers' Houses*, which is pretty well known, but also in half-a-dozen other instances (*B* 7: 481–6).[5] Moreover, the letters of the 1880s contain a number of references to playwriting, and toward 1890 these become more intense, patently protective of an emerging desire. In 1889 he tells one correspondent that he will write a 'suggestive comedy of modern society, guaranteed correct in philosophic & economic detail, and unactably independent of theatrical considerations' (*CL* I 222). Early in 1890 he tells another: 'My next effort in fiction – if I ever have time to make one – will be a play' (*CL* I 241). In a music review shortly afterward he jests: 'If I ever take to playwriting (one never knows how low one may fall), I shall do a London Bourgeois Gentilhomme' (*SM* 2: 23). Shaw must have sensed too that, as he put it a few years later, one is spurred to ambitious literary achievement by a 'dissatisfaction with existing masterpieces' (*OTN* II 248), and accordingly, in 1889, he was reviewing the ending of *A Doll's House*.[6] The question of Shaw's late start should take into account as well the fact that the relatively unknown author of the 1880s could hardly hope to command the expense of mounting a theatrical production, and probably turned to novel writing on prudential grounds. Shaw is disingenuous when he says in 1898 that he wrote *Widowers' Houses* in 1892 to save English honour, manufacturing evidence for the New Drama that everyone, including himself, was talking about (*B* 1: 371). But he was franker about the matter when he wrote to Daniel Macmillan in 1943: 'I wrote novels because everyone did so then; and the theatre, my rightful kingdom, was outside literature. The coterie theatres in which I first reached the public as a playwright did not then exist' (*CL* IV 675).

Shaw's 'first' play, not surprisingly, is rather clumsy dramaturgically, especially before it was revised for publication in 1898, but it already clearly incorporates a dimension of significance lacking in the commercially successful drama of Pinero and Jones, and is indeed reminiscent of Ibsen. Some higher moral ground (a Socialist ideal hinted at by titular allusion) shadowily passes judgement on the characters, who have all repudiated it.

The central figure, Sartorius, a better-defined Trefusis, is a slum landlord who unmasks the 'idealist' illusion of the young man engaged to his daughter. The young man, Dr Trench, would like to think that he can separate his fiancée, Blanche, from his own income, which derives mainly from the investments of his aristocratic aunt. But he is disillusioned. The play's finest surprise is his discovery that his aunt's income derives from investment in real estate which Sartorious manages, gouging the poor to get the highest rent at the least cost. The disillusionment exposes not simply the truth about a contrived complication of circumstances, as would be the case in a conventional play, but about how an economic system works; specifically, the truth that money circulates in a society the way blood circulates in a body, and cannot be freer of taint than the system itself is. In one mood Shaw boasted that he had accomplished the implausible feat of getting the bluebook across the footlights, in another that *Widowers' Houses* was a work of art as much as any comedy of Molière. Certainly the latter description is more accurate. This is a drama, not a sermon.

The educative function of Sartorius is credibly linked to his character. Although he has a strength that comes from knowing he is doing society's dirty work, he is yet anxious to be accepted by the aristocratic aunt and therefore is motivated to win over the young man; his name, Holroyd (1988) plausibly comments, 'suggests society in its formal dress' (p. 280). When Sartorius explains that he serves Trench just as he is served in turn by his unsavoury rent-collector (with the Dickensian name of Lickcheese[7]), the disillusioned Trench asks, 'Do you mean to say that I am just as bad as you are?' (*B* 1: 94). To which Sartorius coolly replies, 'You mean that you are just as powerless to alter the state of society.' Trench is not at all prepared to imagine a reformed, socialist society, merely mentioned as an unlikely possibility by his instructor who, unlike author and audience, is unaware of the titular allusion to Christ's condemnation of men who devour widowers' houses while clothed in respectability. When his hand is forced, Trench accepts the hypocrisy, is reunited with his angry fiancée, and exits with her and the others, conspiratorially, to dinner.

The play, then, seems to make a cynical point – hardly an improvement on the sentimental drama Shaw disliked and shrewdly criticised. But Sartorius's hypocrisy is principled and, up to a point, convincing. I doubt that Shaw quite persuades us, in or out of the play, that his landlord could make no humane modification within the given system, but he is not shown to be a rascal – or he is 'a rascal only in his indifference to the defects of our social system' (*CP* 678). We already find in this first play the mixture of tragic and comic that Shaw much admired in *The Wild Duck* (*OTN* III 138), but the tragic aspect is less horrifying than in Ibsen's play, and the comic laughter at ignorance is buoyant enough to imply a possible solution.

The suddenness of Trench's turnabout has sometimes been criticised, but that kind of peripeteia is really inherent in Shavian comedy, and is justified by the fact that the error involved is an aspect of social rather than individual pathology and therefore not too deeply repressed. (Actually, in this case, there are stages of disillusionment neatly marked off by changes of scene and season: from garden restaurant on the Rhine in summer to a rented villa downriver at Surbiton in autumn to a flat in Bedford Square in winter.) What is far more curious, and requires a moment's attention here, is the sudden and intense outburst of Blanche.

Even in act 1 Shaw had trouble keeping her in check and toned down an earlier version of her lovemaking with Trench.[8] But when she is finally enlightened (by a bluebook left behind on the table!) about her father's work and reputation, she becomes ferocious. Resenting secrecy and rejecting gallantry, she first throttles her maid and later attacks her lover for not telling her at once about her tainted money, whereupon, '*in a flush of undisguised animal excitement*', she '*crushes him in an ecstatic embrace*' (*B* 1: 119, 121). If her name first suggests innocence, it finally suggests the power to appal.

Shaw has given her greater strength than the scene requires so that she seems to leap beyond the frame that contains the others. Trench is paralysed by her outburst and we are puzzled by it. William Archer confessed that the character of Blanche, in particular

the violent lovemaking, 'filled me with despair'. No lady he knew
was like that (Ervine, 1956, p. 173). This is doubtless too fastidious
a judgement, as in the complaint of a correspondent who witnessed
Man and Superman that Ann was 'bestial' (*CL* ɪɪ 474). A dramatist
is entitled to a preference for vital and energetic over delicate and
refined women if he can make the context support them, and for
Shaw it was a matter of principle to try to do so: 'We want more
women of the clever positive type on the stage' (*OTN* ɪɪ 112). The
problem in *Widowers' Houses* is that he doesn't quite know what
Blanche is about.

The role of Blanche suggests that there was a hidden connection
in Shaw's mind between sexual and creative power on the one
hand, and the power of money on the other. In his fascination
with the positivity of his heroine, the dramatist seems to want to
say something about his hatred of the poor. When her father
catches up her statement that the poor make her suffer, Blanche
shifts her ground and says, 'I hate the very idea of such things. I
don't want to know about them' (*B* 1: 110–11). This is more than
the voice of social snobbery. One seems to hear also Shaw's
own hatred of poverty, or hatred of his own sense of poverty,
compensated by a creative exuberance that is hard to distinguish
from a sublimated sexual exuberance. But in this early play, the
voice of devouring desire is as seemingly causeless as it is unde-
niably compelling. In the original version of the play, Blanche was
to have no family, as if she embodied an inexplicable and underived
force.

The Philanderer, though somewhat loosely constructed, introduces to Shavian drama a good deal of comic sparkle, a quality
almost absent in *Widowers' Houses*, where it is confined to the weak
figure of Cokane who stands for 'tact', a euphemism for snobbery.
Writing it must have educated Shaw rapidly in the craft of comedy,
for within the next two years he composed works as elegant as
Arms and the Man and *You Never Can Tell*.

One might say, in fact, that *You Never Can Tell* is the play *The
Philanderer* is trying to be. The old comic irony of theoretic lovers
who are not as immune from amorous need as they suppose is
better handled in the later play. So is the old comic irony of children
who expose the presumptuousness of parental claims of filial duty.
You Never Can Tell really makes these conventions dance, a point
especially well made by Margery Morgan (1972, pp. 83–90) and by
A. M. Gibbs (1983, pp. 90–103). Stanley Kauffmann considers it

the most seriously underrated of Shaw's plays, indeed 'the greatest high comedy in the English language after Sheridan' (1986, pp. 34–6). Harry Levin (1987, pp. 19, 23, 121) and Frederick McDowell (Turco, 1986, pp. 63–83) demonstrate its archetypal affinities with comic tradition, with *commedia dell'arte*, Shakespeare and Restoration comedy. More than any other of his works, I think, it justifies Shaw's claim (alternating with the claim to be nothing more than a propagandist) to be nothing more than a dramatist in the classic tradition of Aristophanes, Shakespeare and Molière (*CL* IV 783). I neglect it here only because it is less dependent on his distinctive vision, less illustrative of the comic sublime. Interestingly, according to Henderson (1932), Shaw sometimes spoke of it as 'the best play that was ever written' and sometimes as 'the greatest trash' (p. 708).

By comparison with *You Never Can Tell*, *The Philanderer* is self-consciously cute. The parental generation find the New Drama abhorrent because it rejects 'scenes of suffering nobly endured and sacrifice willingly rendered by womanly women and manly men' (*B* 1: 159), whereas the filial generation belong to an Ibsen club whose business appears to consist of being facetious precisely about those stereotypes:

> GRACE. I will never marry a man I love too much. It would give him a terrible advantage over me. I should be utterly in his power . . . .
> CHARTERIS. You must marry someone else; and I'll come and philander with you. (*B* 1: 185–6)

It is fitting that the male lead is idiosyncratically named Charteris (reminiscent of Trefusis) rather than, as in *You Never Can Tell*, Valentine.

The Philanderer is an unpleasant play in more than the rather superficial sense designated by Shaw, and it is to the credit of his critical judgement that he (sometimes) spoke of it derogatorily (Dent, 1952, p. 81, but see *CL* III 838). Charteris both attracts intimacy and rebuffs it. He talks of marriage to Grace while suggesting she 'marry someone else', and he gives the unwomanly, jealous and stormy Julia hope to feed on while passing her off to another man. Augustin Filon perceptively observed, '*Que veut-il? S'amuser. Seulement*' (Henderson, 1932, p. 461). The dramatic effects are often coy and prurient. Philandering, in this instance, seems to mean something like peek-a-boo.

But the climactic scene deserves attention here because, though awkward, it makes an honourable effort to accommodate the image of the powerful woman, that lodestar of the Shavian imagination.

Charteris makes a coy speech about the doom of the philanderer ('no fireside, no little ones'), but when Julia savagely mocks him and herself, he remains *'amused and untouched'* while the others – and this receives terminal emphasis – *'look at Julia with concern, and even a little awe, feeling for the first time the presence of a keen sorrow'* (*B* 1: 227). More clearly than in the case of Blanche, Julia becomes at last a scapegoat figure on whom is put the burden of something pushed aside from the general movement of the play. The strong woman is belatedly foregrounded and invested with importance.

Shaw would soon devise three effective means of accommodating the strong woman in dramatic form. One was to soften her force with charm, as he did with Raina, Cleopatra and Lady Cicely. Another was to invest her with philosophic importance, as he did with Ann Whitefield and, later, with Lilith and Joan. A third way, the first to be employed and not necessarily exclusive of the others, was to create a heroine rather than hero who resists the egotism of sexual romance and the concomitant ethic of capitalism. Shaw's next heroine, Vivie Warren, is usually discussed, at his suggestion, as a 'new type in modern fiction' (*CL* II 34), the 'independent young woman of the governing class' (Berst, 1973, p. 7n). In the use made of her reactive resistance, her play is also the first of Shaw's to illustrate what I have called the comic sublime.

I agree with Eric Bentley (1960) that the two long scenes between mother and daughter, in acts 2 and 4, 'are emotional playwriting such as England had not seen for a couple of centuries' (p. xxvi), a judgement the more cogent if we compare *Mrs Warren's Profession* to the various earlier workings of the same plot material (Meisel, 1963, pp. 133–59). In *The Philanderer* the conflict of generations was rather facile, impudence set against fatuousness. Here it is subtle and serious. Faithful to the dynamics of the sublime, the seeker's exalting energy is released from a substantial, serio-comic resistance – in this case, from the very plausible hypocrisy of Mrs Warren, who is right from her own point of view yet, like Sartorius, implicitly self-condemned for her indifference to the defects of our social system, 'a hopelessly Private Person' (*B* 1: 255). The energy of Shaw's approval of her, however limited ultimately, is palpable: 'Though it is quite natural and right for Mrs Warren to choose what is, according to her lights, the least immoral alternative, it is none the less infamous of society to offer such alternatives' (*B* 1: 255). He advised an actress in 1926 to play Mrs Warren as a 'victorious vindicator' of her career, 'morally wiping the floor with Vivie' (*CL* IV 15).

Mrs Warren is brilliantly established in act 1 as a mixture of the easy comrade and the bossy sentimentalist, attractively free of ordinary social scruples yet unscrupulously self-seeking too, a combination epitomised by the clever and charming Frank Gardner in the phrase, 'a good sort but a bad lot' (*B* 1: 324). The first act curtain captures it neatly. She has just recognised an old lover, the pompous Reverend Gardner, who has told his irreverent son (and us) of having written infatuated letters in his youth that could not be bought but were, mercifully, never used:

MRS WARREN [*swooping on the Reverend Samuel*]. Why, it's Sam Gardner gone into the Church! Well, I never! Dont you know us, Sam? This is George Crofts, as large as life and twice as natural. Dont you remember me?

REV. S. [*very red*]. I really – er –

MRS WARREN. Of course you do. Why, I have a whole album of your letters still: I came across them only the other day.

REV. S. [*miserably confused*]. Miss Vavasour, I believe.

MRS WARREN [*correcting him quickly in a loud whisper*]. Tch! Nonsense! Mrs Warren: dont you see my daughter there? (*B* 1: 291)

Mrs Warren's pleasure in embarrassing a former lover and her motherly concern for her daughter's innocence make a wonderfully grotesque combination and are rendered with colloquial ease.

We do not dislike Mrs Warren – the fact that she treats Vivie as a child seems more ignorant than malicious – but we wouldn't suppose from act 1 that her conduct was capable of a moral defence. In act 2, however, she is able to show her daughter that, given exiguous circumstances, it was the result of a defensible choice: 'The only way for a woman to provide for herself decently is for her to be good to some man who can afford to be good to her' (*B* 1: 314). The argument is backed up by a strong story about an impoverished childhood, the miserable fate of 'respectable' sisters, and the escape of one sister and herself by way of prostitution. Her opportunistic immorality thus appears to be pragmatic wisdom, and wins Vivie's tender admiration as the curtain falls.

But there are from the first indications of potential strength in Vivie that will make this admiration only a stage of growth – her recent achievement in Cambridge's maths tripos, along with her unwomanly forthrightness of manner and conviction. Indeed she tells Praed that she expects one day to take her mother by surprise. By the end of the play she is ready to move beyond complicity with an immoral society, and, in the climactic confrontation, rejects her mother not for having become a prostitute, or even for having continued as procuress after gaining sufficient means, but because her mother remains at heart a conventional woman and a conventional moralist. It is a finer surprise than the cynical–sentimental capitulation of the daughter in the antecedent versions of Maupassant and Augier.[9]

Vivie's is not an easy victory. Mrs Warren makes a strong point in exclaiming, with an irony sharpened by a seasoned sense of reality, 'Lord help the world if everybody took to doing the right thing' (B 1: 355). She is not heroic enough to stand against society herself, but she knows, as we do, that it is dangerous to do so. As John Tanner will wittily put it, 'It is dangerous to be sincere unless you are also stupid' (B 2: 796). Vivie is not stupid, but she is heroic. She risks the danger of repudiating a supportive but unjust social morality, one that sanctions double standards for men and women, for parents and children. But her repudiation acknowledges the partial truth of her mother's way, the parallel of her own opposition to it, and thereby establishes the dynamic of her sublime spring: 'I am like you: I must have work, and must make more money than I spend. But my work is not your work, and my way not your way' (B 1: 353). The hyperbolic allusion to Job is earned and strong. Elsewhere Shaw wrote of the 'ignoble irrelevance of the retort of God to Job' (B 4: 131). (Indeed, his Black Girl, searching for God, asserts: 'It isn't an argument: it's a sneer.') But, true to the romantic tradition of naturalising the supernatural, the retort becomes for him noble and relevant when fitted to an entirely human confrontation.[10]

Vivie's rejection of her mother is enforced by her rejection of other temptations: Praed's temptation of artistic beauty, Croft's of moneyed marriage, Frank's of romantic love. Charles Berst (1973) calls this work a moral allegory that might well have been entitled The Battle for the Soul of Vivie Warren (p. 6). Shaw did take pains to make these tempters plausible from their own points of view, even the egregious Crofts. When Vivie rejects him, she attacks not so much the man himself as the corrupt social values to which he is unconsciously loyal: 'When I think of the society that tolerates you and the laws that protect you!' (*B* 1: 332). Praed is a sympathetic if weak figure, boyish in his love of art. (Shaw has put into his mouth one element of his self-portrait, the feeling of having never grown up.) And Frank, 'an agreeable young spark, wholly good-for-nothing' (*CL* I 404), is genuinely charming, wittily impudent and keen. He earns at the end an unrhetorical goodbye.

But it is precisely in presenting the romantic relations between Vivie and Frank that Shaw had the greatest difficulty in managing the material of his play. Mrs Warren implies at one point, in line with a letter Shaw wrote to Janet Achurch (*CL* I 404), that she is uncertain who Vivie's father is, opening up the possibility that it could be Frank. At another point she tells Vivie that she knows 'at least' it is not either the Reverend Gardner or Crofts (*B* 1: 308). When Crofts stuns the two young people with the statement that they are half-brother and -sister, we must presume, then, that his spite is based either on uncertainty or on the definite knowledge that he is lying. In any case, we do not see him, according to the Achurch letter, 'restrained by a continual doubt as to whether the heroine may not be his daughter'.

There is further fudging on Shaw's part in the fact that their first reaction to Crofts' revelation, at the end of act 3, is shock and bewilderment: she asks Frank to shoot her, they regress to childlike intimacy, and she announces she will bury herself in an actuarial job 'for the rest of my life' (*B* 1: 334–4), whereas in act 4 they are healthily contemptuous of the incest taboo, agreeing that it makes 'no real diffierence' (339). But earlier she indicated that embracing Frank would now make 'all my flesh creep' (334), which is itself a toned down version of the original speech.[11]

Shaw's indecisiveness makes itself felt in an otherwise strong final tableau. The stage directions indicate that, after reading Frank's note, Vivie *'tosses the pieces into wastepaper basket without a second thought'* and *'goes at her work with a plunge'* (356). But if she is rejecting Frank only because of his fecklessness, without the scruple of consanguinity that she has declared her independence of, we would like to see some distinction implied between romance with Frank and all possible romance. It seems as if she has suddenly jumped from a specific to a general repudiation, and is gaining freedom from her mother's world at too high a price. I would rather not say, however, as do Berst and Ganz, that the final impression is of Vivie's not facing reality, for Shaw indicates without irony that he wants her finally to appear buoyant. If her isolation strikes us as chilling, this is to some extent inherent (as the third act of *Man and Superman* shows) in the extravagant idea of marching to the plains of heaven. The sublime is purchased by the renunciation of the beautiful. The end result is an exemplary consciousness that should not be subjected to a realistic curiosity about the day after. Despite the play's realism, the final tableau is, in large part, symbolic gesture.

3
Development of the Comic Sublime

Arms and the Man (along with *You Never Can Tell*) is the most fluent of the early comedies, and was the first to be something of a commercial success. (The hard-working, 38-year-old author opened a bank account for the first time in his life.) Like *Pygmalion* it has proved to be very adaptable to popularisation, partly because it cleverly exploits so many well tried comic conventions. Indeed, as Maurice Valency (1973) observed, the whole plot of a soldier returning to claim the lady and defeating the local rival is an old story (p. 107). Later, Shaw himself turned upon the play, calling it 'a bag of the oldest stage tricks' (*ST* 132).

None the less, it is an important and characteristic performance, and Shaw was justified in being distressed by the broad farcicality of the early productions. In this first of the so-called pleasant plays, he had learned, as Arthur Nethercot (1954) put it, that 'he can create romantic situations and sympathetic characters in an ostensibly anti-romantic play' (p. 55). This fusion accounts for the charming light irony sustained from the opening scene indication ('a lady's bedchamber in Bulgaria') to the buoyant finale. The influence of opera, in which Shaw was steeped from childhood, makes itself felt here for the first time. Herbert Lindenberger's (1984) observation is apt, that opera served him 'as a means of transcending the limitations of a narrowly representational form . . . the late nineteenth century well-made realist play' (p. 66).

The heroine Raina may have been conceived as a female Charteris, for in a draft of the play she informs Bluntschli that 'the man who marries me will have to put up with my heroics with other men' (British Library Additional MS 50601). Traces of this conception remain in her eavesdropping and resourceful machinations. But Shaw also invests her with charm by making her vulnerable because of her untenable idealism of love – 'the noble attitude' and the 'thrilling voice' (*B* 1: 446). She discards the pretence of 'the higher love' and bestows a not unromantic tenderness upon an apparently prosaic man.

The forceful role of Bluntschli, known to have been modelled on Sidney Webb, is similarly softened by charm. The hero is finally no more unromantic than the heroine, though they start from different points. Given his name, the description of his person and his prosaic attitudes towards love and war, we judge him at first as his aristocratic rival does, 'bourgeois to his boots' (422). (For Cecil Lewis's 1932 film scenario, Shaw recommended a dry voice for Bluntschli, a ringing one for Sergius – see *ThC* 38.) But as the play progresses, his straightforward efficiency attains the dimension of the marvellous. Not only does he climb a drainpipe to a bedroom rather than escaping enemy fire by ducking into a cellar. Not only does he return a borrowed coat in person in order to catch another glimpse of the lady who saved his life. He also organises with great dispatch the complex task of sending soldiers home, to the bafflement of Majors Saranoff and Petkoff, and sweeps up the daughter of the house in hyper-prosaic fashion.

Charm, however, does not quite obscure an ironic point about the heroic mentality. The last words of the play are Sergius's uncertain tribute: 'What a man! Is he a man!' (472). Originally they were simply, 'What a man! What a man!' (British Library Additional MS 50601). The change incorporates a suggestion of inhumanity in the idea of a super-man. Interestingly, Cecil Lewis in the film changed the phrase back to its original form, as if to spare his popular audience an ambiguous fillip.

Sergius does not accept Bluntschli's pedagogical disillusionment as gracefully as Raina does. He becomes a curious combination of life-is-a-joke cynic and I-never-withdraw romantic, which leads him to marriage with the Petkoffs' aspiring maidservant. Shaw liked to think of him as someone who takes himself seriously but cannot be taken seriously by us, like Torvald Helmer of *A Doll's House*, and was distressed that his role in particular was played so farcically. His conversion from romance to realism is, after all, parallel to Raina's, and his marriage to Louka can be understood as a symbolic realignment.

The Petkoff parents must, of course, be played broadly, and are very funny. So must the super-servants, though Nicola in particular, with his *'low but clear and keen intelligence'* (B 1: 412), is not merely conventional. Having perfected the art of service, blandly agreeing with Louka that he has the soul of a servant, he conducts himself in trying circumstances with such self-possession that he earns from Bluntschli the tribute of being thought 'the ablest man . . . in Bulgaria' (466). His freedom from illusion at an unheroic level reminds us in one way of Mrs Warren, in other ways of the super-servant William in *You Never Can Tell* and of Burgoyne, the admirable but unheroic gentleman of *The Devil's Disciple*. Shaw was learning to discriminate several levels of articulate 'lower realism', and thus several modes of comic resistance to heroic aspiration.

The heroic aspect of *Arms and the Man* is never quite separate from the comic and is especially well fused with it toward the end. If it is a question of putting the credentials of a bourgeois suitor on a par (at least) with those of a gentleman, how grandly absurd an invention is a hotelkeeper-father's will with its thousands of sheets, blankets, dessert spoons and so forth. When it is necessary to modify Bluntschli's omnicompetence and at the same time make the girlish heroine more womanly so that the two can conclude as approximate equals, Shaw cleverly exploits the device of having him boast to a friend on whose discretion he could rely about his extraordinary adventure, miscalculate the young lady's age, and clumsily forget to look in the pocket of the returned coat where she had put an inscribed picture of herself, a device improved by their having to co-operate, once the discovery is made, to deceive the others.

In view of the serious theme of transvalued values, Walkley's contemporary assessment, 'second hand Gilbertism' (Berst, 1973, p. 21n), is not quite fair. Yet there is on balance something soft about *Arms and the Man*. (Holroyd, 1988, calls it 'a nursery play' – see p. 297.) The realistic romance of hero and heroine is from the beginning too childlike and at the end, when marriage looms, becomes coy and evasive. Having learned suddenly that Raina is of eligible age, Bluntschli swiftly makes up his mind, formally proposes, is accepted with a momentary tenderness, gives a quick boyish laugh, and immediately announces his leavetaking and return in a brisk, businesslike way. Although the abruptness is exaggerated enough to be amusing, Shaw evades the suggestion of a mutual flame by letting his couple regress into a chocolate-cream cosiness, ignoring the fact that a point has been made of Raina's growth into a more mature view of life. Lacking the resources of *Man and Superman* where the lovers meet strenuously at a higher level, the play in its very charm leaves us with a hint of authorial discomfort.

Eight months after the opening performance of *Arms and the Man*, Shaw was reading to friends a new play that continues to be his most controverted. We shall probably never consensualise our view of *Candida* because the three major characters are all presented with a peculiarly unstable ambivalence; a further brief may always be filed for or against any one of them. But this very unresolvability helps the play retain a special fascination. Shaw was trying to work more directly than heretofore with the most potent icon of his imagination.

In a preface written three years after the play itself, Shaw describes its primary conflict as one between a 'higher but vaguer and timider vision' and a 'clear, bold, sure, sensible, benevolent, salutarily shortsighted Christian Socialist idealism' (*B* 1: 374–5). This neatly outlines his ambivalence toward Marchbanks and Morell, but it implies more firmness of definition than we actually find.

The strength of the young lover is supposed to be a poet's strength, but it is mainly evident to us as a certain keen contempt for his rival's naïvete. Although his longing for love is authentic, his poeticity consists in too large part of fastidious recoilings from the mundane world and of verbal posies for his lady in weak imitation of Rossetti, hardly doing justice to his creator's admiration for De Quincey and Shelley on whom he is modelled.[1] Until the end, and then only tentatively, we do not perceive in him an authentic 'higher . . . vision'. The true Shavian poet, it seems, must be assigned the congenial subject of salvation rather than the uncongenial subject of love.

The strength of the married rival is supposed to consist of an effective and worldly goodwill, which is merely a certain honourableness beneath a veneer of complacence. Shaw complicates the role by trying to suggest that Morell is a poet too: his eloquence awes his curate and secretary, and he himself tells Marchbanks, 'my talent is like yours insofar as it has any real worth at all. It is the gift of finding words for divine truth' (*B* 1: 543). This is the first play in which Shaw opposed two potentially heroic strengths, though the contrast is somewhat muddled. It is not until *The Devil's Disciple* that these strengths are distributed into truly contrasting roles, that of saint and soldier.

None the less, the first two acts are well constructed as a contest of respective strengths. In the first, Eugene's thrusting intelligence penetrates the complacent confidence of his older rival, leaving him visibly shaken as the curtain falls. In the second, Morell regains the advantage by rising above the temptation of jealousy (much as Napoleon would do *vis-à-vis* the Strange Lady in the soon-to-be-written *Man of Destiny*), and at the curtain leaves Eugene impressed and Candida puzzled. The element that most disturbs the balance in the first two acts, and fractures it in the third, is Candida herself.

The calming protectiveness implied by her *'serene brow'*, ennobling *'largeness of mind'*, *'dignity of character'* and *'amused maternal indulgence'* (B 1: 532) are in practice difficult to distinguish from manipulation and even contempt. 'James is master here', she tells Eugene (588). 'Eugene's always right', she tells James (564). 'My boy [i.e. husband] shall not be worried', she warns Eugene (581). But she hurtfully teases James with such remarks as: 'It seems unfair that all the love should go to you, and none to him; although he needs it so much more than you do' (563). At times the contempt is overt. Her husband is told that his sermons are 'mere phrases that you cheat yourself with' (565). Her young lover is pointed at with the words, 'Do you call that a man?' (582).

From her coaxing and commanding first words – 'Say yes, James' – to the climactic auction scene, she teases and controls. Valency (1973) comments: 'Candida mothers everyone and loves no one. She is completely self-sufficient. . . . As Shaw shows her to us, Candida is readily accessible but impossible to please' (p. 126). This perceptive judgement cannot fail to remind us of Shaw's mother who 'did not hate anybody, nor love anybody' (*SSS* 29). His imagination was powerfully and ambivalently drawn to such a woman, requiring and despairing of her approval, and his art was challenged to work out ever new forms to accommodate her.

Bentley (1947) compares Candida to a catalyst, disillusioning Morell, educating Marchbanks, herself unchanged (p. 110). One might elaborate upon this apt remark by saying that the disillusionment of Morell is so thorough that we can hardly imagine the future of his marriage. As for Marchbanks, we have grounds for questioning whether his sudden attainment of higher vision, his leap into the night, really does leave Candida quite behind, mired in the prose of domesticity: *'She takes his face in her hands; and as he divines her intention and falls on his knees, she kisses his forehead. Then he flies out into the night'* (B 1: 594). The implication is not exactly, as Shaw later claimed, that he is repudiating the 'stuffy fireside warmth of mothers and sisters and wives' (*CL* II 33). Rather, he seems to be accepting a sort of knighthood in order to carry her spirit with him. Despite her limitedness (and the character and name of her father, Burgess, functions largely to establish that limitedness), Candida is capable finally of being incorporated by the emergent poet as a muse, the Virgin Mother as muse. The subtitle, A Mystery, suggests a religious dimension to her role.

To be sure, the subtitle is often understood as a reference to the much debated 'secret in the poet's heart'. But this creates a difficulty. Shaw's final words tell us that Candida, along with her husband, does not know this secret. But how can that be true? Although Candida has earlier proved herself indifferent to poetry, her understanding that Marchbanks 'has learnt to live without happiness' (593) must essentially be the secret that Shaw had in mind, for it is tantamount to his own later explanation: 'what business has a man with the great destiny of poet with the small beer of domestic comfort and cuddling and petting at the apron string of some dear nice woman?' (Stanton, 1962, p. 169). Candida, then, can hardly be said to be ignorant of it. One may guess that Shaw meant to keep her ignorant, and later asserted she was, but was still rather under her spell on the last page of his play.[2] So much so, in my view, that the secret should really be understood in another way of which neither she nor Marchbanks nor Shaw himself is fully conscious. The secret is that the poet – Marchbanks or Shaw – will continue to carry a Candida-figure in his imagination. His vision requires the presence of a muse as much as the absence of a wife.

In stage directions Shaw associates Candida with Titian's 'Assumption of the Virgin', a painting which, he noted in a review of that period, represents 'a union of the flesh and the spirit . . . triumphantly beautiful' (*OTN* I 82). To Ellen Terry he admitted, 'One does not get tired of adoring the Virgin Mother . . . and Candida, between you and me, is the Virgin Mother and nobody else' (*CL* I 623). Within the play he offsets this idealisation, unevenly as we have seen, by showing her to be, and even speaking of her as, unscrupulous. Outside the play he turned increasingly against her, to the point of imagining in 1944 that he had written 'a counterblast to Ibsen's *Doll's House*, showing that in the real typical doll's house it is the man who is the doll' (Rattray, 1951, p. 102). There is a kind of truth in this judgement, but only as an admission of the weakness of Morell.

Marchbanks seems even weaker, partly because he talks about his weakness, but, as performances are likely to prove, there is more animation in his role. He is subversive, more explicitly sexual than any other character in Shaw,[3] and the only character with a modicum of irony. The play's strongest moment may be his bid in the auction scene: 'My weakness, my desolation, my heart's need' (*B* 1: 591). Shaw is here allowing Marchbanks some of his own insight into the human cost of literary power.

In the years immediately after 1895, Shaw wished to see Marchbanks as a clear precursor of the new hero delineated in Siegfried of *The Perfect Wagnerite* and Caesar of *Caesar and Cleopatra*. He is, in fact, the first character to think of the rejection of happiness specifically as a spur to something nobler. In a preface of 1898 Shaw refers to Candida as an opportunity 'to distil the quintessential drama from Pre-Raphaelitism' by dramatising its 'conflict with the first broken, nervous, stumbling attempts to formulate its own revolt against itself as it develops into something higher' (*B* 1: 373). This, of course, reminds us of the dialectical function of Wotan in *The Perfect Wagnerite*, published in the same year, the god whose function is to create the hero who will supersede him. But the play of 1895 does not break new ground quite so confidently.

Since a weakness of the sublime always corresponds in Shaw to a weakness of the comic, another way of expressing one's dissatisfaction with *Candida* is to say that all its characters lack a sense of humour. The only comic character is Candida's father Burgess, a coarse butt. It may be that Shaw degrades Burgess because he was trying, clumsily, to offset a perceived idealisation of Candida.

Before we comment on *Three Plays for Puritans* in which the development of the comic sublime is matured, it is helpful to step back and consider Shaw's changing conception of the heroic that we touched on in connection with Marchbanks. The altered conception underlies the imaginative logic of the plays in that volume and clarifies its preface's adoption of Puritanism and Diabolonianism as progressive or dialectical concepts.

Shaw's interest in moral evolution or social Darwinism goes back at least to 1887 when he wrote a review of, and was much impressed by, Samuel Butler's *Luck or Cunning*. Butler declared that Darwin's theory of natural selection 'banishes mind from the universe', a phrase Shaw quoted throughout his life. In so far as his Butlerian (and Larmarckian) counterview hardens into a doctrinal theology – according to which God is identified with a general will to perfectibility and evil is merely the trial-and-error of creative evolution – it is tedious. It is too palpably a protest against fear of disorder, chance, uncertainty, chaos. But this hardening occurs only occasionally. Of the plays, only *The Shewing-Up of Blanco Posnet* and perhaps *Back to Methuselah* are marred by doctrine, and even they dramatise more than they sermonise. The airing of some such theology in the third act of *Man and Superman* seems to me wholly absorbed by the dialectical energy of the debate. And in the work of the 1890s it is always the psychology of moral elevation that interests him and us.

From the pioneers of *The Quintessence*, to Marchbanks, Napoleon, Dick Dudgeon, Siegfried and Caesar, heroic strength is conceived as arising dynamically from an act of renunciation. Marchbanks is propelled into the night by 'fierce . . . disgust' in reaction to Candida's temptation of incestuous intimacy ('Am I your mother and sisters to you, Eugene?'). Since 'out . . . into the night' is a rather vague gesture of self-definition and since Candida's question is a rather mischievous temptation, we may say that Dudgeon's recoiling spring from the lulling passivity of Judith Anderson's home to a noble act of self-sacrifice on her husband's behalf is a more successful realisation of the sublime, though the explanation of his deed requires some questioning. Siegfried exemplifies the hero in evolutionary or, more exactly, Hegelian terms. Interpreting *The Ring*, Shaw puts aside the amoristic theme involving Siegfried and Brünhilde and the grand plangencies of *Die Götterdämmerung* to focus brilliantly on two elements: the layered allegory of greed in *Das Rheingold* and the dialectical relation of Siegfried and Wotan, hero and god. The god imagines something better than himself and the old law, bringing into existence the human hero who will destroy him. But this dialectic, for all its Hegelian appearance, is essentially a psychological conception. Shaw describes 'the philosophically fertile element' in the conception of Wagner's hero in such a way as to make clear that his interest lay in the resolution of intrapsychic conflict rather than in the unfolding of a world soul:

> [Siegfried is] a type of the healthy man raised to perfect confidence in his own impulses by an intense and joyous vitality which is above fear, sickliness of conscience, malice, and the makeshifts and moral crutches of law and order which

accompany them. Such a character appears extraordinarily fascinating and exhilarating to our guilty and conscience-ridden
generations, however little they may understand
him. (*SM* 3: 471)

The description is a blueprint for Shaw's Caesar who interests us
throughout *Caesar and Cleopatra* because his mind works differently
from the minds of more ordinary persons and makes possible a
different sort of morality.

By choosing an historical figure as the culmination of the type,
Shaw is implying the realisability of his myth of progress. But he
does not suggest that history itself or a collective will is the agent
of moral improvement. His vision of the future, even at its most
abstract in *Back to Methuselah*, is filtered through anthropomorphic
figures and individual perceptions.

The Devil's Disciple re-establishes the triangular situation of
Candida with much clearer definition, bringing forward the heroic
potential of the two men and subduing the unmanageably seductive
woman.

The Reverend Anthony Anderson of colonial New Hampshire
begins like the Reverend Morell of prosaic modern London as a
comfortably married man, but in him there is undiscovered strength
rather than weakness. '*Shrewd, genial . . . strong, healthy . . . capable
of making the most of this world*' (*B* 2: 58), he is from the first not
hurt by Richard Dudgeon's ironic insults or by Mrs Dudgeon's
envious spite. As a husband he is more considerate than affectionate
(he frequently addresses his wife as 'my dear', a locution said in
an earlier work to be a sign of coolness between spouses – *UN* 60),
which may be taken to signify his potential freedom to change.
When at the end of act 2 he realises that Richard has gone off to
accept death in his place, Anderson is suddenly transformed into
a man of war, and, with an eagerness not unmixed with relief,
puts down the wifely guardian of hearth and home as a restrainer
of heroic action. He charges out of the house without explanation,
leaving her perplexed and disappointed. (She supposes he will
abandon Richard, whose nobility has converted her hatred into
love.) But in act 3 he caps his success in saving Richard and the
town at the last minute by asking her with pride what she thinks
of him *now*. After which, he asks Richard to see the abashed Judith
home while he manages the official business with Burgoyne.
Anderson remains technically married at the end (and, since in

this lighthearted melodrama Shaw does not probe the marriage to any depth, we are not tempted, as with Morell, to wonder about his future state), but in spirit he is like the unmarried Richard, a man 'impassioned only for saving grace, and not to be turned aside by wife or mother' (B 2: 35).

The awkward young lover of Candida is transformed in *The Devil's Disciple* into an authentic ironist who in Blakean fashion wittily scorns those who live by conventional notions of virtue and vice, and finds his true purpose in rising above selfhood. But the mode of his unselfing, martyrdom, though one of the natural termini of heroic aspiration, is not one that Shaw the vitalist felt comfortable with. Like another vitalist, D. H. Lawrence, he resisted the form of tragedy, all the more perhaps because it corresponded to an underlying temptation.[4] And so the dramatist's confidence in Richard's role becomes less certain as the play proceeds.

In act 1 Shaw merges Blakean intellectual satire and Dickensian farcical satire as he brings the devil's disciple into confrontation with a group of more conventional moralists. As William Irvine (1949) suggests, Richard is a little tame as a diabolonian (p. 225), for he is really attacking a degraded Puritanism, but the attack is deftly managed and a considerable challenge for an actor, requiring rapid modulations of tone to indicate both the gaiety of his mind and the underlying seriousness of his convictions. His knowledge of the will that is about to be read makes him contemptuous, but his contempt must be expressed without a trace of his mother's spite.

Along with the Pumblechookian hypocrites Uncle William ('Would it comfort you, sister, if we were to offer up a prayer?') and Uncle Titus ('Or sing a hymn?' – B 2: 701), the spectrum of types includes Richard's oafish brother Christy who is too innocent to be resentful about the disposition of the will; he is only sorry that the will assigns him the stuffed birds rather than the china peacocks. He is a naïve literalist regarding ethical matters, permitting Shaw a wonderful drollery in act 3 when Christy is brought into the Town Hall to identify the prisoner. The question whether the man before him – his brother – is the Reverend Anderson utterly confuses him. How could anyone fail to distinguish the minister, a 'good man', from the devil's disciple, a 'bad' one (126)? At the less farcical end of the line of degraded Puritans we get the rather complex portraits of Judith Anderson and of Richard's mother.

Judith is also caught up in conventional valuations of good and bad but is altogether sincere, a purely unconscious hypocrite. Her ignorance makes her fearful and vulnerable, and Richard strikes another note when he addresses her: he affronts her gallantly, telling her that, though she deserves her reputation for good looks, he is sorry to see by her expression that she's 'a good woman'. She is of course shocked but her husband *'remains perfectly good-humoured'* (B 2: 72). Only Anderson can parry Richard's thrusts. His self-possession implies an ability to move on a plane beyond conventional good and evil where, like a Blakean angel, he can become a devil's spiritual comrade.

Mrs Dudgeon, modelled on Mrs Clenham in *Little Dorrit* as well as Mrs Joe in *Great Expectations*, combines the unconscious hypocrisy of the Shavian idealist with just enough awareness to make her errors of ignorance partly a corruption of will. Her motives of envy and revenge are near enough to the surface for us to perceive her righteous rationalisations of them as comical, though we can also see that her reasoning is serious to her. She has been hurt and wants to hurt, she has suffered and wants others to suffer. Sometimes she is close to outright farce, as when she rouses Essie, the 'irregular child' of Uncle Peter Dudgeon: 'Wake up; and be ashamed of yourself' (55). Or when she hears the minister's news of her husband's death: 'Well, I do think this is hard on me' (57). Or demurs from his reminder that punishment in the afterlife is 'not in our hands': 'Why should we do our duty and keep God's law if there is to be no difference made between us and those who follow their own likings' (60). At other times she is nearly a tragic figure, as when she complains of the injustice that women suffer under the law, confesses that her heart had always belonged to her husband's brother, or expresses her resentment to Anderson for having followed his own inclination to marry: 'Go home to your pretty wife, man, and leave me to my prayers' (62). Shaw wants her seriousness in the scene but recognises, I think, that it could make Richard's sallies seem too frivolous. His solution is to have her say very little after Richard enters, yet remain on stage as a dour presence.[5]

One must include also Richard's relation, the seventeen-year-old Essie, the only awkward note in act 1. It is a nice irony that, adoring Dick, Essie should be dismayed to hear him ask if she is a good girl. Effective too is the fact that public discussion of her irregular birth shocks him into sincerity. But her cringing before

Mrs Dudgeon is too slight a thing to be linked to his Blakean–
Shelleyan denunciation of the God to whom the world cringes,
and there is something sentimental in his desire to make his
mother's house a home where no child shall cry and no soul shall
cower. Richard sounds huffy when he angrily asks who has been
ill-treating her, as he does in act 3 when he throttles Major Swindon
for causing Judith to cry.

In the key scene of act 2, set in the Anderson home where
Richard and Judith are supping tea together after Anderson has
been called away to attend the dying Mrs Dudgeon, Richard on a
sudden impulse substitutes himself for the minister whom the
British soldiers think he is and want to hang. This beau geste was
the germ of the play's conception and remains its primary turning
point, but it challenges the interpreter.

In the preface to *Three Plays for Puritans* Shaw commented on
the enigmatic motivation of the deed. In the Anderson home,

> Dick looks round and understands the charm and the peace and
> the sanctity, but knows that such material comforts are not for
> him. When the woman nursed in that atmosphere falls in love
> with him and concludes (like the critics, who somehow always
> agree with my sentimental heroines) that he risked his life for
> her sake, he tells her the obvious truth that he would have done
> as much for any stranger – that the law of his own nature, and
> no interest nor lust whatsoever, forbad him to cry out that the
> hangman's noose should be taken off his neck only to be put on
> another man's.   (*B* 2: 35)

Would he indeed have done as much for any stranger or, as the
play itself has it, 'for any other man in the town, or any other
man's wife' (*B* 2: 113)? The motive actually dramatised (and implied
even in the first sentence of the passage quoted above) is a specific
renunciation of domestic beauty for the sake of marching to heaven
with the only man in town whom he respects – as Shaw himself
understood in a late letter to the actor Robert Donat advising him
to 'make as much as you can of the impression that Anderson's
magnanimity makes on Richard before the supper scene. That is
why he finds it impossible to betray him' (*CL* IV 581). When Judith
bursts into tears in act 3, Richard cries out that her husband 'wrung
my heart by being a man. Need you tear it by being a woman?
Has he not raised you above my insults, like himself?' (*B* 2: 93). If

Shaw wished to suggest that he was motivated only by a 'law of his own nature' (a phrase used also in the play) would he not have convinced us more effectively by presenting a less worthy beneficiary and a less pointed rejection?

I am in some disagreement with the prevailing critical view of this crucial motive, well expressed by Louis Crompton (1971):

> Man, in his best moments, is for Shaw in the grip of a transcendent racial will which has the force of moral necessity. . . . It is close to a kind of religious determinism conceived in Hegelian terms, by which the agent becomes, in a phrase Shaw adapted from Wagner, 'the Freewiller of Necessity.' . . . Dick is simply not the sort of man who can save himself by endangering Anderson.   (p. 54)

This statement corresponds pretty well to what Shaw thought he was doing in *The Devil's Disciple* but not so well to what he actually did. I press the point because Shaw did not characteristically reify the will in such a fashion. He was more a 'scientific historian' (read: psychological moralist) than a metaphysician. Dick can represent an improved type of humanity and still be governed by the dynamics of the Shavian sublime. Shaw merely toyed with the notion of a transcendent racial will both in *The Perfect Wagnerite* and elsewhere, and we would do well not to take it very seriously.

In act 3 he added another motive for his hero's choice of martyrdom, a patriotic intention to 'send Burgoyne back across the Atlantic and make America a nation' (111), indicating how uncertain he really was about the matter. At a performance of the play I heard a London audience laugh at these words as if they were mockery. I don't think that is quite its intention, but an audience with some knowledge of Shaw can hardly be blamed for supposing that it is. And indeed he himself was apparently not satisfied with it because Judith follows with: 'Oh, what does all that matter?' To which Dick adds, 'True, what does it matter?' We may suppose that Shaw was embarrassed by this attempt to account for his hero's perseverance, especially in view of the opening stage direction which announces in Swiftian fashion that both sides were highmindedly determined to kill as many of one another as possible.

Shaw's trouble with Dick in act 3 seems to derive from his own ambivalence toward martyrdom. We cannot help noticing his hero's complacence on the gallows, nor can Judith, who says, 'I believe you *want* to die' (112). The fear of death is never effectively imagined by Shaw, yet the image of martyrdom attracted him because it gave simultaneous expression to his horror of killing and his love of victory. And in this case the logic of melodrama doubtless induced him to let his would-be martyr dangle to the last minute before the inevitable rescue. Yet he is clearly not as comfortable with Dick's brand of heroism as with Anderson's. At the end, the soldier pays a condescending tribute to the courage of the saint.

In short, Shaw's devil's disciple is most convincing in act 3 when he is resisting the blandishments of Judith Anderson and, with wit and scorn, the official, military procedures of Burgoyne, Swindon and the Chaplain; and least convincing in the role of patriot and martyr. His 'Thou shalt not kill' in prompt response to the Chaplain's 'Man that is born of woman' resounds forcefully whereas his 'My life for the world's future' does not (134, 137).

The role of Judith may seem to lack the strength I have suggested it has. I believe Shaw himself underrated it, and critics have followed him here. It provides, in fact, along with that of Burgoyne, much of the resistance to the heroic, hence the comic irony, without which the Shavian sublime loses its peculiar character and force. Her illusion about her husband was a natural mistake since she had no reason to suspect that her Tony would change from mild minister to aggressive soldier, and, though she remains sentimental (falling in love with Richard because he acted nobly and believing he did so for love of her), she protests tellingly against the heroism of both husband and lover, allowing us to measure its cost and appreciate its underlying energy.

When the British soldiers knock on Anderson's door, the reck-lessness of the two men and the life-affirming quality of the woman begin to emerge. The exchange of coats strikes Dick as humorous but horrifies her. When both of the men reject her – first Dick by going off to his certain death and then Tony by going off to save himself (as she thinks, but she knows in any case he could not save Dick directly without sacrificing himself) – her voice acquires some moral authority. Watching her husband depart determinedly, she cries out: 'I know you will take your own way as he took it. I have no power . . . I'm only a woman' (102). When she goes to visit Dick in the Waiting Room of the Town Hall, she protests not only his indifference to her love but also his complacency as a condemned man. Dick himself admits that 'men have these strange notions . . . and women see the folly of them' (111). In the subsequent dialogue, Shaw plays off the seriousness of her claim, however selfish, against the flippancy of his, however selfless. Perhaps her strongest protest on behalf of a sane 'lower realism' is her interruption of the elegant exchange between Richard and Burgoyne in which the two, each following a principle rather than a spontaneous impulse, discuss the imminent hanging as if it were a social engagement: 'Oh, you are mad. Is it nothing to you what wicked thing you do if only you do it like a gentleman?' (123).

Shaw is obliged by his happy ending to reduce Judith once more to the abashed and dutiful wife, but his difficulty in finding the right tone for her final words testifies to the enlargement of her role in the latter half of the play. The published text leaves the impression of Judith as a merely sentimental character who understood nothing, omitting any hint that she serves as a vehicle for a certain moral weight. Originally he expanded her speech to suggest her moral education: 'I never really loved him before. I only pretended to like most wives. He never could have taught me himself what love is. But you taught me. And now I love him. Isnt that funny?' (British Library Additional MS 50606). This attributes the wrong sort of complexity to Judith, and was wisely dropped, but was not replaced by a more satisfactory closing.

The strength of Judith's adversary role is much enforced by the surer presence of another voice outside the orbit of heroic action, General Burgoyne's. Self-possessed unlike Judith, Burgoyne sees no charm in the extravagant deeds of Dudgeon and Anderson. Practically his first words are a memorable quip about the one: 'Martyrdom, sir, is what these people like: it is the only way in which a man can become famous without ability' (115). And his attitude toward Anderson's triumphant return and request for safe conduct is pragmatic and businesslike rather than amazed and admiring.

The wit and vitality invested in Burgoyne is even more obvious on the stage than on the page, and the part is likely to steal the show. But its dramatic function is complexly dual: to show, on the one hand, through Burgoyne's superiority to the duty-minded Major Swindon and even through his sparring with Richard, the dignity and personal force of a purely worldly philosophy; and, on the other hand, the moral inferiority of any mere worldly position however confidently held. Gentleman Johnny is a type

Shaw created many times, the urbane pragmatist who takes the world as he finds it, accepts human weakness as inevitable, scorns most people as fools, slaves and idolators, is detached from the prejudices of his age yet lacks the itch for any higher vision. Earlier and simpler versions of the type were the conscious hypocrites, Sartorius and Mrs Warren, and the blandly clever servants, Nicola and William. Given greater power of articulation in Burgoyne, the type develops into the Devil of *Man and Superman* and into Andrew Undershaft.

Dramatic interaction in *The Devil's Disciple* is thus richly discriminated, involving the two contrasting moral geniuses, the protesting victim of their exalted egotism, the witty gentleman who assesses idealism coolly, and a range of voices conceived in a more or less farcical spirit. I do not want to suggest that it is one of Shaw's greatest plays, for in richness of thought it is no match for several soon to be written, but formally it is the first that might be called fully mature, the first to sound the full scale of his instrument.

Caesar and Cleopatra suffers from stilted language, postured scenes and gestures, and a certain 'scatteriness' of structure which Shaw himself thought was inherent in the form of the chronicle play, though he later handled this form more deftly in *Saint Joan*. Yet it has some original strength. Judging his new work quite candidly, Shaw points us in the right direction: 'there is no drama in it because Caesar was so completely superior to his adversaries that there was virtually no conflict, only a few adventures. . . . Of course the main feat to be performed was to . . . present Caesar as a great man with a genuine differentiation of character & view. . . . It is true that I have done this by making rather small beer of the protagonists; but I think he dwarfs them fairly and that his eminence is something more than an illusion produced by the flatness of the surrounding country. That achieved, I give up the rest as hopeless' (*CL* II 94). The conception of Caesar is interesting in itself, and becomes sufficiently dramatic not so much through unfolding action as through clashes of perspective. The incidents or adventures serve the rather static and allegoric drama of differentiated points of view rather than the other way around, much as they do in Conrad's *Lord Jim*, written a year or two later.

Shaw's world-historical hero, adumbrated in *The Perfect Wagnerite*, has come to replace the old laws of vengeance and atonement associated with the god-figures of the Judeo–Christian tradition, and he does so simply by being himself, that is, by challenging us to understand what natural greatness or natural virtue consists of as a psychological phenomenon. In his notes to the play, Shaw comments: 'Goodness in its most popular British sense of self-denial, implies that a man is vicious by nature, and that supreme goodness is supreme martyrdom.' Rejecting that opinion, he puts his Caesar beyond even the temptation of jealously and revenge, of merely personal desire. The hero can therefore be entirely 'selfish' and still produce an impression of magnanimity and disinterestedness.

We have seen such a conception anticipated in the matter-of-fact superiority of Bluntschli, whom Shaw acknowledged as a Mommsenite figure like Caesar, though his Bulgarian caper is hardly on the world-historical scale. The historical Napoleon in *The Man of Destiny* is another sketch for Caesar, especially in his superiority to personal revenge, but his belief in himself is presented somewhat farcically and his sense of humour is sardonic. Vivie, Marchbanks, Dudgeon and Anderson have all been discussed as ascenders to a superior plane of being and are thus incorporated in Caesar. He is both soldier and saint, both doer and dreamer. But instead of an active renunciation and leap, we find in him mere traces of a renunciation of self that is almost coeval with his being.

A consequent impression of inhuman coldness, though not totally averted, is reduced by his pervasive boyishness[6] and by two humanising limitations that afford a measure of poignancy. One is the middle-aged regret for the loss of sexual charm so vibrant in Cleopatra. The other is the premonition of assassination, for he knows, like Christ, that the world is not ready to understand him.

At fifty-four, Caesar is too old for sixteen-year-old Cleopatra (though Shaw has here tampered with the historical record according to which he fathered a child and brought both mother and child to Rome). He necessarily adopts an avuncular role toward her, not without a touch of chagrin at her allusions to his ageing appearance. A premonition of his famous end also humanises a little this extraordinary hero: 'I shall finish my life's work on my way back; and then I shall have lived long enough. Besides: I have always disliked the idea of dying: I had rather be killed' (288). Poignancy is checked here by a quip but emerges in another speech, often quoted: 'If one man in all the world can be found, now or forever, to *know* that you did wrong [referring to Cleopatra, who ordered the slaying of Pothinus in the spirit of revenge], that man will have either to conquer the world as I have, or be crucified by it' (277). In linking his conquering hero with the crucified Christ, Shaw is not warming to the idea of martyrdom but suggesting that the exceptional man is fundamentally not at home in the world as it is, however admired he may be or however natural and even boyish his manner. His superiority isolates him from his fellows.

Making the central interest of his play the mystery of character rather than the movements and turns of an action anticipates the discussion form of Shaw's middle plays. Caesar's acts and judgements are exempla to be discussed and interpreted by others who only partly understand. But this perspectival drama is, in fact, combined with a slim plot turning on the degrees of Cleopatra's (and to a lesser extent Rufio's) understanding of his nature.

In act 1 Cleopatra imagines power only as childish revenge, ordering Ftatateeta peremptorily about. In act 2, her sophomore phase, she tries to play the part of a queen but is perplexed by the idea that leadership entails a readiness to work and the putting aside of jealousies. Act 3 is given over to spectacle, though some symbolic weight may be assigned to the incident of the carpet in which Cleopatra nearly drowns in her effort to join Caesar. And in act 4 she uses power with some control, having talked to Caesar for six months and having learned to listen opportunistically to the chatter of those around her. She recites what she has learned about renouncing revenge like a catechism, but the speech is ironic because she soon vengefully commands the death of the plotting Pothinus. But she can appreciate Caesar's disappointment in her, and comes to accept her need for a man like Mark Antony rather than a human god. Rufio too has learned to rise above some of his egotism, is duly rewarded, and accepts with sorrow and grace his moral limitations. All the others, in fact, watch the departure of Caesar with mingled regret and relief.

But the dramatist's resourcefulness does not erase the impression of a certain makeshift quality about *Caesar and Cleopatra*, especially in the operatic third act, which was omitted in some productions with Shaw's consent. In the silly battle with the Egyptians and sillier escape by water, the boyish spirit of adventure gets out of hand. All Shaw can do is have Caesar acknowledge that it is the first time he has run an avoidable risk.

There are inherent difficulties in the idealisation of historical figures. Shaw idealises the record when he makes his Caesar shudder at the 'wise severity' with which he had justified the slaughter of Vercingetorix, and, perhaps because he committed himself that far, the dramatist draws too fine a distinction between Ftatateeta's murder of Pothinus and Rufio's murder of Ftatateeta. We feel the pressure of idealisation also in the rhetorically strained prologue of 1912, which compares Caesar's supercession of Pompey to the supercession of the Catholic by the Protestant idea in the sixteenth century as symbolised by the defeat of the Spanish Armada. But it would not be easy, in any case, to create a character who can make the grand revolutionary gesture and still come across as eminently reasonable and practical. When the library of Alexandria is in flames, the scholar Theodotus laments the loss of 'the memory of mankind', giving Caesar the opportunity to say, romantically, 'A shameful memory. Let it burn.' A moment later, however, he hurries Theodotus off to get help (*B* 2: 219–20).

The peculiar quality of the play is epitomised in the curious figure of Apollodorus. He is so frankly an aesthete and a worshipper of art and beauty that we are surprised at first (knowing Shaw) to find him treated so admiringly. It becomes apparent that art for Apollodorus is indistinguishable from the joyously romantic gesture (like ferrying the carpet-rolled Cleopatra in the midst of the battle), and Caesar's admiration allows us to see that the Shavian ideal is meta-Roman. In releasing his romantic impulse so freely, however, Shaw has dissipated the tension usually found in his comic sublime, and has created what might be called An Enthusiasm.

My chief discomfort with *Caesar and Cleopatra* concerns its complacency with regard to authority and power, a complacency not particularly evident in Shaw heretofore but destined to become conspicuous in his later work. There is too much invoking of the great name of Caesar, too easy a satisfaction in its awe-inspiring effects: standing *on* the plains of heaven is a tricky business. The unsatisfactoriness of the role of Britannicus is symptomatic here. The comic aspect of the role is reduced to facile jesting about the English. The serious Britannicus is presented, without discernible irony, as an idolator: 'only as Caesar's slave have I found real freedom' (287). This is not the sort of freedom that Shaw celebrated best. The creation of a human god insufficiently checked by comic resistance is self-indulgent.

The theme of rising above vengeance is dramatised again in *Captain Brassbound's Conversion* (1899) within the framework of a well-made play. Brassbound '*is set to one tragic purpose*' (*B* 2: 342), to avenge his mother's ruin upon her husband's brother, Sir Howard Hallam, 'the hanging judge' who condemned her to prison (and thereby to death) when the crazed woman threatened his life. But the Captain's powerful temptation is defused by the subtle pedagogy of the judge's niece, Lady Cicely Wayneflete. Shaw brings them together in exotic Morocco, where Lady Cicely expresses a bold wish to visit the interior. Dour Brassbound and his men are hired as their guides to protect them from predatory Arab chieftains. Sir Henry thereby falls into the Captain's power, but after Lady Cicely's exposures, the tables are turned. At an official inquiry, the strongest scene of the play, Lady Cicely – half witness, half counsel – skilfully tells an edited story of their history and relationship, knowing that the whole truth is damaging to both men yet that each has enough excuse on his side to be acquitted by an unofficial conscience.

Like Caesar, Lady Cicely has raised herself above the needs of personal satisfaction, and is therefore able to disarm the egotism of others, to confound their set convictions and purposes, and, at the same time, win their respect. Because she is a woman and is expected to be weaker than a man, her triumphs take on a more ironic appearance than Caesar's. Like Candida she does rather patronise her men (she prescribes baths, sews buttons, dresses wounds and talks to them as if they were children) but her behaviour is more principled. Her deliberate hypocrisy is based on her recognition of the fact that real justice will not be obtained through institutions. She perceives with calm acuity that Judge Hallam and Captain Brassbound, seeming opposites, are much alike, that the insider's belief in punishment as a deterrent to crime is very similar to the outsider's belief in honourable revenge. She cleverly exploits the insight, as Major Barbara will, that the conduct of people depends in great measure on how they are treated, that very few are absolutely bad or good by nature. And she saves herself from sentimentality by understanding that the rascal Drinkwater (who had been, as he himself admits with wonderful blandness, 'wrorngfully hacquittid' – 333) is likely to remain unscrupulous.

The play does not have the scope of *Caesar and Cleopatra*, but the restricted focus makes it, as a parable on the theme of revenge, neater and clearer. And it is a bit more searching than its predecessor in one important respect, exploring the connection between the protagonist's moral superiority and his/her renunciation of egotistic sexuality.

Shaw boasted that Cicely was the first heroine he had created in whom our interest is not 'partly a sexual interest' (*CL* II 99). One sees what he means, but in fact he has given her some power to resist, and therefore to have felt, sexual temptation. She declares: 'I have never been in love with any real person; and I never shall. How could I manage people if I had that mad little bit of self left in me? Thats my secret' (*B* 2: 416). This admission is fleshed out by the fact that she is attracted to Brassbound, who in turn pleads with her to be his commander as Gordon of Khartoum once was. But the temptation is marred by 'archness' (Nethercot, 1954, p. 96). When Brassbound discovers that he has learned her own secret of command and no longer feels rudderless, Cicely cries out, ending the play, 'How glorious! And what an escape!' (417).

His next play, *Man and Superman*, applies a much bolder strategy to the sexual theme that Shaw was struggling with. But to write it he had to create a new form, not merely heighten a thematic stress. In the use of time and space, the three plays for Puritans – set in colonial New England, ancient Egypt and modern Morocco – already evince a remarkable freedom from realistic constraint – a gaiety of structure, so to speak as well as of language. Perhaps the defects of *Caesar and Cleopatra* are partly the result of Shaw's making a clumsy first step in the direction of opening up his plots, breaking down the well-made form to allow for extended discussion. Certainly the perspectival sublime gains prominence in the middle period, and correspondingly the sublime moment tends to become assimilated to a larger action rather than constituting the chief peripeteia.

At the end of the century Shaw changed his pace. He had written ten plays in seven years, not to mention his energetic weekly columns for *The Saturday Review*, book-length works of criticism, prefaces to published plays and ceaseless efforts on behalf of the Fabians. Now he resigned his column, married his Irish millionairess (thus relieving himself for the first time in his life of financial anxieties) and devoted several years to the writing of one play. He not only changed his pace (the previous pace, he admitted, nearly killed him – see *OTN* III 384–6) but also gathered new strength. He drew back in order to jump higher.

4
The Big Three

Looking back on his career to date in 1915, Shaw commented that *Major Barbara* 'is the third of a group of three plays of exceptional weight and magnitude on which the reputation of the author as a serious dramatist was first established, and still mainly rests' (*B* 3: 193). He refers of course to *Man and Superman* and *John Bull's Other Island*, along with *Major Barbara*, which were written in sequence between 1901 and 1905. They are all highly original and together explore the heights and depths of Shaw's sensibility. No play is more central to the canon than *Man and Superman*, whose crucial third act both enacts and discusses the comic sublime. None is more committed to the sublime in its basic overall structure than *Major Barbara*. And none is more despairing of attaining the heights than *John Bull's Other Island*.

One of the reasons *Man and Superman* seems so central is that it transvalues or sublimes not only romance, like *Arms and the Man*, but marriage itself, that most persistent of Shavian concerns. Since its composition followed hard upon the author's own marriage, commentary might appropriately begin by way of biography.

Around the time that Shaw began to think of marrying Charlotte Payne-Townshend, whom he had met through the Webbs in 1895, he suffered a remarkable series of 'accidents', culminating in a foot infection that would not clear up. 'My objection to my own marriage', he wrote characteristically, 'had ceased with my objection to my own death' (*CL* II 51). In fact, he and Charlotte settled into their new state rather comfortably, having mutually agreed that it should exclude sex. This biographical tragi-comedy of 1895–8 seems in retrospect like a warm-up for *Man and Superman* (1903), the story of a Shavianised Don Juan who carries matrimonial reluctance to fantastic lengths before capitulating on special and agreed-upon terms.

After a period of recovery he did a sketch called 'The Superman, or Don Juan's great grandson's grandson', which evolved into the extraordinary dream sequence of the new play.[1] For the first time he could afford to ignore theatrical limitations and the style of a particular actor-manager or a particular actress. (He had shaped the role of Caesar for Forbes-Robertson and of Lady Cicely for Ellen Terry.) *Man and Superman* was the first play to be published before the consideration of a performance, and it included accordingly extensive non-dialogic commentary and a 'philosophy' along with a 'comedy'. 'My next play', Shaw wrote to a correspondent in 1900, 'will be a Don Juan – an immense play, but not for the stage of this generation' (*CL* II 174). Of course, his theatrical instincts by this time were pretty well educated, and when the Court Theatre under the management of Barker and Vedrennes did perform the work in 1905 and 1907, not only did acts 1, 2 and 4 make very successful comedy but act 3 itself, separately mounted, proved to be a brilliant *coup de théâtre*. Occasionally since 1915, the whole work has been performed at one time, and the result can be exciting.[2]

One of the first actions that Shaw took, after coming to an agreement with Charlotte, was to arrange for a sum of money to be settled on his mother if he should predecease her. The fact that he himself was soon to become a commercial success does not render the action insignificant. His duty must have been felt as a burden. Shaw would continue to wrestle artistically with the mother-image, but the financial arrangement must have eased his spirit so the fight could be carried out all the more energetically on the page. He could malign his dutifulness with great gusto, excoriating the artist who exploits his mother for the sake of his art. He could mock his new, unearned wealth with a splendidly sustained jest about a millionaire socialist – Member of the Idle Rich Class.

A new form was required for the new scope of the dramatic conception. In the 1913 edition of *The Quintessence*, Shaw cited 'discussion' as the prime technical novelty introduced by Ibsen, and certainly the expanded use of discussion is the most obvious feature of the plays written after 1900.[3] In one of his *Saturday Review* pieces, he had pleaded for wider use of discussion: 'We shall never get the drama out of its present rut until we learn to dispense on occasion with dramatic aim . . . and allow feeling to flow without perpetually working up to points and situations' (*OTN* II 138). But he added, no doubt appreciating the difficulty of this anti-climactic technique, 'that sort of freedom must be conquered, not begged'. It is *Man and Superman* that first conquers this new freedom.

A more discursive style is incorporated to some degree even in the comedy of acts 1, 2 and 4. It is accommodated rather easily, in fact, because of the elegant strength of the plot line – the parallel stratagems of the two women to combine money (present for Ann, absent for Violet) and man (present for Violet, absent for Ann), each skilfully manipulating the vulnerabilities of others without breaking the social bond. Thus, although act 3 inverts the situation of the other acts, making Tanner/Juan a pioneer on the march to the plains of heaven instead of a destined prey, the philosophy and the comedy are diffused throughout; the topic of moral passion is discussed in the 'comic' acts and the ironic view of it is dramatised also in the 'philosophic' act.

But it is, of course, the third act, written first, that most dazzlingly extends the meaning of a drama of ideas. It is not just discursive freedom that is involved here but the kind of conceptual concentration, freed of time–space limitations, that we associate with poetry. The ascent-to-heaven metaphor, though already climactic in Shaw's previous plays, had to be worked up to. Here it is essential, the ore to be mined. One might say that act 3 shows us language as action whereas the other acts, like most drama, shows us action as language. That is, act 3 is really about the quintessential metaphor of springing to the plains of heaven; the rejection or transformation of conventional happiness into creative vitality, of the beautiful into the sublime, is Don Juan's very *raison d'être*. 'By virtue of Act III, *Man and Superman* must be classified as the first example in Shaw's work of the play of ideas that may be considered his most characteristic invention' (Morgan, 1972, p. 118). 'With *Man and Superman* Shaw leaves behind such popular forms as melodrama and domestic comedy to enter a kingdom peculiarly his own' (Crompton, 1971, p. 75).

The prefaces of the post-1900 plays assume a proportionately new magnitude. The subheadings expand in number and variety, until in some cases, notably in the prefaces to *Androcles and the Lion* and *Back to Methuselah*, Shaw is writing virtual monographs. Yet the first of these expanded forms remains unique, not only by virtue of its discontinuous third act but also because of the supplemental Revolutionist's Handbook and the brilliantly Blakean Maxims for Revolutionists, both understood as composed by Tanner and hence not incidental to the structure of the whole.

The impression persists in Shaw criticism that *Man and Superman* is central to his achievement, despite a widespread lack of enthusiasm (which I share) for the notion of breeding an improved quality of human being. I have suggested that one reason for this justifiable impression is its central use of the metaphor pivotal to the comic sublime. Another reason, also indicated, is the play's scope, its synthesis of two kinds of drama and several kinds of discursive material. In the context of this study a third reason emerges and deserves particular comment.

We have seen that, in his earlier plays, Shaw had difficulty keeping his stronger male and female figures in balance with one another. The force of Candida tended to diminish the force of her two men, and in turn Judith Anderson was diminished by hers. *Man and Superman* is the first play – and no later one achieves this so perfectly – to give full scope both to a powerful woman and an equal opposite. Shaw charges the figures of both Ann and Tanner with heroic energy, making the biologic and instinctive vitality of the one a match for the creative and intellectual vitality of the other. (One must concede, however, in the light of a later feminism, that Shaw, reflecting his age, is subtly derogatory to the female mind in making this division.) We are never required to consider whether their superiority will have specific eugenic implications. Their vitality, evident in every speech and gesture, asks for no further justification.

Their final union is simultaneously comic and sublime as no other dramatic climax in Shaw quite is. The comedy is completed by a joyous and socially cohesive marriage. The sublime is completed by our understanding that the marriage takes places under the sign of greatness rather than (or at the expense of) happiness. The principals have transformed a hell into a heaven but have done so mundanely, for hell is a city much like Seville (Shaw's adaptation, of course, of Shelley's 'much like London'), and heaven, also an aspect of this world, is a state of creative activity. Tanner realises that the Life Force, which he has only dreamt, is behind their conjunction – an idea that is equally comic (another name for it is feminine manipulation) and sublime (it remains, irony notwithstanding, a power larger than the self that makes for individual and hence racial improvement).

Ann is the most glittering of those hypocrites whom Shaw admires for getting what they want within an oppressive society, in this case a society prejudiced against bold, assertive women. (Violet is another such hypocrite who succeeds by means of a blunter but also witty style: 'You can be as romantic as you please

about love, Hector; but you mustnt be romantic about money' –
B 2: 607.) But unlike Mrs Warren, she needn't lose out finally
because her goal coincides with a desirable and realisable social
goal. Her energy is unmistakably sensual and morally justifiable
at the same time.

Tanner himself appears to be defeated at the climax of each act,
but this is only part of the truth. Although he is usually said to be
merely a bumbler, his keenness in unmasking others and even
his theories regarding marriage and the artist are not really
undermined. It is only in his personal relations to others, or in his
misunderstanding of their motives, especially those of the women,
that he is exposed as a comic butt. In act 1, Violet, having been
married privately, accepts her unborn child without shame or guilt,
and finds Tanner's approval of her as a free woman, and his theories
themselves, merely distasteful; in the throes of his passionate
theorising, he has neglected to consider that there is a practical,
worldly equivalent to his own Nietzschean transcendence of
conventional good and evil. In act 2 all that Tanner has said about
the pitched battle between the mentally creative male and physically
creative female is shown to be true, but, unlike his chauffeur, he
has failed to perceive that it is he and not Octavius who is the
male in question, the destined prey, just as he fails to foresee the
practical consequences of his enthusiastic speech to Ann about
asserting her independence from her mother. In act 4 he seems to
have been finally overcome by Ann, who swoons half in calculation
and half under the strain of her concentrated will, eliciting from
him a pledge of marriage. But he promptly and uncontestedly
states the conditions for a higher kind of marriage (somehow
beyond domesticity though not beyond sex) and, not lacking '*a
sense of humor*' in spite of being a '*megalomaniac*' (541), joins in
the good-humoured mockery of his everlasting talk as the play
concludes in '*universal laughter*' (733). Wisenthal (1974) infers from
the comic climaxes that 'Tanner neither converts nor even slightly
influences anyone . . . [his] victories are merely verbal' (p. 38). But
a merely verbal victory is not trivial in a work of literature. Tanner
is not contradicted and our final awareness of his solidarity with
the others should be taken to mean that his voice is inextricably
part of the general discourse.

Just as philosophy may be said to resist comedy in acts 1, 2 and
4, so comedy resists philosophy in act 3: it does not merely function
as relief. I cite one key instance. Ana for the most part is more

conventional than Ann and weaker in relation to Don Juan than Ann is to Tanner. But this weakness is somewhat deceptive. She offers a resistance to the sublime other than the devil's. As Wisenthal (1974) observes, she is different from the devil, both less sentimental and less cynical, in the prosaic view she takes of marriage, and she becomes 'a spokesman for the earthly, for the real, tangible world of flesh and blood' (p. 28). Moreover, her resistance fuels her own spring to the heights. At the end of the dream sequence, indeed after Juan has left Hell to return to Heaven, she is seriously enough beguiled by the debate she has heard to inquire about this 'Superman'. 'He is not yet created', the Devil informs her, taking an urbanely cynical view of the human capacity for self-improvement. But the word 'created' may be understood in a more commonplace sense, and Ana seizes on that implication in a speech that superlatively fuses the comic with the sublime:

ANA.   Not yet created! Then my work is not yet done. [*Crossing herself devoutly*] I believe in the Life to Come. [*Crying to the universe*] A father! a father for the Superman!   (689)

Despite her conventional beliefs she is suddenly alive with instinctual purpose and flies after Juan, just as in the realistic plot framing the dream sequence Ann is flying after Tanner. In fact Ann catches up with him at last upon his awakening in the Spanish Sierra Nevada. In other words, Tanner comically dreams his own capture yet heroically dreams its occurrence on the plains of heaven. Ana is comic by virtue of her philosophic naïveté (her pursuit could be confused with vulgar husband-trapping) but at the same time she is shown to be motivated by the same vital energy, the same will to improvement or Life Force that is driving Juan. Her 'I believe in the Life to Come' is an exquisitely poised ambiguity, allowing itself to be understood equally well as orthodox Christian and unorthodox Shavian doctrine.

Ana's vertical chase of Juan provides the necessary and sufficient gloss on Ann's horizontal chase of Tanner, helping us imagine, as completely as we need to, the idea of a marriage that is neither disembodied on the one hand nor merely mundane on the other. The quasi-mystical eugenics lightly implied in act 3 and made more explicit in the Handbook are not basic to the play's structure. The debate about the Superman is almost entirely a debate about the possibility of educating moral attitudes by psychological means. The crucial terms are cowardice and courage, inertia and will, fear and faith. The Life Force is, to be sure, a concept with theological significance for Shaw, but it is conceived as working through human will and it is directed primarily at reforming the ethics of gentility. It is worth remembering that the germ of the play's conception was the exchange between Tanner and Mendoza that parallels the gentleman and the brigand (*CL* III 837). An assertion in Tanner's Handbook is also pertinent to our understanding the Superman in naturalistic, essentially political terms: 'The overthrow of the aristocrat has created the necessity for the Superman' (780).

None the less, as many have observed, Shaw's introduction in this play of the idea of a Life Force reflects a certain discouragement on his part with the possibility of political and psychological change. As Wisenthal (1974) points out, the very conception of Hell is based on the premise of the impossibility of human progress and the consequent wisdom of living only for the pleasure of the moment (p. 25). That is, Shaw allows us to suppose that the Devil's pessimism about progress is realistic, not merely cynical – a supposition we are more likely to take seriously than he could have realised. Probably the most cogent speech in the whole astonishing debate is the Devil's account of the endless human capacity for destruction, and the most cogent sentence may be his quiet rejoinder: 'Beware of the pursuit of the Superhuman: it leads to an indiscriminate contempt for the Human' (687). Of course Juan – and Tanner – strive energetically to wrest the word destruction away from the connotation of murder so that its vital antithesis, creation, can be saved from dilution, and his effort is only intensified by the very considerable measure of diabolic or human resistance.

The intense intellectual struggle of act 3 is a matter of personal urgency for all its broadly cultural reference. The Devil represents the dangerously passive charms of beauty and pleasure which Juan seeks to sublime by a gospel of energetic work. I am more than a little beguiled by Harold Bloom's (1987) intertextual reading of this debate whereby the Devil is aligned with the doctrines of Wilde and Pater, and Juan with those of Carlyle and Ruskin (pp. 1–13). Certainly Shaw is struggling here with strong influences, and trying to put up the right resistance to what he recognises as his bias.

There are other resistant voices, too, conceived in a more relaxed comic spirit but contributing to the rich tension of the work. Roebuck Ramsden may not be the most formidable antagonist – he was an advanced thinker of sorts a generation earlier than Tanner – but he puts up enough resistance to his co-executor's ideas to create opportunities for a cutting wit. Then there are four distinguishable varieties of sentimentalist – Octavius, Hector, Malone Senior and Mendoza (who becomes as the Devil a much more sophisticated spokesman). They too spark Tanner's wit and expose themselves unconsciously to the edge of Ann's and Violet's keen practical sense. The comic role of Straker, Tanner's chauffeur and New Man, is a composite of the conventionality of the men, the shrewdness of the women, and a droll insouciance regarding the whole business of social change. An equally effective comic insouciance (more truly philistine than Ann's because it lacks any heroic potential) is attributed to Mrs Whitefield who readily perceives her daughter's hypocrisy but is at ease with inconsistency, commenting with motherly dutifulness that Ann must after all marry someone and that Tanner, because he can take care of himself, will do very well. We have also the witty political caricatures of Mendoza's brigands, who, for example, find the phrase 'friend and chauffeur' contradictory. And there is the fine irony, important to the structure of act 3, of the attractively worldly Statue first choosing Heaven as a matter of course, then shedding his sense of duty and finding his proper niche in Hell. Representing another version of the gentleman earlier worked out in Burgoyne, the Statue provides important ballast in act 3 since the Devil's hedonistic doctrine must, for the sake of the needed rhetorical energy, be dealt with harshly.

One of the most striking features of *Man and Superman*, belying to some extent the theme of the impossibility of progress, is its festive and joyous tone, the friendliness of its antagonisms. Ramsden at the end is somehow sufficiently disarmed to speak of the man whose book he threw, unread, *'violently down on the table'* (538) as 'one of our circle' (713). Octavius embraces his successful rival no less warmly than before. The marriage, in fact, brings everyone together in spirit, and even in voice: universal laughter. Surely one of the reasons for this festive spirit, despite an under-lying despair in the conception, is the pervasive imagery of wealth, privilege and luxury. (We shall notice a similar phenomenon in *Major Barbara*.) The hero is a millionaire; his freedom from all but intellectual pressures is made evident; a startling new motor car (the year is 1903!) is conspicuously on stage. This sustained glitter helped Shaw a good deal, I believe, in keeping the sensual vitality of his protagonists before us while, at the same time, sublimating it to an extraordinary degree. They are about to enter a marriage not specifically companionate like his own yet lifted above the usual chagrins of the married state by whatever it is that distinguishes strength from happiness. Really the whole play lifts the idea of marriage to a higher plane, as *Arms and the Man* lifts the idea of romance.

Shaw set the second of his 'big three', *John Bull's Other Island*, in Ireland – the real, present Ireland, poor and oppressed, the place of his devilish childhood and lonely boyhood, defiantly not the Ireland of Yeats's *Cathleen ni Hoolihan* and of the Celtic revival generally.[4] In sharp contrast to the other two, it is permeated by images of poverty and discouragement. This underlies the two aspects of the play that are most original and important. One is the intense emphasis on Hell rather than Heaven – not Hell as we found it in act 3 of *Man and Superman*, presided over by an urbane humanist, but a Hell all-too-human, invoked (principally by Peter Keegan and to some extent by Larry Doyle) with bitter energy. The other new aspect is a change in the presentation of the heroic figures.

We have earlier encountered several kinds of heroes: the unmaskers like Bluntschli and Tanner whose romantic shortsightedness was merely the result of their general farsightedness; the heroes of a climactic conversion experience like Vivie, Marchbanks, Dudgeon, and Anderson; and the heroes of an accomplished higher consciousness, like Caesar and Lady Cicely, who seem to descend among mortals in order to set things straight. *John Bull* is the first of the plays – and certainly not the last – to present not so much heroes as a group of several major figures who may be said to possess differentiated portions of heroic virtue, the first, as Wisenthal (1974) puts it, 'in which characters are overtly symbolic' (p. 87). Broadbent possesses the power of efficiency without wisdom, the means of good without the knowledge of good; Keegan has wisdom without the power to make it effectual; and Doyle adheres in action to the one, in thought to the other, giving his speeches a uniquely savage and corrosive irony. The play is a darker comedy than any Shaw had yet written, as if he had lost confidence in the vision of an ascent to heaven but clung to it anyway.

Keegan evokes an ideal state of things but does so out of despair of our ever attaining it. (Nothing, by the way, illustrates better why it is important to see Shaw's politics as vision, not praxis, than Keegan's speeches about an ideal theocracy, three in one and one in three. This would be repulsive in the actual modern world, as the present-day example of Iran attests. But it is genuinely eloquent as a prophetic fusion of power and morality.) The sublime, then, is present in *John Bull* only through visionary words – as something unattainable – and the comedy of the play is accordingly harshly ironic, more so than any other work by Shaw with the arguable exception of *Heartbreak House*.

In both preface and play, Shaw attempts to make his characters both individuals and types, typically English or typically Irish. Broadbent is particularly vulnerable in this respect because he is the play's single, composite Englishman with representative qualities: he is self-confident but lacking in tact, '*eager and credulous . . . buoyant and irresistible, mostly likeable, and enormously absurd in his most earnest moments*' (B 2: 894). Shaw's didactic intention – 'to teach the Irish people the value of an Englishman as well as to show the Englishman his own absurdities' (British Library Additional MS 50615) – is not in this case quite concealed by art, but the wonder is that, in the enactment, the personality of Broadbent makes as plausible an impression as it does.

His objective is to bring his Land Development Syndicate to Ireland. The fact that this requires foreclosing the mortgages of some small landowners who are old familiars of the Doyles seems to him merely the cost of progress, and he lacks the vision to perceive that a golfing hotel may be something less than a foretaste of heaven. Thus he misunderstands Keegan's oblique charge of hypocrisy, even after his friend Larry calls attention to the ex-priest's 'peculiar vein of humor' (B 2: 989). Broadbent succeeds in spite of his human insensitivity because of his blindly well-meaning confidence in the ideals of progress and efficiency. 'Much as I like him, I object to being governed by him', Shaw wrote in the preface (811), and showed in the play that the Irish have little choice except impotently to deride him.

The half-dozen Irish characters are well differentiated and individualised (excluding Tim Haffigan of act 1 who is used diagrammatically to challenge the stereotype of the stage Irishman.) And the portraits of Keegan, Larry Doyle and Nora are exceptionally fine and sensitive. Together, the Irish figures exemplify in their different ways a keen psycho-political truth: namely, that the citizens of a conquered nation, unable to be honourably indignant, are led into self-incrimination. They learn to sneer and deride, like Corny and Matt who laugh at the hapless Patsy Farrell and at the story of Broadbent's accident with the pig; or to become excessively fastidious like Nora and Doyle; or impotently visionary like Keegan. Keegan's eloquence draws on more depth of feeling that Juan's or even Joan's, and Shaw never wrote better in the realist vein than with Nora and Doyle. As a rule, he is not stimulated by imagining persons of restricted or choked vitality, but the hard-won freedom from illusion in these two gives them dignity and elicits from us a considerable though cool sympathy. Unconsciously snubbed by one lover and bullied by another, Nora would seem destined to become a pitiful or else risible figure, but she is neither: she is 'drawn with great tact and careful neutrality' (Morgan, 1972, p. 127). We are shown Larry's hopelessness about his own idealism (a country 'where the facts were not brutal and the dreams not unreal' – B 2: 919), yet we respect uneasily his penetrating, sometimes cynical perception of fact. Shaw's Irishmen, contrary to caricature yet credibly, are much less victims of self-deception (the 'dreaming' mocked by Larry is not delusional thinking but merely passive, wishful thinking) than of poverty and powerlessness, forcing them into attitudes of ironic realism. The preface describes Wellington as a typical Irishman on the grounds that he was 'an accomplished comedian in the art of anticlimax' (816).

A pervasive mood of grim fact-finding is the chief reason why *John Bull's Other Island* lacks the brilliant surface of *Man and Superman* and *Major Barbara*. Yet Shaw was able to find imaginative sustenance in the very defeat of Keegan's idealism. Inverting the sublime, he found strength in anger and disillusionment themselves.

Although *John Bull* is a rather talky play that stops and starts several times, its set moments are strong. The expository first act functions as a kind of prologue yet establishes well Tom Broadbent's naïveté about the Irish and Larry Doyle's contrasting reluctance to revisit his homeland. The second act, though it does not advance the action (except for Broadbent's somewhat absurd courtship of Nora), is memorable for Keegan's bitter, hillside rumination, ably assisted by a sentient grasshopper, on this world as a place of torment (Purgatory in the draft, Hell in the finished version of the play) and his pertinent application of this view to the situation of Nora and Larry, who are destined, for all their decency, always to inflict pain on one another. The third act is the most dramatic, and the most political – although its theme is in a sense anti-political.

The apparent issue is a seat in Parliament, which his father's cronies offer first to Larry Doyle himself. But he discredits himself in their eyes by claiming to be neither liberal nor conservative but radical. Taking a higher point of view, he understands that the present Rosscullen landlords are morally no better than the landlords they replaced. Like Keegan, he would have everyone morally accountable, which is hardly favourable to his father and friends. (For both Keegan and Larry the Church too is to be accountable; hence they are opposed to disestablishment.) Broadbent offers instead the Gladstonian Liberal platform of Peace–Retrenchment–Reform, which means little on examination, and really offers his prospective constituency the reassurance of no fundamental change while power is shifted again, in the name of progress and efficiency, to other landlords. The issue is brought to a kind of resolution in the first part of the fourth act with the vivid, curiously resonant story of the pig crushed under a wheel, first told derisively by Barney Doran, then with naïve dignity by Broadbent. The Englishman wins a grudging respect in spite of being thought ridiculous.

After the pig story, the last act moves into a thematically inevitable confrontation between Keegan and Broadbent, the man of vision and the man of efficiency:

KEEGAN.   You feel at home in the world, then?
BROADBENT.   Of course. Dont you?
KEEGAN [*from the very depths of his nature*].   No.   (*B* 2: 991–2)

Broadbent's optimism about the corrigibility of man-made evils is found in Shaw's non-dramatic writings but so is Keegan's feeling of spiritual homelessness. In an autobiographical preface of 1921, Shaw wrote movingly: 'Whether it be that I was born mad or a little too sane, my kingdom was not of this world: I was at home only in the realm of my imagination, and at my ease only with the mighty dead' (*C* 1: xlvii). Despite some lasting friendships, he continued to feel like a man who has 'no companionships, only occasional contacts' (*CL* IV 87). To fail to see that he identified himself as much with the visionary outsider as with the practical insider is to miss the perdurable undertone of desolation accompanying the prevailing robustness. I can believe with Frederick McDowell that the play derived from the desire 'to use the efficiencies of capitalism in the service of a new socialism and a new religious awakening' (Bloom, 1987, p. 84). McDowell goes so far as to call this 'the direction of the play', but the actual enactment works against this desire. His comment helps us to understand why the intrusive presence of Broadbent in this Irish milieu is so important, but Shaw emphasises equally the impossibility of assimilating and using him properly.[5]

The voice of Larry in *John Bull* assesses the cost of efficient progress: 'The real tragedy of Haffigan is the tragedy of his wasted youth, his stunted mind, his drudging over his clods and pigs until he has become a clod and a pig himself. . . . I say let him die, and let us have no more of his like' (1013–14). But Larry's offended idealism is tainted by cynicism. This sense of realism is mixed with disgust because he has associated himself with the party of 'progress'. It is through Keegan especially that Shaw turns upon his own well-loved dream of efficiency, christened 'executive power' as far back as *Cashel Byron's Profession*, revived and distrusted to the end of his life. Giving a long speech astonishing for its exact knowledge of how Broadbent's mercantile steamroller will grind down any obstacles in its path, Keegan concludes: 'For four wicked centuries the world has dreamed this foolish dream of efficiency; and the end is not yet' (1018).

The harshly ironic dénouement supports this pessimism. Broadbent's hotel is symbolically a move from the unreality of the deserted Round Tower on the hillside to the reality of the tilled and populated valley below – but what a reality! English egotism has simply displaced Irish egotism. For the Irish really to learn the value of an Englishman, not simply to follow bitterly along like Larry Doyle, they would have to change their nature. And for the English to profit from learning the absurdities of one, they too would have to be capable of fundamental change. Inasmuch as the play implies that such changes are not likely, it undermines at the least Shaw's didactic statement of its intention. If *John Bull* refuses a final despair, it does so chiefly through the visionary intensity of Keegan's language. No character in Shaw speaks quite so eloquently about the 'commonwealth of saints' that the preface to *John Bull* refers to: the ideal harmony of Church, State and People –

Three in One and One in Three. But, like Aubrey in the late *Too True to Be Good*, Father Keegan is speaking into a void.

The enormously buoyant *Major Barbara* is perhaps a reaction to the preceding effort. Turco (1976) comments that, if *John Bull's Other Island* can be said to find a deep dualism between wisdom and power, *Major Barbara* 'ventures a resolution' of the polarised conflict (pp. 199–200). To this I would add that the reason the play runs into trouble after two exceptionally brilliant acts (in the view of almost every critic, beginning with Shaw himself) is that it is so fascinated by Undershaft's power that it cannot make enough room for the counterclaim of wisdom. To put it another way with a psychoanalytic slant, it is so hypnotised by money-as-power that the erotic component of this fascination is not recognised and hence not built upon to create a strong sublime. Sexual interest, always important in Shaw if only for its negativity, is in this instance too far backgrounded.

The first act is pervaded, more even than in *Man and Superman*, by the imagery of wealth, luxury and privilege. The scenic opulence of the Wilton Crescent drawing room is enhanced by the mention of grand titles and very large sums of money: Lady Britomart's father, the Earl of Stevenage – 'the Stevenages are as good as the Antonines, I hope' (*B* 3: 75) – has only £7000 a year, and of course her husband is 'simply rolling in money' (72). In accordance with her own great sense of dignity, Lady Britomart considers that the sums needed as marriage settlements for her children and their prospective spouses are all the greater because – due to oafishness, highmindedness or priggishness – they are unable to earn sufficient incomes. Even in the second act, set in the plain, cold Salvation Army shelter, we are made aware of immense wealth and power by way of the dazzling donations of Bodger and Undershaft, which prove that, although highminded persons cannot be bought, the institutions of which they are a part can be. And of course, the third act advances this fantasy-in-reality atmosphere (though a somewhat different feeling takes over when the subject of power is submitted to discussion) by the actualisation (verbal in the play, scenic as well in the film) of a glittering, Garden City ideal.

This imagery helps to account for the joyousness of *Major Barbara* but does not take us far in understanding its great distinction.

(*Major Barbara* is, I would say, the most brilliant of Shaw's comedies, *Man and Superman* the most central, and *Pygmalion* the most humane. These three along with the three searchingly dark comedies – *John Bull's Other Island*, *Heartbreak House* and *Saint Joan* – are my candidates for the big six in the canon.) Shaw's buoyancy is sometimes shallow, especially in his later phase where it may seem a reflex optimism, a nervous froth at the top of a depth of discouragement that is not being engaged. But *Major Barbara* is charged with dialectical energy. Three superior souls wrestle for high ground while a variety of distinctly conceived comic characters are played off against them, making for wonderful concentrations of effect.

Lady Britomart is not a self-possessed conscious hypocrite like Mrs Warren, mistaken but worthy of respect. Nor is she, on the other hand, like Ann Whitefield, someone whose calculation serves higher ends than she herself is aware of. Best compared to Wilde's Lady Bracknell (we shall see the type again in Ariadne Utterword), she raises complacent moral snobbery to a level at which we may say that she herself seems to conduct her creator's satirical purpose: 'It is only in the middle classes, Stephen, that people get into a state of dumb helpless horror when they find that there are wicked people in the world. In our class, we have to decide what is to be done with wicked people' (*B* 3: 73). Or again: 'I should not have minded his merely *doing* wrong things: we are none of us perfect. But your father didnt exactly *do* wrong things: he said them and thought them' (76). Such speeches can hardly be described as ironic defences of hypocrisy. Their command of style and tone minimises the question of the speaker's limited understanding. There is no way of constructively disillusioning Lady Britomart and thereby educating her to a higher level of awareness. Like Alfred Doolittle whom she prefigures, she is impregnable in her comic perfection.

Her son Stephen and prospective son-in-law Lomax are almost as good, perhaps the best prig and oaf that Shaw created. Almost every one of their speeches is funny in itself and contributes as well to a developing structure. Their conventional dismay regarding the cannon business is absurdly shortsighted but still helps us to see that money is power and that power is potentially spiritual.

In the comic situation of the first act – a father revisiting his family after so long an absence that he doesn't recognise his own children or even know for sure how many there are – these figures are played off skilfully against Cusins and Barbara, whose cleverness and magnanimity, respectively, are effortlessly established, leading directly to their elevated alliance with Undershaft. Within two or three pages of his entrance, the 'Prince of Darkness' is able, along with the expression of some droll embarrassment, to perceive that his daughter Barbara and her suitor Cusins (whom he had mistaken for his son, a pleasant symbolic touch) are authentic rivals. Undershaft and Barbara quickly establish the structure of the subsequent action by making a bargain. He will visit her workplace if she will visit his, each challenging the other to be converted to a new way of life. Their neat exchange promises us a dialectical wrestle between antithetical meanings of salvation represented by the cross and the sword, just as the parallel between the physical descriptions of Cusins and Undershaft (one is *'sweet'* but *'fierce'*, *'capable possibly of murder, but not of cruelty or coarseness'* – see pp. 79–80; the other is *'patient'* but with *'formidable reserves of power'* – see p. 84) promises us a stimulating struggle of civilised ironists for the meaning of words as well as for an appropriate course of conduct.

In act 2 Shaw draws in additional points of view and, at the same time, intensifies the several confrontations. He described the act fairly enough to the actor Louis Calvert as 'MAGNIFICENT' (*CL* II 599) – using the upper case, immodest letters in an uncharacteristically straightforward way. As late as 1915 he noted that 'The second act, the Salvation Army act, was a play in itself. Regarded in that way, it may be said to be the most successful of all the author's plays' (*B* 3: 194).

Three successive stages of interaction – marked by the introduction of Snobby and Rummy, of Peter Shirley and of Bill Walker – work up to the exalted quintet that climaxes the act. Snobby and Rummy explain to each other the rationale for their hypocritical manipulation of the Army, claiming some sympathy in doing so by virtue of their sense of fair play and their appreciation of those they exploit. The irony screws up a notch with the entrance of Shirley, who unlike Snobby and Rummy is conscientiously honest, to the point of being unable to receive anything without feeling obliged to make return, but who is out of a job and embittered. He hardly understands Barbara's superiority to class resentments, nourishing as he does the fixed idea that the rich are dishonest and the poor honest (rather like the brigand in *Man and Superman* who wants to know whether Straker is Tanner's friend *or* chauffeur). Denouncing Undershaft ('I wouldnt have your conscience, not for all your income'), he elicits from him the memorable repartée: 'I wouldnt have your income, not for all your conscience, Mr Shirley' (111). Finally, the rough customer Bill Walker comes in looking vengefully for the girl who left him, and proves to be captive in his way to the same morality of repayment. Provoked by frustration to hit Rummy and then gentle Jenny, he is distressed enough by Barbara's skilful prodding of his conscience to want to make amends – not to Rummy who plays the old rough game he knows but to Jenny whose turn-the-other-cheek response has overburdened his conscience. His case carries forward the motifs of the bribe of bread, introduced by Rummy and Snobby, and of the false ethic of humility, introduced by Shirley. It thus exposes the vulnerability of the Army's morality as Undershaft is about to undermine Barbara's adherence to it.

In the struggle for Walker's soul, which is the central incident of the play – though of course the conversion of Barbara and Cusins is the climactic action – Barbara steers him away from the game of atonement that he wants to play so that he cannot simply return with a cleansed conscience to his former behaviour. Barbara's Christianity attempts to drive out his Crosstianity, a point driven home in the preface, which seeks to reform Christian morality itself: 'You will never get a high morality from people who conceive that their misdeeds are revocable and pardonable, or in a society where absolution and expiation are officially provided for us all' (43). A severely Protestant point of view but a stirring one.

Walker will manage to get off the hook, partly because he sees his expiatory coin, refused by Barbara, pinched by Snobby Price, and partly because he witnesses the virtual buying out of the Army itself by those two princes of darkness, Bodger and Undershaft. So Barbara 'loses' Walker and her faith too. She knows too well that the Army needs money to continue its work, and acknowledges Mrs Baines's right to accept it, but for her it is a capitulation to the world, the flesh, the devil. To Cusins it seems so too. In seeking to win Barbara, Undershaft appears truly diabolical because he would replace a passion for good with a passion for power, including very pointedly the power to kill. The stage is now set for a concentrated interaction of five tones of voice: Mrs Baines's sturdily naïve 'Come, Barbara, I must have my dear Major to carry the flag with me'; Jenny's sweetly naïve 'Yes, yes, Major darling'; Undershaft's diabolical 'My ducats and my daughter'; Cusins's bitterly ironic 'Money and gunpowder'; and, finally, Barbara's sublimely heartbroken 'Drunkenness and Murder! My God! why hast thou forsaken me' (135–6). Jenny and even Mrs Baines, who make less moral demand on the world than Barbara does, will never quite believe that they have been bought. The exhilaration of Cusins is, of course, the consciously ironic reaction to an acutely wounded idealism but will later come to seem a necessary step toward a sobered acceptance of what now he regards as diabolism. It is different from the quiet, conscious irony of Undershaft's sly allusion to Shylock, which is based on a confident knowledge of what must come and is therefore (like Marx's view, according to Shaw) self-possessed amid the tumult. And Barbara's anguished disillusionment is even more emphatically an instance of proleptic irony than Cusins's anguished joy. She must taste bitter ashes before she can truly understand that good is of little use without the means of good.

It appears from act 3 that Undershaft has a nobler goal in mind that anything Shaw has let us see in him earlier – not only to teach the absolute importance of power in itself but to teach the potential moral efficacy of power. In altering him thus from a diabolist proper to a dialectical moralist, Shaw has created a problem in act 3 which is not finally resolved – though his extensive rewriting of the act, primarily for the purpose of strengthening the role of Cusins, prevents the play from ending with any sense of abruptness. The preface tells us that Undershaft's conduct, unlike Peter Shirley's, passes the Kantian test (letting every action become a universal law), which is certainly not the case if we are to take him at his word that the manufacture and indiscriminate distribution of armaments is justified in itself without regard for the morality of ends. Even the 'gospel' that poverty is the worst of crimes only really makes sense in so far as we can imagine the kind of Utopian society discovered for us in Perivale St Andrews. The truth is that Undershaft is essentially a pedagogical agent. After he has completed the teaching of his lesson he should somehow fade out and allow his vital but partial truth be absorbed by Barbara and Cusins.

But he continues to dominate through act 3, a mixture of unrepentant diabolonian and philosopher-king. If we honour the former role, we must see the new society as a false hope since it continues to exploit, and even depend upon, the unregenerate baseness of the outside world. If we honour the latter, we must see the new society as a pretty island in a sea of greed and cruelty. Clearly neither implication is intended. Shaw wants both a total society and an ideal one: every starving child is to be forcibly fed and fattened. Such an idea can seem attractive in so far as we think of Undershaft as mystic or religious, heeding a 'will of which I am a part'. But he is quite as likely to assert this will in the manner of a tyrant: '*I* am the government of your country' (151). Undoubtedly Shaw was trying to imagine an ideal fusion of religion and politics, but the dramatised result is very uncomfortably close to what we know as totalitarian dictatorship. It is the forcing of one man's vision down everyone else's throat. Undershaft's advice to his daughter is to think of her broken-down religion like a broken-down machine, and to pick up a new and improved religion to replace it – advice so patently impatient that it is hard to know how seriously Shaw was presenting it. I agree with Wisenthal (1974) that the profession of armaments is different from a profession like distillery in that it implies not just money but also power (pp. 60–1), but directing cannons at moral evils is rather fanciful and the concentration of power is always dangerous. Elsewhere, in *John Bull's Other Island* and especially in *Heartbreak House*, Shaw is much less enchanted by the idea of a plutocratic leader. And he came in time to be less charmed by his Andrew Undershaft (*B* 3: 198–200).

The climax of the action is evidently the moment of Barbara's conversion, the sublime spring from her grim acknowledgement of the power of money (act 2), following her idealised confidence in wisdom alone (act 1). In act 3 she discovers that worldly power is not necessarly at odds with her high idealism and in fact can endow it with far more effectiveness than it had before. And the discovery is characteristically dramatised as a metaphorical ascent, sudden and comprehensive:

CUSINS. Then the way of life lies through the factory of death?
BARBARA. Yes. Through the raising of hell to heaven and of
    man to God. (*B* 3: 184)

But this particular sublime moment in Shaw, it is widely felt, is not quite satisfactory, although its eloquence extends over several longish speeches. One line of explanation, taken by Eric Bentley and Anthony S. Abbott, is that the idea of a synthesis between Barbara's idealism and Undershaft's realism, as represented by Cusins, comes too late (Zimbardo, 1970, pp. 56, 103). Another,

suggested by Bloom among others, is its subordination of the
divine to the human: 'When I die, let him [God] be in my debt,
not I in his; and let me forgive him as becomes a woman of my
rank' (*B* 3: 184) – such a speech almost reduces religious faith to
bourgeois decorum but is nevertheless important, as Joseph Frank
pointed out (Zimbardo, 1970, p. 45), because it stresses the value
for Shaw, finally, of individual responsibility; elsewhere in the
play and preface, progress is made dependent upon a *collective*
reformation. To these explanations I am adding another – the
deficiency in this sublime moment of irony, comic resistance,
palpable temptation. Not surprisingly, therefore, we find irony
supplied by the querulous critic. Arthur Ganz (1980) finds Barbara's
role in act 3 'unclear' because 'the men are already religious' so 'it
is hard to see what she can do in Perivale other than go from
house to house, like the unhappy hero of *The Wild Duck*, presenting
the inhabitants with a "claim of the ideal"' (p. 74). If we are looking
for poetic rather than practical truth here, the question at issue is
really the authenticity of Barbara's heightened consciousness. The
trouble, perhaps, is that we hardly see her tempted by money –
or by sex as an erotic component of greed – and *resisting* the
temptation.

Nor do we see Cusins thus tempted:

BARBARA.   . . . There are larger loves and diviner dreams than
the fireside ones. You know that, dont you?
CUSINS.   Yes: that is our understanding. I know it. I hold to it.
Unless he can win me on that holier ground he may amuse
me for a while; but he can get no deeper hold, strong as he
is.   (*B* 3: 142)

It is not made clear why the acceptance of Undershaft's offer
should require Cusins to consent to a rarefied marriage. Domesticity
has not been presented as a restriction on the morality of the choice
to be made, though elsewhere in Shaw it is so presented. Here
the economic theme dominates, and the sexual motif, which should
be integrated with it, is undeveloped.

More precisely, the sexual motif is expressed not as a complex
irony but as a simple sentimentality. Barbara caps her new exalta-
tion with peculiarly infantile gestures: she *'clutches like a baby at her
mother's skirt'*, and, crying 'Mamma, Mamma', wants help in
choosing 'a house in the village to live in with Dolly' (185).

Wisenthal (1974) compares Undershaft's relation to Barbara with Wotan's relation to Siegfried (in *The Perfect Wagnerite*); in each case a god, unable to achieve his own goal, creates a hero who can (p. 75). Although this is conceptually plausible, the dramatic realisation of the idea remains weak. It should have been stronger, for the three principals clearly enough represent spiritual, intellectual and practical power, and their interaction is a crucial Shavian theme. In fact, their interaction *is* vibrant in acts 1 and 2, as the three communicate above the crowd. But in act 3 Shaw's language loses touch with the repressed energy that, in release, fuels the sublime.

Money was to a considerable extent a repressed subject in Victorian England, as if the fascination of it were understood to contain a sensual element. E. M. Forster (1938) testifies: 'I remember being told as a small boy, "Dear, don't talk about money. It's ugly"' (p. 54). Some of that taboo remains. That is why Shaw's enthusiastic embrace of the subject – 'The universal regard for money is the one hopeful fact in our civilization' – still makes us laugh, still seems refreshing and liberating. The ability to say what others were afraid to say in this regard was deservedly a source of pride for Shaw. But he was an imaginative writer, not an economist, and he could not help encountering the anxiety that prompted the repression. We see him backing away from this anxiety in the peculiarly antiseptic third act of *Major Barbara*, with its emphasis on cleanliness, order and childlike sexuality. Significantly, Shaw's main reaction to Freud consisted of a fastidious objection to his indelicacy. Significantly too, at his most searching, in *Heartbreak House*, money and sensuality are linked together in Shotover's invective and even associated with darkness and disorder. Shotover asks grimly at the first act curtain for 'deeper darkness. Money is not made in the light' (*B* 5: 105). We are far, at that moment, from the airy brilliance of *Barbara*.

5

Compromise and Negation of the Comic Sublime

No dramatic work after *Major Barbara* is quite so committed to the logic of marching to the plains of heaven and discoursing thereupon. But the comic sublime continued to compel Shaw's imagination through the compromise structures of 1906–12, the powerful negation of its logic represented by *Pygmalion* and those extraordinary baffled apocalypses, *Heartbreak House* and *Back to Methuselah*. The best work of the raggedy 1906–12 period is, in fact, the most artificial – the contrived dilemma of *The Doctor's Dilemma*, the fable of *Androcles and the Lion*, the frame device of *Fanny's First Play*. The freer forms, particularly *Getting Married* and *Misalliance*, are less successful, though they are, as the artifices are not, serious preparations for the later and greater *Heartbreak House*. *Getting Married*, moreover, introduces the third version of the comic sublime (though it was adumbrated in the role of Caesar), the lonely standing on the heights in search of the shadowy embrace that promises to complete, to totalise, the ego.

It is difficult to know why Shaw imaginatively retreated for a while after *Barbara*. Perhaps the difficulty of resolving that play prompted him to realise that the dream of human perfectibility was a bit hollow. Perhaps he was becoming more sensitive to his advancing age, a possibility suggested by the plot of *The Doctor's Dilemma* (which may owe something to his unsettling flirtation with young Erica Cotterill in 1905) and by the fact that there are many more references to his age in the letters of this period than in those of the seven preceding years. In any case the point to stress is the writer's resourcefulness. If he could not in 1906 seek the heights, he could dramatise the tragi-comic compromises we make in attempting to be honourable. He could, for example, write a play about doing the right deed for the wrong reason.

We cannot really call *The Doctor's Dilemma* a tragedy, although it is so subtitled and although it features a scene about the early death of a genius. A reluctance to find error inherent in the human

131

condition rather than in shortsighted, theoretically corrigible human judgement leads the author to create here what is more accurately termed a dilemma. Or, rather, two dilemmas, awkwardly joined together.[1]

The overt dilemma of the play (and presumable reference of the title) involves the physician-protagonist, Sir Colenso Ridgeon, in the question of whether to use his newly discovered cure for tuberculosis (which for certain reasons only he can safely administer) to save a humble but decent colleague named Blenkinsop or a thoroughly caddish but brilliant artist named Dubedat. We are not to question the idea that there is only enough serum left over from the cases already selected to save one man or the other.

This is one of those ethical dilemmas sometimes concocted as a parlour game, as in Balzac's report of Rousseau in *Père Goriot* – would you press a button if, by doing so, you make a large gain yet at the same time cause the death of an obscure Asiatic? Actual life seldom if ever allows us to arrange such a neatly controlled ethical experiment.[2] The schematic aspect of this dilemma is hardly modified by the role of Dubedat, which is rather pat and theoretic, based really on the preconceived idea, earlier dramatised in *Man and Superman* (not to mention the novels), that the man of genius is humanly impossible – an idea that will be most fully dramatised in *Pygmalion* but remains little more than a notion here. Dubedat's ability as an artist and his contempt for those traditional points of honour, money and women, are crudely imagined. The jesting is also crude: 'I dont believe in morality. I'm a disciple of Bernard Shaw' (*B* 3: 393). I cannot agree with Max Beerbohm (1930) that Dubedat exemplifies Shaw's insensitivity to art (vol. 2, pp. 570–1), for there is too much evidence of appreciation in his musical, literary and theatrical criticism, but it is true that he never depicted an artist effectively. Like Marchbanks, Dubedat is only effective when he is catching up his opponent's words, when he is exposing the self-deceiving logic of moral compromise. The deathbed scene, which Shaw crowed over to Archer who challenged him to write one, is bathetic, with its insensitive clichés and its romantic credo adapted from a story by Richard Wagner.

The doctors who come to congratulate Ridgeon on his knighthood, and later assemble at a dinner where they will meet Dubedat and be consulted on the decision to be made, are conceived with Dickensian gusto[3] and are considerably more interesting: the sagely cynical Sir Patrick Cullen; the self-mocking Schutzmacher who knows that his advertisement – 'cure guaranteed' – will be accurate nine out of ten times independent of his own skill; the monomaniacal BB who, riding the craze for serum-cure, believes that the secret to medical treatment is 'to stimulate the phagocytes'; and Cuthbert Walpole who, riding the craze for surgery, believes instead that the secret is to 'extirpate the nuciform sac'. Despite their absurdity, however, Shaw meant his doctors to be well-meaning men.[4] And that brings us to the second dilemma, sufficiently more interesting than the first that Roger Boxhill (1969), in his book-length study *Shaw and the Doctors*, considers it the 'real' dramatic subject (pp. 134–43).

Cullen asks Ridgeon whether he intends to save the decent doctor or the blackguardly artist. Ridgeon responds that it is a dilemma with a complication: 'if I let Blenkinsop die, at least nobody can say I did it because I wanted to marry his widow' (377). He has been established for us as *'a man of fifty who has never shaken off his youth'* (325), and, though at the height of his career, he is depressed in a way that suggests he fears his chances of romance are fading. In this state of vulnerability – what we would call a mid-life crisis – he is confronted by the very beautiful young wife of Dubedat, whose Welsh charm and name (Jennifer) as well as her uncritical devotion to her rascally husband touch his imagination. Convinced that she's interested in him despite Cullen's warning that he's going to make a fool of himself, he finally decides to turn Dubedat over to the eminent but, as he knows, riskily wrongheaded BB and save Blenkinsop. It is an ethically defensible decision given the premises, but the reasoning behind it is exposed as a self-deluding rationalisation: Ridgeon would protect Jennifer from ever having to be disillusioned in the character of her husband.

Some time after Dubedat's death, Ridgeon visits the gallery where Jennifer is helping to exhibit the artist's work. There he learns that she not only harboured no personal interest in him whatever but has also remarried, as Dubedat advised. Acknowledging the determining force of his covert motive, he observes with chagrin in the closing line of the play, 'Then I have committed a purely disinterested murder' (436). This is to recognise a miscalculation rather than a flaw in one's nature (though Jennifer implies at one point that a man whose profession condones the torture of animals might well be prone to such an error), and the play attains an ironic rather than tragic climax. Ironic too is Ridgeon's discovery that Jennifer was never ignorant of her husband's blackguardliness but accepted it because she believed in his work and her love. One might add that this subtle finale has proven to be more effective on the page than the stage, a rare instance in Shaw of a lapse in theatrical instinct.[5]

An important reason for the partial obscurity of Shaw's irony here is his ambivalence toward Jennifer. Outside the play he commented that she was a type he hated (*CL* III 823; *CL* IV 609), but, inside, he made her presence compelling. Like Candida, she seems to overshadow and dwarf the men – in Valency's (1973) view she is the Shavian Virgin Mother who pronounces judgement though she is unable to have what she loves (p. 278) – yet, like Candida, she is supposed to incarnate a vision that is valid up to a point. This ambivalence helps to explain why Dubedat is so badly done. Shaw must have sensed that he was investing Jennifer with more charisma than his purpose called for, and so degraded the man who was her religion and *raison d'être*.

Perhaps because the play in its ironies denies us a higher vision, the preface is a sustained, eloquent polemic against an age of littleness – mired in concupiscence, greed and fear of death – on behalf of the 'vital dogmas' of 'honor, liberty, courage, the kinship of all life' (*B* 3: 317). It is not an attack on the medical profession as such but on professional exclusionism of any kind. 'All professions are conspiracies against the laity', it says, and the words are echoed in the play by Sir Patrick Cullen. Equally, it is an attack on the credulous idolatry of the laity without which such exclusionism could not be sustained.

To the highminded Shaw it seemed a manifest absurdity to give a group of men who were morally no better than other men a pecuniary interest in disease, especially if they were poorly paid, as doctors were in England. Mocking the ease with which a physician could rationalise unethical conduct ('my wife – my pretty ones'), Shaw snorts, 'It is enough to make one despair of political humanity' (226–7). Being merely decent men they are bound by custom, and so, without a sense of wrongdoing, they commit acts of cruelty, like vivisection, without even thinking them cruel. They do not even seek out alternative, humane methods of investigation. Darwin to his credit at least knocked out the belief promoted by the Catholic Church that men were essentially distinguishable from animals by virtue of having a 'soul'. But his natural selection – which for Shaw becomes 'so-called Natural Selection', 'mere dead luck and accident' (278) – may well have been responsible for creating a moral atmosphere in which we can no longer think of living things as sacred at all.

The Shavian knife, of course, turns easily around to ourselves, the laity. Doctors are insufficiently critical of their own conduct because we want to believe in them. It is we who enable someone like Dr Bonnington to retain his faith in a panacea like stimulating the phagocytes despite a margin of error wide enough to send a serious scientist back to the drawing-board.

Shaw is particularly vigorous in exposing the fallacies of the statistical logic that allows us to believe so uncritically in vaccination, carrying his attack to the point of saying that until public hygiene is greatly improved, no cause and effect relation between vaccination and the prevention of disease can be validly established.

As long as his argument remains critical and analytic, exposing the kind of logic that helps to maintain the status quo, it is usually effective despite its crankiness. But when it becomes constructive, rising to the challenge of the inevitable question 'What Then Is To Be Done', it rests too complacently on the premise that political states can force moral improvement upon individuals and should therefore exercise more control over their conduct. The socialisation of medicine is, arguably, a constructive result to which the Fabians contributed, but one might have predicted that the legislation of the Socialist government of the late 1940s would seem prosaic to the aged Shaw, failing to nourish his dream of a commonwealth of saints.

We can discern a new degree of impatience, amounting to jitteriness, in the next major effort of the dramatist who would soon be acting out his own version of a mid-life crisis in a serio-comic affair with Mrs Patrick Campbell. *Getting Married: A Disquisitory Play* (including its preface, written two years later in 1910) is not careless work exactly, although its subtitle seems to acknowledge its diffuse structure, but its paradoxes tend to be flaccid. It presents with diminished tension a theme that continued to obsess Shaw, the reasoned wish to accept prosaic marriage in conflict with the subsistent yearning for the splendid and heavenly.

On the one hand, it recommends a sensible acceptance of the institution of marriage as a more or less distasteful necessity: marriage, after all, is not likely to be legislated out of existence, and it is inconvenient and undignified to rebel against it beyond a certain point. Shaw perceives that the economic equality of women with men would relieve the curse of jealousy and make for juster laws, but his chief interest, especially in the preface, is to warn against the strain of trying to pitch marital happiness too high, of glamourising it with romance and sentiment and libertine pleasure. He perceives that the sex instinct 'clouds the reason and upsets the judgment more than all the other instincts put together' (*B* 3: 498), but his own common sense seems clouded, or he is in the grip of a theory that blinds him to psychological realities, when he argues that energetic spirits should be allowed polygamy and polyandry: if they are not, their pursuit of pleasure will depopulate the race or at least rob it of its more promising experiments.

The most sensible speakers in the play, Collins the grocer and Mrs Bridgenorth the Bishop's wife, talk of accepting marriage with a superficial blandness, but there is a peculiar edge to their remarks. Collins sounds like William the waiter when he observes that 'marriage is tolerable enough in its way if youre easygoing and dont expect too much from it'; then he adds, 'but it doesnt bear thinking about' (603). Mrs Bridgenorth sounds like Mrs Whitefield when she says, 'Of course people must get married'; but adds, not altogether rhetorically, 'Will somebody tell me how the world is to get on if nobody is to get married?' (597, 600). In the two couples who are debating respectively whether to marry or divorce – Cecil and Edith, Reginald and Leo – we see, accordingly, a measure of rebellion and a more or less grim retreat to conventionality, eased by a contract in the first case and by a spiritless acceptance of a lover-on-the-side in the second.

On the other hand, especially in the play, we see a peculiar straining for the emotionally absolute. (In the preface this takes the form of political dogmatism, of scorning democracy as a means and recommending stronger leadership.) Lesbia scorns her merely real suitor for the heroes of her imagination; Shaw uses her name not to hint at alternative sexual preference but to suggest her interest in having children without that reduced form of humanity known as a husband. Soames, the Bishop's chaplain-lawyer, is a fiercely celibate Christian for whom marriage is only honourable in the context of a primitive communist society freed of associations with property. Hotchkiss, to whom Shaw has given some of his own recognisable stigmata, like the nickname Sonny and a special interest in Mahomet, is infatuated with the demon–goddess– mayoress (and coal merchant's wife), Mrs George, a mother whose charismatic force compels him into her household. The Bishop himself, whose splendid twelfth-century Norman kitchen provides the single scene of the play, functions conveniently as the focus for Mrs George's own intense idealisations and correspondingly intense frustrations. He is, in a sense, her John the Baptist, and his authority yields to hers, rhetorically at any rate, after her entrance.

The vatic pronouncements of Mrs George are the play's highest rhetorical pitch and verge on ineffability, as if to compensate for the constricted sexuality of his two previous heroines, Barbara Undershaft and Jennifer Dubedat. Earlier, a letter from Mrs George (pseudonymously Incognita Appasionata) is quoted, telling us that she seeks 'some great man who will never know her, never touch her, as she is on earth, but whom she can meet in heaven when she has risen above all the everyday vulgarities of earthly love' (578–9). On stage she announces that she has 'become a voice for them that are afraid to speak, and a cry for the hearts that break in silence' (647) – a phrase re-used and given political resonance in *Heartbreak House* – and she intones a message of 'intensely sad reproach', beginning, 'When you loved me I gave you the whole sun and stars to play with. . . . A moment only; but was it not enough?' (645). Her pseudo-poetic eloquence, along with her flaccid responses to Hotchkiss and the others, prevents us from agreeing with Shaw when he told Stella Campbell that 'Mrs George contains the most wonderful of all my serio-tragic woman's parts' (*CL* III 335). Certainly the speeches of Ellie and Hesione about the longing of women and the restlessness of their sons are better done and contain more dramatic charge. But Mrs George's long message, only a third of which I have quoted, affords us one of the fullest illustrations of Shaw's dialectic of desire.

We have noticed that a central characteristic of Shaw's imagination is the alternative idealisation of self and other. Perhaps nowhere else in his work can we see so plainly the vulnerability of the latter choice, exposing a painful incompleteness inherent in the very act of idealisation. The all-giving Mother cannot give or receive enough to feel complete. And it is dangerous to be loved by her. Mrs Collins's children have left home because they would otherwise be destroyed by cuddling. Mother-love is objectionable as well as infinitely desirable. If the elusive object of desire can be said to be the symbiotic fusion of self and other, this must remain as inaccessible and unrecoverable as Eden before the Fall, leaving both self and other forlorn.

The tendency to absolutise desire, shown by Mrs George in the play and in the preface by an authoritarian tendency to stanch muddle by scorning democracy as a political means, assumes a theological cast in *The Shewing-Up of Blanco Posnet* (1909), which is worth comment here because it indicates so clearly what in my view militates most damagingly, in middle and late Shaw, against the interaction of ironic and idealising elements that constitutes his best efforts.

The comic effects in the play are easy ones, used mainly as a lead-in for the 'sermon' (as the subtitle calls it) to follow. Shaw has some fun with a group of frontier women whose judgements of the horse-stealer Blanco are absurdly limited by their conventional habits of thought. And perhaps good enough to bear comparison with Mark Twain's Pap is Blanco's elder brother, whose justification of drinking has a droll plausibility much like Pap's justification of racism. In fact, the central irony of the play – Blanco performs a deed considered immoral by his society but noble by us – is similar to the irony of Huck Finn's famous decision to free his enslaved friend and go to hell. But it degenerates into sentimentality. Blanco's decision to help the desperate woman with a mortally sick child by stealing a horse is perceived by him as 'going soft', not as going to hell. The impression of sentimentality is not exactly weakened by the fact that tough Feemy Evans, who had no love for Blanco, goes so soft herself that she tells a lie which will save him from hanging. Nor by the fact that the sheriff seems like a Sunday-school teacher rather than the law enforcer of a community that sanctions hanging for horse-stealing.

But what is most troublesome, and most revealing, is the dogmatic aspect of the sermon itself. Tolstoy was pained by its theology (*CL* II 902); so was Yeats (Hone, 1962, p. 233); and so am I. Jumping on to a table in order to preach a sermon on the moral of the day's proceedings, Blanco himself explains that his action was motivated by God, an emerging will-to-perfectibility operating by trial-and-error. He tells all assembled that he had been playing the 'rotten game' but that God tricked him or showed him up by means of 'the little Judas kid' so that he found himself playing the 'great game' instead. Even this weak irony is dropped when Shaw, with pride, wrote about his play to the aged Tolstoy:

You will also see that my theology and my explanation of the existence of evil is expressed roughly by Blanco. To me God does not yet exist; but there is a creative force constantly struggling to evolve an executive organ of godlike knowledge and power: that is, to achieve omnipotence and omniscience; and every man and woman born is a fresh attempt to achieve this object. (*CL* II 901)

Such a theology leaves nothing whatever to fear, nothing in us to be resisted or confronted or remade. A child killed by croup is merely the necessary error involved in a worthy experiment. John Tanner had told us to beware of a man whose God was in the skies. We might say that, in Blanco Posnet, Shaw has taken God not only out of the skies but out of the human mind as well and identified him with some sort of transcendent historical will. Yet he speaks for his deity with a confidence amounting to complacence. How can Blanco be so sure that 'It was early days when He made the croup' (*B* 3: 797)? He and his creator are too certain of a providential plan (trial-and-error does not hide the progressive thrust of the plan), and too certain that 'despair' must be the only alternative to a belief in it. This is not to conquer fear but to deny it, and the result is an art whose thinness may be said to be proportionate to its dogmatism.[6]

In *Misalliance* (1910), Shaw has regained some of the vivacity of his best work by allowing his fears of political and sexual disorder more scope for expression. The two fathers of the older generation (much more effectively than their counterparts in the early *Philanderer*) are sympathetically bewildered as well as a bit ridiculous in their uncertainties and sentimental infatuations. Their children are less sympathetic but their anti-sentimental claims and defiances are to be taken with some seriousness. And the disciplinarian-goddess who falls from the skies and confronts all this disorder is both severe and charming.

What *Misalliance* chiefly lacks is concentration of effect, an impression strengthened when we compare it to *Heartbreak House*, for which it is in many ways a preparation. The vivacity is jittery, almost frenetic; Tarleton's rapidly associative monologuing is of a piece with his daughter's chasing about the stage. The gaiety of *Misalliance*, its rapid talk and situational turns, does not seem sufficiently responsive to a darkness of any kind. A programme note for a 1977 production of the play compares it to Ingmar Bergman's film *Smiles of a Summer Night*: in both, a civilised weekend houseparty explodes into an erotic roundelay (Lawson,

1977). But the comparison really points up the lack of underlying gravity in Shaw's play: consider the comparative seriousness of Shaw's Mrs Tarleton and of Bergman's bedridden mother. The original title, *Just Exactly Nothing* (CL II, 871), is somewhat too apt for comfort.

None the less, an authentic theme is, I think, latent. The play is not about misalliance in the usual sense of an unsuitable spousal partnership. It is about the unsuitability (or, one may guess, the danger) of *any* tie based on personal liking. Hypatia Tarleton rejects Bentley Summerhays not because he is an aristocrat (her father manufactures underwear) nor even because he is effete (she is hyperactive) but because their friendship is personal. She takes up with Joey Percival instead, not because they are equally vital like Tanner and Ann but because their attraction to one another is animalistic and thus averts the danger of love-slavery. Lina Szczpanowska, the acrobat-aviatrix, rejects the amorous advances of the two fathers whom she personally likes (as well as the lovemaking of Johnny Tarleton whom she personally despises) and gathers up into her death-risking airplane the least likely person on stage, the frightened Bentley Summerhays.

What makes these incidents seem thin is that the play hardly addresses the reason *why* affection is dangerous. But at least at one point it gives an adequate clue. Tarleton declares: 'Believe me, Summerhays, the relation between the young and old should be an innocent relation. It should be something they could talk about. Well, the relation between parent and child may be an affectionate relation. It may be a useful relation. It may be a necessary relation. But it can never be an innocent relation' (B 4: 187). So *this* is what the play is trying to be about, the psycho-sexual burden of the parent–child relation.

The preface, written later, does explicitly address the question of Parents and Children, though it is only moderately candid and self-confrontational. Based on the premise that every new-born human being is 'an experiment: A fresh attempt to produce the just man made perfect . . ., to make humanity divine' (B 4: 20), Shaw's argument (like that of Rousseau and of D. H. Lawrence) is that any attempt to discipline a child according to personal biases and emotions, especially by a system of penalties and rewards for which divine sanction is claimed, is the warping and desecration of a soul. His most emphatic advice is to let the child's character alone since 'nobody knows the way a child should go' (23). Yet to suspend a truly religious education would be 'Rationalism gone mad' (125–6). We need belief, though all belief is provisional.

Taken at face value, the argument pretty much cancels itself out since it is much too vague on the subject of a truly religious education and how it would escape the danger of every other programme. But regarded more shrewdly, it is disheartening; it approaches and then evades self-knowledge. Shaw apparently suffered all his life from surfacing incestuous fantasy, and this preface, as much as any single piece of his writing, tells us so. He himself did not experience the kind of possessiveness he deplores in these pages. On the contrary, everything we know suggests that he suffered from too little love, from the emotional neglect of a remote mother whom he idealised but could never please. To be let alone as a child is the opposite of what he really must have wanted. He fails to recognise, in other words, the nature of his attachment. At one point he does refer to the peculiar attachment of the child to the parent but only in order to say that familiarity destroys all romantic charm and hence any possibility of incestuous desire (113).[7]

The play curiously links the strength of a maternal parent with the vagueness of a paternal one through the business of Joey Percival's 'three fathers', recognised by Shaw as an echo of his own situation in which the biological father was supplemented by the mother's brother and by Vandeleur Lee. It is a common enough perception in psychoanalytic literature that the replication of father images indicates an underlying anxiety about really having any father. A silly playlet of the same period as *Misalliance*, called 'The Fascinating Foundling' (B 3: 899–914), brushes across this insight by presenting orphanhood as an advantage, a charm in a young woman that should compensate a young man for her bullying and other apparent disadvantages.

The preface to *Misalliance* stresses political discipline, even a kind of absolutism, offsetting the recommendation of extreme laissez-faire in childrearing. The child must be left alone because no adult can know the natural bent of his divine spirit. But when adults are in question, this endorsement of spontaneity turns into advocacy of an intensely purposive will. Shaw impatiently and humourlessly drives his idealism hard. Not surprisingly, this preface defends the political need for capital punishment, and denounces even so serious a moralist as Samuel Johnson for 'trifling with literary fools in taverns' instead of 'shaking England with the thunder of his spirit' (37).

Shaw himself seemed to have realised that it was time for imaginative retrenchment, for more concentration of effect. His next three plays – *Fanny's First Play*, *Androcles and the Lion* and *Pygmalion* – all achieve originality by working within formal limits: a play within a play, a fable-like scheme and a humanistic critique of the sublime mode itself involving his most candid acknowledgement of the psychological basis of the incest taboo. These plays mark an important pause before Shaw's last significant effort to break new ground, in *Heartbreak House* and *Back to Methuselah*.

One remembers best about *Fanny's First Play* the witty induction that establishes the frame. Fanny O'Dowda has persuaded her father to mount a production of her maiden effort and invite leading theatrical critics, whose guesses as to authorship, specifically whether the play is by Shaw or not, bandy what were becoming the stock negative responses to the now famous playwright: brain without heart, incapacity for passion, puppetlike characterisations. The epilogue that completes the frame, in which Count O'Dowda expresses his dismay at the indelicacy of his daughter's invention, is less effective because what we have seen is very mild.

The son of one bourgeois family and the daughter of another break from respectability to the extent of assaulting a policeman and getting themselves gaoled. The son returns home with a not quite respectable girl whom he met in prison and the daughter with a married French lieutenant whom she found smoking a cigarette, after which they drank champagne and went dancing. (The lieutenant will deliver a droll final speech about the charming 'unconventionality' – that is, hypocrisy – of the English bourgeoisie compared to the French.) The daughter is asked by her mother how she could do it, and replies that she was stimulated to her rebellion by attending a prayer meeting where she was 'set free for evil as well as good'. But this self-styled 'heroine of reality' is merely playing at Nietzscheanism. I agree with Valency (1973) that the play betrays a certain shallowness because 'the revolt of the young people' doesn't 'cost them something, psychically speaking' (p. 300). Fanny was considered bold by her father, but her creator seems old-maidish to us. He has not invested respectability with enough adversarial weight. The very phrasing used to describe the daughter's moment of conversion travesties Shaw's favourite metaphor: exalted by the prayer meeting, she felt herself 'climbing up the golden stairs to heaven' (*B* 4: 392).

Imaginative curtailment works to better advantage in *Androcles and the Lion*, thanks in part to the childlike tenderness that Shaw brings to the fable form, unlike the adolescent coyness in *Fanny's First Play*. The Prologue is trebly charming. A dangerous lion is converted into a waltzing companion by the humanitarian Androcles, who 'is unafraid . . . not because he is brave but because he is compassionate' (Kauffmann, 1986, p. 38). A shrewish wife is reduced by fear to pleading and then becomes shrewish again as she observes the lion dancing with her husband. And the waltz itself sets up the delightful reprise in the arena where the recognition scene between the starving lion and his old friend the terrified tailor amazes the bloodthirsty multitude. Shaw sports to fine effect with his fantasies of, and defences against, oral incorporation.

In the main plot, the substantiality of historical fact grounds a drama of worldly vs. religious commitment, and moral discriminations are generated by a quasi-allegorical form.

Shaw's heroine Lavinia is no mere martyr. She says, 'Do not think it is easy for us to die' (*B* 4 595), just as Shaw's Christ, in the preface, did not 'see any more sense in martyrdom than Galileo did' (463). Rather she is someone for whom an exalting faith is an end in itself, powered by the renunciation of the world and the flesh presented as palpable temptation in the person of the Roman captain. But the sublime potential of this confrontation is stiffened by historical formality. Perhaps more effective are the neatly planned climaxes of the second act, set in the Coliseum where the Christians are confronted by lions and gladiators. At one extreme is the pointedly unedifying example of the 'Crosstian' Spintho, who fearfully tries to believe that we are promised salvation in heaven no matter what we do, that martyrdom pays all scores, that immunity of conscience can be purchased by token repentance. Convinced of original sin and merely frightened by guilt into joining the new religion, he is fundamentally a cynic and jeered at on all sides. (Regrettably, the playwright too relishes the death of the coward who, trying to escape, runs directly into the jaws of a lion, though the postscript makes the good point that revolutionary movements attract not only superior souls but also those who are not good enough for established institutions – 637.) At the other extreme is the happy fate of Androcles, the holy fool or 'humanitarian naturalist' (636), who is not aware of his own spiritual power and is sincerely frightened by the prospect of death. His reputation for sorcery is based on his fellow-feeling for animals and will, of course, be justified when he encounters his old leonine friend in the arena. Shaw improves on the pleasant jest by having Androcles, a mere tailor, save the Emperor from the hungry lion by advising him to appear to be *very intimate* with so humble a person as himself.

Between these extremes there is the complex case of the Pauline figure Ferrovius, a powerful, choleric man whose self-control is uncertain but whose conversion has been a sincere, though premature, attempt to shame himself out of an inclination to use force in states of righteous indignation. He mangles six armed gladiators, to the delight of the Emperor who invites him to join the Pretorian Guard, but feels very bad afterward about his lost soul. The preface of 1915 would have us understand him as a transition between two historical phases of faith, the warrior's and the Christian's. Like Ibsen's emperor in *Emperor and Galilean*, he is not quite ready for a God-idea that is itself just emerging. As such he is an effective foil for Lavinia, who chooses, in her hour of decision, 'to strive for the coming of the God who is not yet' (634).

In portraying Ferrovius, Shaw candidly compromises. The prospect of his mutilating a gladiator excites even Lavinia, who calls such a deed 'splendid' and adds, more soberly, 'I am not always a Christian. I dont think anybody is' (606). In having her admit that 'Something wilful in me wants to see you fight your way to heaven' (621), Shaw seems to discern that a repressed instinctual energy empowers his questing for the heights. But of course, the repression, momentarily lifted, remains in place: the figure of Paul in the preface is handled quite harshly.

Like the later and greater *Saint Joan*, *Androcles and the Lion* is supported by our retrospective historical knowledge. In neither case is present knowledge engaged passively, as in middlebrow costume dramas. The postscript to *Androcles* makes a particular point of telling us that the conflict in the play is not between the false and true religions of one age but between the Have-and-Holders and the spiritual vanguard of any age. 'My martyrs are the martyrs of all time and my persecutors the persecutors of all time' (636). If this is too neat, it is nevertheless true that Lavinia's

striving for the God who is not yet works better than Blanco
Posnet's similar striving because it engages the recognition of a
particular history. Which is not to say that Shaw was content with
a simple, onward-and-upward view of the Christian era. The
lengthy and frequently brilliant preface is a strenuous attempt to
separate the retrograde from the salutary components of the
Christian ethic.

It is launched with the salvo, 'Why Not Give Christianity a
Chance?' Most of what passes for religion is merely a defence of
Have-and-Holders, conspicuously including 'salvationism', the
false doctrine of atonement and propitiation that Shaw considered,
as did some other impassioned Protestants including Ibsen, the
antithesis of a true sense of moral responsibility. The argument to
this point recapitulates what was said in the preface to *Major Barbara*.
But it proceeds to demonstrate, with considerable ingenuity, that
the essential doctrine of Jesus, self-transcendence, is yet untried,
obscured by centuries of worldly interest.

This doctrine consists of repudiating money and property, the
practice of revenge and punishment, and the entanglements of
wife and family. Shaw is more cogent than we might expect
in undertaking the extraordinary task of showing that these
renunciations are not only supported by the biblical text but are
also consistent with the goals of Fabian Socialism. A reader of
Major Barbara may be puzzled by his endorsement of 'You cannot
serve both God and Mammon', but it is important to understand
that, in theory, Undershaft should self-destruct; to put it another
way, the goal of Shaw's Socialism is to allow us to forget about
money and property, to set 'our minds free for higher uses' (529).
As for revenge and punishment, his objective is not to commend
anarchy but to show that social discipline is possible without the
motive of revenge; that is what 'Judge not lest ye be judged' really
means, and what the *lex talionis* does *not* mean. The argument
against marriage, not surprisingly, gives Shaw the most trouble.
At times he seems to suggest that sexual conflict is inherent in
human nature rather than in a capitalist society: 'In our sexual
natures we are torn by an irresistible attraction and an overwhelming repugnance and disgust' (539). But finally he emphasises the
idea that the institution of marriage locks in this conflict, associating
gratification with both virtue and sin, and he imagines reasonably
that Socialism will alleviate the conflict by granting more economic
independence for women. What Jesus perceived was 'that nobody

could live the higher life unless money and sexual love were obtainable without sacrificing it' (540).

Shaw's Jesus, in short, must have been a highly civilised man who saw no merit in asceticism (unlike John the Baptist) or in martyrdom. He emphasised conduct as well as faith, and was embarrassed and annoyed that his gift for healing was degraded by a thirst for vulgar miracles. His Jesus, like Blake's, became an emblematic figure of spiritual triumph over materialism and selfhood. 'Christ stands in the world,' Shaw wrote in another preface, 'for [an] intuition of the highest humanity' (*B* 4: 74).

But, much like Eliot, Yeats and Lawrence who discovered a Fall within Christian history, Shaw stressed also the degradation of this ideal. Jesus the moral genius has become Christ the martyr, scapegoat and Saviour. The architect of this degradation, and the villain of the preface, is Paul. Paul was driven by 'the terror of sin and the terror of death', which may also be called 'the terror of sex and the terror of life' (546). But 'Jesus, with his healthy conscience on his higher plane, was free from these terrors' (546–7). Under Paul's influence, Christianity became a denial of life, an infernal fatalism that affected even the leaders of the Reformation, even John Bunyan. The spirit of the Reformation is yet to be fulfilled by Fabian Socialism.

Shaw allows his martyrs in *Androcles* to be willing to die for their truth, but none of them does – or is even meant to by the Emperor – except the coarse backslider, Spintho. That unfortunately reduces the essential seriousness of the comedy. The cruelty of the historical emperors becomes a children's game. Moreover, it is difficult to believe that the old martyrs were quite so joyous in their courage. The struggle between entrenched and emerging powers is doubt-less perennial, but *Androcles* is too sure of a progressive outcome.

A fable underlies the structure of *Pygmalion* as well as of *Androcles*, but Shaw has here individualised his characters to a remarkable degree and dramatised their story with exceptional intimacy and directness. In no other of his plays does he show us resistance to the heroic point of view with so much sympathy and expose so keenly what is problematic in that view. I used to question the popularity of *Pygmalion* because it is less ambitious conceptually than the 'big three' written earlier or than *Heartbreak House* and *Back to Methuselah*. But an imaginative writer can sometimes gain an extraordinary strength by turning against his own vision.

Pygmalion is Shaw's major achievement in the mode of the anti-sublime.

It is subtitled A Romance, and certainly it generates thoroughly romantic expectations up to a point. Few literary fantasies are as irresistible as this Cinderellan metamorphosis of the cockney flower girl into the supposed princess at an ambassador's party. It is sometimes said that the momentum of this romance plot is so strong that the romantic dénouements perpetrated by Sir Beerbohm Tree and Mrs Patrick Campbell (to Shaw's disgust) and later by others, including Messrs Lerner and Loewe, are justified. But Shaw was nowhere more faithful to his own distinctive sensibility than in those potent structures of disappointment, acts 4 and 5. The Miltonic mind of Higgins and the eloquent humanity of Eliza are opposed in an absolute stalemate. There can be no compromise between the expectations of acts 1–3 and the disappointment of 4–5, as Shaw himself managed to prove by trying unsuccessfully to write a narrative continuation about Eliza's moderately happy future with Freddy, pages described accurately by Valency (1973) as 'dismally novelistic' (p. 318). Shaw was, at one and the same time, romantic and anti-romantic, and this ambivalence is especially firm in *Pygmalion*. It is right that Higgins is alone at the end, laughing in denial of his failure to hold Eliza. And Eliza must be disappointed too, for the man she cannot help loving is incorrigible. Her whole story – the fantastic rise and its unexpectedly bitter end – is replayed in a farcical key by the story of Doolittle, her father.

Shaw knew that, at the peril of sentimentality, Higgins must be harsh as well as attractive. It is no accident that *Pygmalion* is the most candid of his works on the subject of incest. Higgins's incapacity for sexual love despite his unconscious seductiveness is explicitly traced to his idealisation of a superior mother. Shaw does not resort here to either of his two favourite explanations for the prevailing taboo on incest. One, drily rationalistic, is that early familiarity kills romance. The other comes closer to the truth by being its exact opposite: a mother's love is too much for a child and overwhelms him. *Pygmalion* is unique among his plays in encouraging us to make a connection between a character's early, excessive admiration of a mother and his later resistance to a woman he could otherwise love.

To suggest that Higgins represents Shaw's most direct effort of dramatic self-confrontation is not to say naïvely that he is a proxy for the author, much less a puppet, for we are dealing with an

imaginative configuration, 'the dancing of an attitude' in Kenneth
Burke's nice phrase, not with mere personal characteristics. The
preface adverts us to a brilliant, arrogant phonetician named Henry
Sweet as the original for Higgins, a proud and impatient man who
did not suffer fools gladly. (Milton, Ibsen and Samuel Butler are
also drawn into this portrait by association.) The arrogance of
Higgins is mainly expressed as an amiable bullying, aggressive
enough yet peculiarly innocent in its unguarded directness. The
most important device for distancing him is to make his aggressive
abruptness look comical by virtue of his lack of self-consciousness.
Probably the most effective of a dozen such passages occurs in act
4, after the party:

LIZA.   . . . Whats to become of me?
HIGGINS [*enlightened, but not at all impressed*].   Oh, *thats* whats
worrying you, is it? [*He thrusts his hands into his pockets, and
walks about in his usual manner, rattling the contents of his pockets,
as if condescending to a trivial subject out of pure kindness*] I
shouldnt bother about it if I were you. I should imagine you
wont have much difficulty in settling yourself somewhere or
other, though I hadnt quite realized that you were going away.
[*She looks quickly at him: he does not look at her, but examines the
dessert stand on the piano and decides that he will eat an apple*] You
might marry, you know. [*He bites a large piece out of the apple
and munches it noisily*].   (749–50)

Higgins's speech is a masterly, half-unconscious effort both to
attract and repel. The final stage direction caps his character
beautifully. Shaw's turn of phrase (*'he eats his apple with a dreamy
expression of happiness, as it is quite a good one'*) so neatly justifies
Higgins from his own point of view and condemns him from ours.
    But though we may laugh at him, Shaw insisted that he must
be heroic (Dent, 1952, p. 24). One of the play's insights is that
intellectual or creative achievement may be significantly related to
the continued presence of early idealisations. But heroic need
not mean likeable, and indeed usually does not. The mother's
exasperation with her son and Pickering who are playing like boys
with a live doll and Eliza's anguished slipper-throwing are human
protests, forcefully expressed, against the inhumanity of an heroic
stance.
    The romance of Eliza's rise is given considerable space before

the shadows fall. Her naïveté in the early acts is extremely charming, and her father's comparable casuistry is unusually disarming. But sorrow is drawn *from* the romance. Eliza owes her transformation to a Pygmalion who must, we can see from the first, fail to live quite up to his mythic role at the last. And Doolittle's 'fall' into middle-class morality has, in a sense, been his own doing. We may regret the forlorness, but anti-climax is a central feature of Shaw's sensibility and I can readily understand his impatience with the softened ending. Higgins is so fully and honestly imagined that he really must not be allowed to toss Eliza a kiss or a rose. And bringing Freddy forward as a companion for Eliza has really nothing to do with the story of her romance. Of course, it is reasonable to assume that a young woman, romantically disappointed, will eventually make a new, more prosaic life for herself, but this makes another story.

The strength of *Pygmalion* has much to do with the unresolved tension between the 'higher' consciousness of Higgins and the 'lower' consciousness of Eliza. It is a sexually charged tension that insists on both eternal separateness and eternal reciprocity. Not every viewer or reader finds aesthetic satisfaction in that. But it may help to show how the impasse of acts 4 and 5 is prepared by the romance of the first three acts.

Each of the early acts gracefully develops a romantic situation and at the curtain gracefully turns it away. We start with a wonderful whirl of contrasting voices – the fretful Eynsford-Hills sending off their Freddy to look for a cab in the rain, the broad cockney whine of the flower girl, the nonchalant echoing of the Notetaker punctuated by the remarks of suspicious bystanders – and gradually rising from the mêlée, as the rain unnoticeably stops, the educated exchange of Pickering and Higgins playing out an irresistibly improbable recognition scene. They joke amiably about what Eliza could be and, with godlike condescension, shower her with coins. She goes off self-importantly but alone in the cab that Freddy finally obtained for his family, who have already left.

The second and third acts are constructed similarly, a movement of building up and dashing romance that is half-concealed by the charm of the humour and the expectation of later fulfilment. In the first part of act 2, Eliza arrives at Wimpole Street with her new wealth to hire Higgins as a teacher, and amid a good deal of bullying and scorn, the romantic wager is made. Enter thereupon a sordid complication, the blackmailing dustman. But he so beguiles the gentlemen and us with his casuistic defence of the undeserving poor that we do not realise, until his charismatic presence fades, that the boy-gentlemen have taken on a 'stiff job' of a less technical and more complexly human kind than they are prepared to acknowledge.

Mrs Higgins serves much the same deflationary function in the third act that Doolittle does in the second. Higgins and then Pickering enter her drawing room excitedly, arousing our expectation of a transformed Eliza performing successfully before an audience of Eynsford-Hills. We are struck for a moment by the element of truth in Higgins's statement that a change of class is like a change of soul. Then our Galatea regresses to street talk, charming Freddy and delighting Clara. But Mrs Higgins soberly and forcefully points out to us that the two 'infinitely stupid male creatures' are toying with a human life. The picture of her at the curtain (scorning men! men!! men!!!) registers one of his strongest judgements against his own kind of inhumanity, drawing its strength from his investment in the image of the judging mother.

With the structure of these acts in mind, we see more clearly that, despite further comic moments (notably the tophatted Doolittle complaining about Ezra D. Wannafeller's Moral Reform Society and Pre-Digested Cheese Trust), the fourth and fifth acts dramatise a sustained impasse. Love is in the air but checked, stifled. The fourth act plays off Higgins's triumphant egotism against Eliza's human anguish. Baffled, she throws his gift ring into the fireplace, picks it out again and flings it once more on to a dessert stand.

The fifth act sustains this mood with the addition of other voices – Mrs Higgins's, Pickering's, Doolittle's. Mrs Higgins's role is to explain to the men the full humanity of Eliza. Pickering is now differentiated more clearly from Higgins, as adumbrated by his earlier politeness. Higgins naturally remains incorrigible: 'Get up and come home; and dont be a fool.' 'Very nicely put', replies his mother, 'No woman could resist such an invitation' (767).

He is, in fact, throughout the play, much like the incorrigible Doolittle, both in his chief virtues – utter frankness and freedom from snobbery – and in his chief vice – thinking of Eliza as a thing to manipulate. The difference is that Doolittle blandly resorts to blackmail whereas the heroically minded Higgins wants to make something of her, and scorns Freddy as a suitor because he cannot, in his terms, do so. Higgins is sincere in contrasting his own offer of a life devoted to Science and Literature with marriage to a man who can only offer money, kisses and kicks. But Eliza, though pained by the knowledge that she must give up much of higher value in making a decent, common life for herself, is resolved to do so and to do so with a measure of dignity. A harshly comic mutual rejection stamps the final moment of action. She sweeps out with mock indifference of his need for her; he laughs excessively at the idea of her marrying Freddy.[8]

Shaw makes it clear that heartbreak is inevitable in either the lofty or the common life yet that each is to be respected. He checks his two most characteristic impulses – to transcend and to ridicule – and thus in effect renders judgement on his own vision.

6

Baffled Apocalypse:
Heartbreak House and *Back to Methuselah*

The anti-sublime is not to be found again in any major effort by Shaw. (I say 'major' because the minor late sketch, 'Why She Would Not', captures a little of its spirit.) It is certainly true that the theme of romantic disappointment – heartbreak – informs his next important play, begun in 1913 though not completed until the war was well along and had left its mark upon it. But, despite a certain similarity of theme between *Pygmalion* and *Heartbreak House*, the two plays are fundamentally different in tone.

Two important events (psychobiographically speaking) – the death of his mother and the abortive romance with Stella Campbell – occurred in Shaw's life very shortly after *Pygmalion* was composed, but it is difficult to draw pertinent inferences from them. Arnold Silver (1982, pp. 253–79) is on solid enough ground in showing how the revisions of *Pygmalion* reflect personal bitterness toward Mrs Campbell, who of course played the role of Eliza in the very successful London production of the play. But it would be hard to say quite how Shaw's feelings about her shaped the different approach to disappointment that we find in *Heartbreak House*. We remember that the theme of demonic sexual attraction is an old one in Shaw, and it is apparent also that the terrible war would in any case have challenged his cherished ideals very severely. His completed dramatic work of 1913 consists of two slight farces about demonic sexuality – 'The Music Cure' and 'Great Catherine' – and it looks as if the war, for one thing, deepened and broadened his treatment of the subject.

To the extent that the war itself helped to rescue Shaw's dramatic work from slightness, it created another problem. As we can see in the prolific journalism of 1914–15, he was beginning to miscalculate his audience. The business of wounding complacent idealism was not so well understood by a society faced for the first time in a century with a massive and immediate public danger, and Shaw, who was fifty-eight in 1914, remained committed to a vision of perfectibility. Better a constructive mockery, he seemed to be saying, than a dwindled vision of a just society. These journalistic writings are worth a moment's consideration, the better to appreciate the intelligence with which he stepped aside from the war issue specifically in forging his most apocalyptic play.

In 'Common Sense about the War' and other pieces collected in the Constable edition under the title of *What I Really Wrote About the War*, the essential rhetorical strategy remains to undermine a prevailing view and thereby stimulate a nobler one that is put forward aggressively as the *true* common sense. Thus Shaw attempted to demonstrate that the English were no less warmongering and jingoistic than the Germans; that England's clergymen were preaching the gospel of Mars rather than of Christ; that the real beneficiaries of war were the militarists and plutocrats of all warring countries. After such clearing of the ground, it should become apparent even to non-Socialists that the day of the soldier is past and that humanity's true interests are now internationalistic (C 21 *passim*).

But Shaw's readers, anxious about their survival, were in no mood now to repudiate a morality of revenge or to abrogate in the name of world federation all merely nationalistic interests. To them Shaw seemed, if not positively pro-German, at least pacifist and defeatist. Probably the statement that aroused most hostility among his compatriots was: 'No doubt the heroic remedy for this tragic misunderstanding is that both armies should shoot their officers and go home. . . . But there is no chance – or as our Junkers would put it, no danger – of our soldiers yielding to such an ecstasy of commonsense' (C 21: 24–5). It is easy enough to perceive at a distance that the tone of this statement, so impatient in its exasperation and absurd in its provocation, was hardly likely to result in any practical danger. It was nevertheless seen at the time as inflammatory and flagrantly demoralising. One prominent editor described 'Common Sense about the War' as 'the meanest act of treachery ever perpetrated by an alien enemy residing in generous and long-suffering England' (*CL* III 240).

In fact, Shaw was not a pacifist. In regard to war as to other matters, he prided himself on being practical, a 'possibilist', and so it seemed evident that, once involved in a war, a country had to fight to win. But the motive should always be honourable. The

British should fight the Prussians precisely to prove that fighting efficiency is not the test of a civilisation (C 21: 102). Conscription could be countenanced 'not as a temporary expedient, but as an advance in social organization' (C 21: 229). Before the war Shaw had sought its prevention by a plan that he may have thought of as a form of *Realpolitik* but that seems idealistic enough: since disarmament is not practical (for power is needed to make justice work), England should ask France and Germany to join in a triple alliance, above jealousy and envy, and check any other force that presumed to threaten war.

These recommendations are pragmatic in the sense that they endorse actual and familiar forms of political conduct – fighting, conscripting, allying. But the central stress on honourableness of motivation makes them Utopian as well. Shaw wants political man in all his dealings to be religious man at his most genuine, always alert to the difference between God and Mammon, between spiritual and material struggle.

Much of Shaw's energy as an imaginative writer went into exploring the incongruity between what we are and what we could be, but during these war years the resultant ironies can seem almost cynical. One short play, 'Augustus Does His Bit', mocks 'a distinguished member of the governing class, in the uniform of a colonel', who is easily tricked out of important papers and naïvely reports that a Prussian colonel set him free, declaring 'that nothing would induce him to deprive my country of my services' (B 5: 214). Another playlet, 'O'Flaherty, v.c.', exploits the incongruity (as does Yeats in 'An Irish Airman Foresees his Death') of an Irishman fighting on behalf of the eternal oppressor, England. O'Flaherty's Fenian mother is outraged to discover the truth when her son returns on leave, then squabbles so much with his girlfriend about the golden (and accidentally earned) Victoria Cross that O'Flaherty yearns for the peace and quiet of the trenches. But despite these ironies, Shaw never goes so far as to embrace a reduced idea of the human being. Somewhat desperately perhaps in his last plays, he clung to the idea that what we *really* are is what we *could* be if fired by conviction, courage or faith. Shotover speaks of our need to believe in ourselves, the Ancients have learned not to die of discouragement, and Joan is exalted by faith.

The journalistic writings of the war years, however, often lack the strength of an active tension between the real and the ideal. They tend to be either airy at one extreme, marked by facile proposals as if Shaw couldn't take the war itself quite seriously, or excessively impatient at the other, as if he couldn't any longer take humanity quite seriously. There is an all-or-nothing spirit to his idealism in these years, prompting him to think beyond humanity. Let the war roar on, Shaw seems to be saying. It will clear slums, slay philistines, reduce commercialism to ruins. Either 'the best is yet to be' or 'the sooner we all blow one another off the face of the earth the better' (C 21: 274). Of course, Shaw occasionally found more concentrated expression even in his journalism, but we may fairly say that it was his ability over a stretch to unleash and yet restrain his imagination of disaster that gives *Heartbreak House* its peculiar authority and ambiguity.

The play's various characters are all aware of a permeating, seemingly irreversible sense of disorder, verging on doom, which they indulge, resist, scorn, succumb to or even welcome. Most of them take more than one of these attitudes in the course of the play, for they feel themselves to be in the same boat. The setting, a crazy house which old Captain Shotover has constructed to look like a boat, is frequently alluded to, and functions as a focal symbol of the demoralised drifting of the ship of state (or ship of soul) which will split on the rocks unless we learn individually and collectively the art of steering rather than drifting. The demoralising doubt is expressed that the time is already too late, but on the whole the tone is monitory rather than resigned.

Some of the strengths of the play – the vigour of its repudiations, its probing for the sources of discontent, and its reaching out, with Chekhov's help, for a more impressionistic technique of organisation – are such as to make one wish Shaw had more often sacrificed charm to force, and allowed his imagination of disaster to influence his form as much as his statement. *Heartbreak House* does genuinely bear comparison to *Women in Love* and *The Waste Land*, apocalyptic works of the same period that use the theme of corrupt sexuality as an index to the moral breakdown of civilisation: in all three, the Great War is not specified as a background but is understood as such, establishing an atmosphere of darkening threat.

The preface tries, not quite convincingly, to put the idea of sexual dalliance into direct cause-and-effect relation with that of political breakdown. *Heartbreak House* represents 'cultured leisured Europe before the War', which shrank from political responsibility and filled a moral vacuum with the grace and charm of refined philandering (*B* 5: 12–15). In Tolstoy's ironic phrase, which Shaw appreciated, it exemplified 'the fruits of culture'. The preface suggests, as does at greater length the preface to *Back to Methuselah*, that the ultimate cause of the current moral breakdown was the pseudo-scientific belief, pervading the whole post-Darwinian half-century, that predestination rather than moral responsibility was the central truth of religion. But the play itself, rich to the point of confusion in ambiguity, speaks a less rationalistic and more interesting language.

In a postscript, Shaw suggests that the central image of his play broadens in significance as it develops:

> The house is not Heartbreak House at first: The fly walks into the parlour with the happiest anticipations, and is kept amused until it gets fixed there as by a spell.
> Then the heartbreak begins, and gets worse until the house breaks out through the windows and becomes all England with all England's heart broken.   (*B* 5: 184)

'Happiest anticipations' does not seem quite right because Ellie Dunn, the fly, is anxious at first on several counts – her peculiar reception, her uneasiness about the understanding with Mangan complicated by her infatuation with 'Marcus Darnley', and her justified uncertainty as to Hesione's response to her marriage plan – but her role as *ingénue* is well defined and accounts in act 1 for much of the comedy, as Ellie confronts the slyness and worldliness, variously expressed, of the others. Her plain name is, of course, sharply contrasted to the luxurious names of those sirens, Hesione Hushabye and Ariadne Utterword. But Shaw's comment points to the fact that her heartbreaking disappointment in Darnley, alias Hector Hushabye, occurs on stage before the first act is over and that her sublime repudiation of 'happiness' and ascent to self-sufficient 'strength' is not only realised but fully expressed before the end of act 2. This sublime moment, in other words, is different from Vivie Warren's or Eugene Marchbank's or any other we have seen so far. It initiates a stoic elevation whose strength is directly tested (chiefly by Mangan, Hesione and Hector) and confirmed (by a mystic marriage to Shotover), yet is crossed by a yearning that can only itself find satisfaction in the apocalyptic rumble of the Zeppelin. The Zeppelin's roar and bombing relieve her frustrated sense that life never comes to a point, and leave her (and others) at the end momentary welcomers of doom.

Ellie Dunn's romantic heartbreak is only the most active and heroic expression of a general malaise that Shaw dramatises very effectively, giving the devil of sexual dalliance greater empathetic expression than ever before or after. The ravishing demon daughters with their seductive names – the one brunette and suave, the other blonde and brittle – hold the stage and even the page as compelling presences, and their half-wearied philanderings (along with those of Hector and Randall the Rotter) are exceptionally well done. Despite their futility, they deserve the compliment paid by the comparative outsider Mazzini Dunn, who tells them that they are not simply 'heartbroken imbeciles', as Hector put it, but 'rather a favorable specimen of what is best in our English culture. . . . Very charming people, most advanced, unprejudiced, frank, humane, unconventional . . . and everything that is delightful to thoughtful people' (*B* 5: 173). Where else, after all, could he feel perfectly at ease in pyjamas, talking about a collective malaise? Dunn's innocence, however, is underlined by the fact that he predicts inaccurately that Mangan and the burglar are the ones who will survive the bomb.

Hesione's seductiveness is sensual, playfully refined and maternal – more compelling and dangerous than Ariadne's. In the course of carrying out a plan to prevent young Ellie Dunn from throwing herself away on Boss Mangan, 'the hog of a millionaire' who supposedly befriended her admired father, Hesione, like Candida, distributes an amused maternal indulgence. Much of it is offered to Ellie who heartbreakingly discovers that the object of her romantic adoration is none other than Hesione's husband, who told romantic stories about himself under an assumed name and who will soon be caught in the web of Ariadne's charm. Some is bestowed on her philandering husband, some on the plain and mild Mazzini, and some (for the sake of her plan) on the snarling and whining Boss. If her first name, like her sister's, suggests sexual captivation, her last, Hushabye, suggests motherly comfort, and in climactic moments, notably the end of act 1, these qualities are combined:

What do men want? They have their food, their firesides, their clothes mended, and our love at the end of the day. Why are they not satisfied? Why do they envy us the pain with which we bring them into the world, and make strange dangers and torments for themselves to be even with us.   (104–5)

Ariadne's charm is impressive too but closer to comedy because of its brittleness. Despite her limited moral sense, she puts forward the theme taken up by the others, observing upon return after twenty-three years 'the same disorder in ideas, in talk, in feeling' (66) and, of course, in ordinary housekeeping. From her anti-bohemian point of view, the principal need of the house is for 'stables', there being but two classes of society, the equestrian and the neurotic. In an elegant little exchange with Hector she manages to articulate her particular social and sexual morality:

> LADY UTTERWORD.   I am a woman of the world, Hector, and I can assure you that if you will only take the trouble always to do the perfectly correct thing, and to say the perfectly correct thing, you can do just what you like. . . .
> HECTOR.   I see. You are neither a Bohemian woman nor a Puritan woman. You are a dangerous woman.
> LADY UTTERWORD.   On the contrary, I am a safe woman.   (97)

The wit of the exchange is based on the assumption that 'dangerous' and 'safe' are really only two sides of the coin of conventional morality. To philander without reproach is in her circle quite possible, so she can flirt with the urbane Hector but taunts her more humourless brother-in-law Randall.

Around these sisters spreads a circle of civilised but oppressive dalliance. Hector Hushabye is bound to both, 'married right up to the hilt' to Hesione but soon enthralled by Ariadne. Ellie is initially infatuated by Hector; Mangan for a while by Hesione (despite his presentiment of doom); and Randall Utterword has no other purpose in life than to pay court to his sister-in-law.

Judgement is passed against this way of life partly by Hector Hushabye himself, who, as his curious name implies, is something of a hero as well as a prime example of what Carlyle called the 'heartbreaking nonsense' of laissez-faire (*CL* III 689). Like John Tarleton in *Misalliance*, but with more bitter vigour, he rises in denunciation of the society of which he is a part.[1] It is he who rips the curtains away at the end to attract the destruction from the skies so fascinating to Ellie and Hesione. He cries out 'We are useless, dangerous, and ought to be abolished' (159), as if he were

a character in Chekhov stiffened by anger. This phrasing, by the
way, had been used earlier (in a speech of 1909) in reference to
the poor (*RS* 26), an indication of the degree to which *Heartbreak
House* internalises Shaw's quarrel with the world.

Hector's rhetoric can even approximate Albany's in *King Lear*:

> HECTOR.   I tell you, one of two things must happen. Either out
> of that darkness some new creature will come to supplant us
> as we have supplanted the animals, or the heavens will fall in
> thunder and destroy us.   (*B* 5: 159)

> ALBANY.   If that the heavens do not their visible spirits
>   Send quickly down to tame these vile offences,
>   It will come,
>   Humanity must perforce prey on itself,
>   Like monsters of the deep.
>   (Shakespeare, *King Lear*, IV.ii.46–50)

But the comparison with Shakespeare indicates a limitation too,
conceptually as well as rhetorically. Albany's 'vile offences' refer
to the shaking of a kingdom, even a cosmos; Hector's denunciation
is based more narrowly on the 'damnable quality' of Hesione and
Ariadne that 'destroys men's moral sense'. 'Is there', he asks, 'any
slavery on earth viler than this slavery of men to women?' (156).
Invoking the heavens at the curtain of act 2, he cries out: 'Fall and
crush' (157). Hesione and Ariadne do not frighten us as do Goneril
and Regan.

Primary judgement against the purposelessness depicted in
Heartbreak House is, of course, rendered through the inspired
characterisation of old Captain Shotover. He is something like
Undershaft plus Cusins in that he invents lethal weapons in order
to destroy evil. But his success is decidedly limited. His home,
unlike Undershaft's, is always short of money, and the rascality of
the rich is what he seeks vainly to destroy. Chiefly he functions in
the play as a prophetic figure, though a curiously charming one.
His great age, his half-sly dotage that permits or enables him to
exercise the license of abrupt speech (too disconcertingly direct as
a rule to be considered mere *non sequitur*), and the references to
his adventurous, semi-magical past – all this makes him a more
forceful prophet than Hector and one through whom we can
understand the underlying link between the sexual and the

political resonances of the image of heartbreak. Shotover sometimes denounces the society of 'my daughters and their men living foolish lives of romance and sentiment and snobbery' (146), on the grounds that it is committed to 'yielding and dreaming instead of resisting and doing' (148). And more clearly than Hector, Shotover denounces as well the figures in the drama that represent the sort of *political* misgovernment that Shaw is warning against.

These figures are three in number, and they carry perhaps more weight than they manage to bear, given their importance to the general conception. One is Sir Hastings Utterword, who is said to have been 'governor of all the Crown Colonies in succession' and whom Shotover regularly calls a 'numskull', though he never appears on stage. Apparently Hastings represents the morally blind and physically despotic aspect of imperialism; he is purposeless in the sense that he lacks any honourable goal, as a result of which his efficiency is merely stupid and brutal. The second figure here is the burglar, who makes a late entrance and exploits the liberal sentiments of the group for the purpose of extortion. The role is basically farcical, but the connection between burglar and plutocrat (or gentleman) had been dear to Shaw from early on. The burglar and Boss Mangan are called 'the two burglars' in *Heartbreak House*, and the destruction of only these two at the end of the play, by a bomb that hits the garden pit where Shotover keeps his dynamite, is a hint, doubtless too neat, of apocalyptic justice.

The chief figure of obloquy is, of course, Boss Mangan, the hog of a millionaire, the factotum of plutocrats. Through Mangan, Shaw wants to show both the insidiousness of the commercial mentality ('I dont know what you call achievements; but Ive jolly well put a stop to the games of the other fellows in the other departments' – 164) and the way it dictates the priorities of government itself. It is hard to get all this into one character, and, although Mangan is certainly made unpleasant on stage, his sinister aspect is considerably diminished by the fact that he is abused so roundly and so all-aroundly that he strikes us as more a victim than an oppressor. What Shaw was getting at in Mangan is made clearer if we step outside the play to learn that the model for the role (Lord Devonport) was 'the founder of a national chain of grocery stores who became a member of parliament' whose philosophy Shaw found retrograde (Crompton, 1971, p. 163). Shaw himself admitted to his Swedish translator that his animosity toward Lord Devonport partly spoiled his play (*CL* III 505).[2]

The appearance of conceptual incoherence in *Heartbreak House* derives principally, I believe, from the ambiguous focus of Hector's and especially Shotover's attacks. What is the connection between scorn of sexual dalliance, a theme so well developed, and the scorn of plutocracy, a theme less well developed but in the picture? What is the connection between 'Randall's lovelocks' and 'Mangan's bristles', parallel images in an exchange between Hector and Shotover?

When Shaw commented that Shotover's shiplike house 'becomes all England with England's heart broken', he was doubtless exploiting the ready metaphor, 'ship of state'. Shotover tells us that an Englishman's business is to learn navigation so that he can steer rather than drift. And this, I think, gives us the necessary clue. It is the image of purposeless drifting that indirectly joins the two ideas of political government and self-government, for government comes to mean not only what the state does but also, and perhaps more emphatically, what the individual does to strengthen the too-relaxed will, to spit out the rotten fruit of beauty and move toward the perilous sublime of apocalypse. That is why Ellie is really the heroine of the play and why her mystic marriage to the prophetic Shotover, late addition or no, is highly suggestive.

There was, I think, an unconscious connection in Shaw's mind between sexual libertinism and political libertinism (another phrase for plutocracy or capitalism). He characteristically imposed a strong negative judgement upon both, as if to hold them in check, yet betrayed a fascination with both that emerges in what he shows in spite of what he tells. We know from *Major Barbara* and elsewhere that Shaw was fascinated by the power inherent in wealth, what Undershaft calls 'command of life and command of death', a phrase echoed by Shotover who says 'we must win powers of life and death over . . . both [Mangan's bristles and Randall's lovelocks]' (*B* 5: 100). In *Heartbreak House* the idea of wealth is degraded. It is associated with darkness and with the figure of Boss Mangan who is attacked to the point of being jeered at. But if Mangan is to represent soulless efficiency, we would like to see the same degree of justice meted to him as to Broadbent. It is as if the degradation of Mangan is needed to fortify resistance to the dangerous charm, so convincingly depicted, of Hesione and Ariadne.[3] When Shotover lifts his aim from Mangan particularly to the ship of state in general, we see more clearly that the fear that links the political and sexual themes is the fear of losing control.

But Shaw does not simply run away from this fear. I have said it was associated with the image of darkness, and darkness functions in the play with particular richness, to suggest the making of money, sexual lassitude and, finally, the heavens from which terrible judgement will come. Shotover makes the connection with money at the end of act 1. Gathering darkness is nicely associated with sexual lassitude in the Chekhovian first half of act 3. And at the end of the play, upon hearing the warnings to draw the curtains in order to conceal light from approaching bombers, Hector rips them away and soon there is a stunning illumination as the dynamite explodes in the garden pit.[4] Like Yeats and Lawrence, though perhaps less wholeheartedly, Shaw here takes an imaginative delight in disaster.

Heartbreak House reads like a culmination of earlier work, particularly *Misalliance*. The romance theme is better integrated, language and incident always pointing toward a central cluster of metaphors. The strong heroine, Ellie in comparison to Lina, is less magically conceived, more fully engaged in the action; she gains her altitude by a measure of felt repudiation and not without pathos. The burglar, who is farcical relief in the early play, helps in the later to bring out the symbolic meaning of its most problematic characterisation. And of course, the apocalyptic rumblings heard throughout *Heartbreak House* give it a strange new seriousness.

To some extent Shaw has managed to assimilate Chekhov, whose influence is alluded to in the subtitle ('A Fantasia on English Themes in the Russian Manner') and create a more fluid, poetic structure than ever before, while retaining his characteristic, un-Chekhovian wit, abruptness and impetuosity. Valency (1973) comments fairly enough that the succession of surprises and shocks in Shaw is at the opposite pole from Chekhov, 'who makes us marvel at the ordinary' (p. 339). But Shaw did really adopt a number of Chekhov's most innovative techniques. One is to let potentially climactic moments be dissipated by homely details so that the atmosphere is suffused with a sense of spiritual paralysis and ineffectuality: as Ellie puts it, life never seems to come to a point (*B* 5: 174). Another is to let the characters not only judge themselves but half soliloquise in doing so, thereby linking individual discontent with a general sense of disorder. And another is to use the symbolic imagery of light fading into darkness in a similar fashion; as Morgan (1972) observes, the opening half of act 3 in *Heartbreak House*, where several couples sit or meander languor-

ously beneath a moon, is quite like act 2 of *The Cherry Orchard*
(p. 209).

But it is precisely in the use of this fading-light symbolism that
we can see how Shaw pulls sharply away from Chekhov. Instead
of pathos at the final curtain, the midnight at the end of *Heartbreak
House* is a time of judgement. Resignation was repellent to Shaw.
He shared much of Chekhov's dismay but had to express it in the
form of indignation and irony. The play does dramatise political
powerlessness but averts the poignancy of powerlessness and
shows us instead a sort of embattled self-sufficiency. Through the
final, apocalyptic incident, which includes the tidy death of the
two burglars, Hesione's and Ellie's welcoming the raid as 'a glorious
experience', and Randall's resumption on the flute of 'Keep the
Home Fires Burning' (with the double sense of 'Let the judgement
burn on', 'Let's return now to the old comfortable way'), we can
just make out the survival of the Edwardian country house, and
therefore must describe the play, finally, as a qualified or, in its
incompleteness, a baffled apocalypse.

Disorder does not break and remake the very form of *Heartbreak
House* as it does that of *Women in Love* and *The Waste Land*. The
imaginations of Lawrence and Eliot delighted more boldly in the
abominated idea. Shotover's anger seems directed toward the
exercise of yet tighter control over its objects. For Lawrence and
Eliot, the house is, in effect, already destroyed. Shaw's imagination
would not carry him so far. He is not shoring up fragments or
(beyond a point) seeking like Shotover 'deeper darkness' but telling
us, like a conscientious late-Victorian, that civilisation is in danger.

But to suggest that *Heartbreak House* is less extreme than *Women
in Love* or *The Waste Land* is less a judgement of comparative literary
power than an acknowledgement of the fact that its author was
born a generation earlier and confronted the enormity of the Great
War with a sensibility and style already quite formed. We are
inclined to modernise as much as we can, and so we praise it by
saying that none of Shaw's plays pursued the apocalyptic theme
with more imaginative energy – with the possible exception of *Back
to Methuselah*, which, however, handles it more abstractly.

Despite its clumsiness, Shaw's 'metabiological pentateuch' is informed by an essentially poetic conception. Unlike Bentley and

Wisenthal (perhaps because I am looking for its poetry), I find it weakest in the middle, where it most resembles a contemporary comedy of manners, strongest when it stretches before and after by way of legend and fantasy. More than any other of his works, it deserves to be called, in D. H. Lawrence's phrase, a thought-adventure. Regrettably, Shaw led his critics to compare it to *Man and Superman* by suggesting that it improved upon the eugenic theme hinted at in the earlier play: 'In 1901 . . . being at the height of my invention and comedic talent, I decorated [the theme of Creative Evolution] too brilliantly and lavishly. . . . Now I abandon the legend of Don Juan with its erotic associations, and go back to the legend of the Garden of Eden' (*B* 5: 338–9). *Methuselah* is not as strong a work as *Superman*, but its merits can be better appreciated if we realise that it is a fundamentally different kind of imaginative act.

It abstracts the question of whether or not to marry, which is central to the earlier work, and transforms it into a contest between Body and Spirit. Here, as always, Shaw sided with Spirit, but there is enough resistance to this ultimate version of the sublime, enough irony, to make effective drama. Consider, in Part I alone, Adam's dismay at the idea of immortality; Eve's combination of intense interest and overwhelming repugnance;[5] Cain's felt pleasure in blood lust, male superiority and slavery; the subtly paradoxical idea that the Fall was initiated by the choice of mortality. These are all inventive turns upon a familiar topos, and in different ways register Shaw's own scepticism about the final vision of Lilith toward which the play leads. At the same time Part I is driving past its own ironic resistance. Shaw usually took the Augustan line that we should not quarrel with nature or the human condition itself, but Part I of *Methuselah*, like Byron's Cain, verges on doing so, and is none the worse for this audacity.

Similarly, at the other end of this extensive work, we find forceful confrontations between the spiritualised superpersons known as Ancients and the resisting representatives of the glories of our blood and state. The vocabulary of the Elderly Gentleman in Part IV is not quite intelligible to his 56-year-old 'flapper' of a nurse, and his eloquent defence of the dignity of threescore years and ten is reduced: 'in this land of discouragement the sublime has become the ridiculous' (551). Gulliver-like, he tells the Oracle that he 'cannot go back among people to whom nothing is real', but as she offers her hand and looks steadfastly in his face, '*He stiffens*

. . . *and* . . . *falls dead'* (563). In like fashion, the Napoleonic General Aufsteig, a descendant of Cain who says he must pursue *la gloire* in order to live, is told that, although his 'mesmeric pull is strong for a short-lived person', 'If I were not veiled and robed in insulating material, you could not endure my presence'; she unveils: he shrieks, staggers and covers his eyes (533).

Part V also contains confrontations of this kind made starker by the fact that, 30 000 years of development later, the resistance comes from children whose insistent immaturity is being seized from them by a force of greater power. Strephon, aged two, whines for Chloe, who is four and no longer responsive because she is outgrowing her need for sexual love. The Newly Born, bursting dramatically from her large egg, demands love immediately and exclusively, and is regarded with a mixture of amusement, pity and contempt. Both are late additions, severe but inventive.

More poignant and complex are the calibrated responses of the sculptors, still partially implicated in the human attachment to image-making, to art. Arjillax recounts how he has come to prefer making realistic studies of the Ancients to portraits traditionally considered beautiful, and compares his developed taste to the practice of a 'legendary' artist named Archangel Michael whose powerful images of prophets and sybils represented the 'majesty . . . of the mind alone at its intensest' (586). Martellus reports that making images even of the Ancients has become unsatisfactory because, ultimately, 'art is false and life alone is true' (588). Pygmalion has gone one step farther. Taking a hint from an old 'scientific document' known as Genesis, he has breathed a vital force into a male and female figure. But they lack conscience, the capacity to choose. In a mechanical reflex, the female figure bites and kills her maker. The Ancients, however, despite their scorn for these 'dolls', are able to improve on Pygmalion's work by inspiring in each figure a spark of altruism ('Spare [him/her], kill me') and a capacity for discouragement which, though fatal, implies at least a realisation of their moral inferiority.

We must be careful not to interpret the repudiation of art in this aspect of the fable too literally. It is after all contained within an artistic structure. From the Ancients' point of view, according to which body, 'the last of the dolls to be discarded', approximates pure mind or vortex, art may indeed be imagined as surpassable. But that is only to emphasise, obliquely, its fundamental human importance.

Shaw was not content here or anywhere with the outrightly supernatural. 'Don Juan in Hell' is a dream sequence, and a programme note of 1907 is at pains to explain that its locale is mental. His earnest imagination required that the speculative or fantastic wear a scientific air. Although it was not necessary to believe that 'the thing' will happen, he clearly wanted to believe that it was not quite impossible. 'You imagine what you desire; you will what you imagine; and at last you create what you will' (348). The coerciveness that we sense in this vitalistic credo suggests a straining against naturalistic limits, an imagination seeking release in the finality of an apocalypse.

The premise of *Methuselah* is Shaw's supposition, not in itself a new one, that human beings were politically inadequate animals who seemed unable to learn to govern themselves satisfactorily, who lacked the will to give up their cigars, champagne and golf for serious pursuits. The new twist here is the inference that human beings fail because they only have one short life to live, that conduct is determined not only by how much life we have already lived but also by how much we can yet expect to live. Such a premise should not be less suggestive today than in 1920 because our collective sense of the future is even more grim. But, psychologically, the most interesting thing about it is that Shaw presses the imagined alteration of human nature back into childhood as well as forward into a second and third century of life.

His fable requires not only that the years of mature judgement be greatly extended but also that the years of immature judgement be virtually erased. Growth must be speeded up. Squelching the insistent pleadings for immediate gratification of Strephon and the Newly Born seems to dramatise a compulsion to re-enact the denial of fantasies associated with early pleasures. The Ancients are most themselves when they are annihilating the charms of youth and beauty with a glance. We have seen that the Shavian sublime typically evokes heightened moral consciousness by repressing a seductive but lower level of desire. Carrying that logic to an extreme in *Methuselah*, Shaw imagines repression almost at once, before there is much of anything to repress, not entirely unlike Freud's speculations on the repetition compulsion in *Beyond the Pleasure Principle* (published the same year) which also adopted a metabiological rather than a strictly psychological point of view. I am reminded too – and perhaps this comparison is more pertinent – of Swift's Houyhnhnms who, finally, and like the Ancients, have very little to think about except whether Gulliver, like the shortlivers, shall be destroyed.

Shaw's ambition throughout the work, play and preface, was to fuse a moral or religious view with a scientific one – science being identified here with the biological theory of evolution. The same ambition really informed Shaw's view of every subject he took a special interest in – particularly medicine, criminology and education. In every case, he refuses to separate science/law/knowledge from honour/morality/decency. His objection to juries, for example, is that they must decide guilt on the basis of deeds rather than intentions (C 22: 263). Keegan's dream of a society in which Church and State, God and Mammon are unified may be 'the dream of a madman' for dramatic purposes, but it is one that Shaw took seriously. Statesmen in particular 'must have a religion' (B 5: 327), and *Methuselah* is harshly satiric, especially in its middle parts, about the moral vacuity of political life, the silly parliamentary game of principles without a programme. From the standpoint of the 'tertiary' oracle who is consulted by political leaders, the question of whether Parliament should adjourn or stay in session is too contemptible for a proper answer.

When it came to the doctrine of evolution, then, Shaw hit out hard against the godlessness or 'mischievous heresy' of Darwin's theory of natural selection. This theory postulated an evolutionary leap or jump caused by chance rather than choice. Shaw refused to call it 'natural' – that was to concede too much to Mammon. Evolution was, in the deepest sense, purposeful, and the only genuine science was vital rather than mechanical. The point is that Shaw was willing neither to propound an unscientific thesis nor to call natural (or circumstantial) selection scientific. He imagined a combination of the two. Accordingly, the brothers Barnabas, whose doctrine is dramatised in the play, are respectively a biologist and a clergyman. Their 'gospel' incorporates both 'genuine science' and 'genuine religion', the two being, as he writes elsewhere, 'fundamentally inseparable' (C 22: 381).

The play itself makes a token concession to 'mechanistic' (as opposed to 'vitalistic') science; that is, to the hypothesis that genetic change is brought about not by will or choice but by chance and is then replicated by necessity. The first characters to whom 'the thing happens' are merely a parlourmaid and a clergyman who flirts with her. Yet Shaw cannot help suggesting that these two are obscurely motivated by a deeper will.[6]

Back to Methuselah is essentially similar to Yeats's *A Vision* and Lawrence's *Fantasia of the Unconscious*, all written soon after the First World War. These works are vitalistic mythologies that adopt a mechanistic and even schematic form. Their peculiar literalness seems to be an aggressive way of saying that, if anything is to be called science (for they cannot help recognising the social authority of science), let it be this. The difficulty in reading them is that their very assertiveness inhibits our own imaginative response. We grant Shaw the freedom to use the Eden legend or a futuristic fantasy, but we balk at being told that Genesis is 'a scientific document', that the crucial mutation is 'plain deductive biology if there is such a thing as biology', that a poem is 'a word for what is too wonderful to come true yet came true' (*B* 5: 349).

The wonderfully assured preface discovers with zestful irony the various nineteenth-century enthusiasms for Darwin's theory of natural selection, showing how different ideological camps had their own reasons for welcoming it. (A recent book about Deconstructionism relishes the irony of literary academics canonising their antagonists of the day before and comments, 'Would that Bernard Shaw were living at this hour to do justice to the institutional high comedy of the process' (Felperin, 1986, p. 46). The comment points to the dialectical vivacity that is so important an aspect of Shaw's genius, and of which the preface to *Methuselah* is a fine example.) The Christians welcomed it because it killed off Paley's disorderly designer; the humanitarians because it dispelled Shelley's Almighty Fiend; the Socialists because it stressed the importance of environment; the Marxists because it emphasised inexorability; the Capitalists because it supported their predilection for *laissez-faire* economics; and the Materialists because it made poetry out of matter. All were demoralised, and therefore vulnerable to begin with, because rationalistic science had been elevated into a religion rather than being informed by religion.

It must be added that *Methuselah* stresses not the humanity of religion but its power to judge its inhuman rival: we are to imagine that the twenty-first century brings a general massacre of men of science, after which they are chastened and know their place. Yet this severity creates impressive effects as well, many of which cluster around the Medusa motif.

Repeatedly, it is the faces of transcendently powerful women that destroy, in a quasi-sexual manner, the men who meet their gaze.[7] Yet the author's sympathy seems directed less toward the victim than the judge. In Part III, the first of the female longlivers is revealed grandly as *'a handsome woman . . . with the walk of a goddess. Her expression and deportment are grave, swift, decisive, and unanswerable'* (B 5: 465). One shortliver *'is glad to escape her gaze'*; another, trying to flirt with her, *'suddenly covers his eyes with his hands'* (470). We have already noticed the stunning effect of the Veiled Woman upon the Napoleonic figure. As for the Elderly Gentleman, though he elicits our sympathy to some extent, our interest is directed finally to his severely righteous judge:

> THE ORACLE. Be it so, then. You may stay. [*She offers him her hands. He grasps them and raises himself a little by clinging to her. She looks steadily into her face. He stiffens; a little convulsion shakes him; his grasp relaxes; and he falls dead.*]
> THE ORACLE [*looking down at the body*]. Poor shortlived thing! What else could I do for you? (B 5: 562–3)

More clearly than earlier in Shaw, the figure of the Great Mother is shown to be both infinitely inaccessible and, at the same time, lonely in her self-sufficiency. The first such figure introduced in the play (Mrs Lutestring) scorns those around her and measures the cost of doing so: 'You are all such children. And I never was very fond of children, except that one girl who woke up the mother passion in me. I have been very lonely sometimes' (474).[8]

It seems inevitable in a Shavian work of this imaginative stretch that the climactic judgement should be rendered by a woman of mythical proportions. Lilith is well prepared for. As the picture of mankind 30 000 years hence fades from view, the originators of the human experiment are brought forward for a summary opinion. Farmer Adam sees nothing but foolishness in this evolution toward bodilessness. His vision is comically limited but expressive of a plain man's sense. Eve's view is also limited but in what might be called a bourgeois fashion. Like many a mother who is glad to see her children employed less humbly, though she doesn't understand what they do, she expresses satisfaction that at least the clever ones prevailed. Cain takes a more sophisticated view, with overtones of tragic irony. He perceives that his own sensual way of being has enjoyed a long history but has been finally superseded and comments that it was a great game while it lasted. And the (female) Serpent expresses satisfaction at the Ancients' combination of wisdom and power, the desired end of Shaw's own political idealism.

The concluding speech of Lilith attempts to go beyond this point, to say that even this combination of wisdom and power is not enough. For there is still a corporeal residue, hence still a conflict of desires. Her tone is at first punishing yet at last tolerant, as she reflects that Life, as distinct from Matter, is beyond any conceivable embodiment and thus beyond her own comprehension. Paradoxically, her vision rests finally only in the imagining of a perpetual becoming.

In the last part of *Methuselah*, 'As Far as Thought Can Reach', a preference for Becoming over Being results in an optimism of statement played off against a pessimism of tone. Shaw remains the idealist but implies despairingly that, from any imaginable human perspective, the fulfilment of desire can never be achieved. Thus we have passed beyond the first and second versions of the comic sublime, the saltatory and the perspectival, and are shown here the radical third version whereby desire, extended as far as thought can reach, encounters its own inherent limit. *Back to Methuselah* is finally, therefore, like *Heartbreak House*, an incomplete or baffled apocalypse.

7

The Summing Up

Saint Joan (1923) makes a magnificent coda to the major phase of Shaw's career, gathering together the several versions of the comic sublime. The youthful Warrior Saint, who dares and dares again in God's name, is a perfect emblem of idealised self-sufficiency. Or almost perfect, because it involves the idealisation of a warrior, though this is softened by feminine charm. Shaw senses the difficulty enough to try to compensate for it in the preface. There, Joan is carefully compared to Christ, Socrates and Mahomet, and carefully contrasted to Napoleon who was 'neither frank nor disinterested' (B 6: 18). We are told explicitly that 'it is far more dangerous to be a saint than a conqueror' (17–18), as in the preface to Blanco Posnet we were told that 'Great religious leaders are more interesting and more important subjects for the dramatist than great conquerors' (B 3: 714). The play itself cannot, of course, ignore the business of military conquest, but it does attempt to make Joan's victories represent, however unconsciously on her part, a spiritual advance in the march of civilisation.

This, however, leads to another problem, the dependence of Saint Joan on the advantage of its audience's historical hindsight, in particular its knowledge (by name) of oncoming Protestantism and Nationalism. The memorable discussion between the Bishop of Beauvais (Cauchon) and the Earl of Warwick concerning Joan's significance depends upon that knowledge, as Shaw well knew, for he set about boldly to dramatise their intuitions of political development, though the scene is not free of a certain coyness as a result of the anachronism. One could compound one's uneasiness by calling to mind, as Nicholas Grene does, that Joan is ushering in, not an age of Socialism, but 'terrible eras' of nationalism and capitalism (Bloom, 1987, p. 242). Yet the fascination of her prophetic power overrides these scruples. The scene is a successful tour de force.

Another anachronism is perhaps more bothersome: Joan's very modern explanation, in response to Baudricourt's scepticism, of the authority of her voices:

BAUDRICOURT.   They [Your voices] come from your imagination.
JOAN.   Of course. That is how the messages of God come to
us. (*B* 6: 92)

What is troubling here is not so much the modern idea that
the voices might be understood psychologically as the extreme
readiness of her response.[1] If Joan is really sophisticated enough
to have at her fingertips so self-conscious an explanation, it is hard
to believe in the naïveté on which much of her charm and indeed
her political and military effectiveness depend. A rationalistic
impulse on Shaw's part intrudes, as it does again in the Archbishop's blandly commonsensical explanation of miracles in scene
2. In these cases the mediaeval atmosphere, which the author
boasted he let blow freely through the play, might well have blown
a bit more freely. The robust, no-nonsense attitude demonstrates
the sanity of mediaeval faith too chillingly.
    Nevertheless, there is greatness here. A retrenchment from the
overstretching of *Methuselah* enabled Shaw to draw upon his
submerged sympathy for human limits and to bring it into vital
relation to his idealism. The result is only a little less impressive
because he used an available historical record as a skeleton.[2] For
he made this record very much his own imaginative property; so
much so, in fact, that in no other of his plays can I discern so
clearly the full range of his comic sublime: the spring to the heights,
the perspectival drama of heavenly and earthly points of view,
and the visionary scepticism or dialectic of desire. Possibly the
three phases of Joan could be better integrated, for I cannot take
sharp exception to Harold Bloom's (1987) harsh judgement that
'The figure of the first few scenes has nothing in common with
the heroine who repudiates her own surrender at the trial, or with
the shade of a saint who appears to the King of France in his
dream that forms the epilogue' (p. 25). The inconsistency is less
troublesome if we think of Joan not only as a character but also as
a vehicle for dramatising aspects of the heroic-religious mentality.
    The first three scenes, prefatorily described as 'the romance of
her rise' (*B* 6: 66), dramatise quickly several graduated saltations
in which we can see that Joan's power of working upon others is
attained by the renunciation of private desire. As Hans Stoppel
(1973) pointed out, Joan's choice of the heroic life, for her 'the most
natural and the richest', 'also means the total rejection of what
appears the things most desirable in life to the average person

such as love, family-life, mass-amusements' (p. 178). The erotic component of this renunciation is especially clear in the third scene when, as Joan and Dunois with mutual ecstasy greet the sudden turning of the wind, sexual and religious emotion fuse without embarrassment:[3]

> DUNOIS [*rising*]. Now for the forts. You dared me to follow. Dare you lead?
>
> JOAN [*bursting into tears and flinging her arms round Dunois, kissing him on both cheeks*]. Dunois, dear comrade in arms, help me. My eyes are blinded with tears. Set my foot on the ladder, and say, 'Up, Joan.'
>
> DUNOIS [*dragging her out*]. Never mind the tears: make for the flash of the guns.
>
> JOAN [*in a blaze of courage*]. Ah!
>
> DUNOIS [*dragging her along with him*]. For God and Saint Dennis! (*B* 6: 123)

I must add that my admiration for these opening scenes is qualified because their climaxes (the sudden laying of the eggs, the blind recognition of the Dauphin and the abrupt turning of the wind) work on my emotions too easily and seem a kind of magic. It is comforting to learn that Shaw himself described them to Sybil Thorndike as 'flapdoodle', 'just "theatre" to get you interested' before the play proper begins (Bloom, 1987, p. 239). But they do work, and they prepare us for the more ironic uses of the sublime to follow.

The core and primary strength of the play is 'the tragedy of her execution' (*B* 6: 66), scenes 4 to 6. Here the human interest of Joan's situation is inseparable from an exceptional intellectual energy. Without losing a sense of her humanity, of her isolation in the human world despite her robust faith in God, we see her as a problem for those around her who are wrestling to understand historical change, to reconcile their conservative, egoistic interests with the radical claims of heroic will and to render justice according to their necessarily limited perspective. The double judgement of Joan by her earthbound contemporaries is fully expressed: she is miraculous but unbearable, supremely inspiring yet supremely insufferable, what the preface calls a 'born boss' (38). The ambivalence that underlines that phrase, part of Shaw's later lexicon, is fully dramatised here.

In his later years Shaw often became glib about the legitimacy of suppressing dissent for the sake of disciplined and efficient government, but, in the fine preface to *Saint Joan*, his imagination is humanised by his evocation of the loved heretic, and he speaks with particular eloquence both on behalf of toleration and in recognition of its limits:

> The saints and prophets . . . are always really self-selected, like Joan. And since neither Church nor State, by the secular necessities of its constitution, can guarantee even the recognition of such self-chosen missions, there is nothing for us to do but to make it a point of honor to privilege heresy to the last bearable degree on the simple ground that all evolution in thought and conduct must at first appear as heresy and misconduct. In short, though all society is founded on intolerance, all improvement is founded on tolerance. . . . The degree of tolerance attainable at any moment depends on the strain under which society is maintaining its cohesion   (57, 60).

An admirable statement (despite its too confident trust in progress), born of feeling distributed equally to the superhuman dissenter and to her all-too-human destroyers, a balance of the counsels of heart and head.

Scene 4 touches up the historical record to make more attractive the figures of Warwick (urbane spokesman for the institution of feudalism threatened by the growing spirit of nationalism) and of Cauchon (serious spokesman for the mediaeval church threatened by the growing spirit of Protestantism). But it is very well done. For the sake of their intellectually spirited dialogue, I am almost willing to forgive the coarsely conceived jingoist, de Stogumber, who at least helps to serve as a foil for the sophistication of the principals.

Scene 5, set in the cathedral of Rheims after the coronation, develops neatly yet in an unforced fashion a sharply ironic aspect of the tragedy. Joan simply cannot understand why she has come to be distrusted and even hated. She says: 'I never speak unless I know I am right' (147). Dunois's good sense – 'Do you expect stupid people to love you for shewing them up?' (142), 'God is no man's daily drudge' (148) – falls on deaf ears. Bluebird, La Hire and the Archbishop also express in their characteristic ways their ambivalence toward the fascinating but frightening girl. Yet what is wilful pride to others is merely faith to Joan, and the consequence of such irreconcilable conflict must be tragic.

A fair amount of critical ink has been spilled over the question of whether Joan is hubristic and therefore a genuine tragic figure. Is her presumption the weakness of a noble yet human spirit or the godlike superiority of a saint? It seems to me that Shaw's play invites us to accept an affirmative answer to both parts of the question.

The great trial scene painstakingly presents her accusers as well-meaning men who are wrestling with their own consciences – particularly Cauchon, the Inquisitor D'Estivet, his deputy Lemaître and the Dominican Ladvenu. Desmond MacCarthy (1973) recognised the strength of these characterisations in 1924: 'The extraordinary intellectual merit of this play is the force and fairness with which the case of her opponents is put; the startling clarity with which each of them states it, and consequently our instantaneous recognition of its relation to the religious instinct' (p. 34). Shaw has balanced their right against Joan's in a contest that approximates a tragic impasse. There is no compromise possible between these 'lower' and 'higher' points of view. The self-interest of the judges is indistinguishable from a sincere sense of responsibility to the Church. Joan will obey the Church provided it does not command the impossible which is to disobey the voices of her own judgement: 'What other judgment can I judge by but my own?' (B 6 175). She cannot understand what to them is an essential distinction. And she suffers as humanly as Shaw ever made a character suffer upon hearing the verdict of worldly power.

Yet in this scene she moves the drama a step closer to what Louis Martz (1973) has called a saint's play, by finally judging her judges. Her human willingness to recant, on learning she is to be punished with perpetual imprisonment, is itself recanted. It resembles the momentary dubiety of Christ on the cross before the reaffirmation of a superhuman faith. Although a still more terrible punishment looms, she is sufficiently withdrawn from the spirit of contest and sufficiently identified with divinity to scorn her judges as inferiors rather than contend with them as rivals:

JOAN.   His ways are not your ways. He wills that I go through
    the fire to His bosom; for I am His child, and you are not fit

that I should live among you. That is my last word to
you.   (184)

Taken as a whole, the tragic scenes approximate what I have called
the perspectival sublime, as the romance scenes exemplified the
dynamic type.

The epilogue, described by Shaw as 'the comedy of the attempts
of posterity to make amends for that execution' (66), not only alters
the tone of the work by introducing farce and fantasy but seems
to extend the very notion of a half-tragic saint's play, making us
see it again as a divine comedy. The suffering of Joan, in the light
of the sanctification of 1920, becomes a phase in a larger plot
governed by a divine, evolutionary will. But, as Alfred Turco (1976)
has argued, the epilogue is in a sense more pessimistic than the
tragedy proper. Cauchon's famous line implies that a Christ
must perish in torment in *every* age to save those who have no
imagination, a perpetual defeat of the heroic spirit. Quoting Joan's
moving last words ('O God that madest this beautiful earth, when
will it be ready to receive Thy saints? How long, O Lord, how
long?'), Turco comments that 'the saint foresees a future that will
never escape the bonds of history' (p. 270).

I demur, however, from Turco's conclusion that '*Saint Joan* is a
tragedy, not in spite of, but *because* of, the epilogue'. The pessimism
of the epilogue is different from that of the tragedy, and is
thoroughly characteristic of Shaw. The melancholy of Joan's words,
and of Cauchon's, does not at all reflect the resignation of the
tragic dramatist but the scepticism of a visionary facing once again
the limits of desire. The poignancy of Joan's last words is harsh at
the edges if we remember that, in the preface to *Methuselah*, Shaw
had written that 'How long, O Lord, how long?' is a vain cry, for
'the pitiless reply still is that God helps those who help themselves'
(*B* 5: 266). In that light, Joan's denunciation of her accusers is
indistinguishable from the lethal judgement of the Ancients upon
the all-too-human shortlivers.

The epilogue, then, is a prime instance of the third version of
Shaw's comic sublime, as 'the romance of her rise' and 'the tragedy
of her execution' were of the first and second versions. It discovers
unfulfilment in the very enactment of heroic will. Shaw would
continue in the weaker vehicles of his late years to try to absolutise
self or other, the rebellious or the judging will, and continue to
discover that the very force of desire eventually throws it back

upon itself. He was not a systematic enough psychologist to conceptualise this aspect of his work in terms comparable to the 'always already' formula of the French Freudians, but his imagination leads him finally in that direction.

8

Relaxation of the Comic Sublime

After the composition of *Saint Joan* there was a five year pause (August 1923 to November 1928) in the writing of plays. During this time, Shaw put his major effort into *The Intelligent Woman's Guide to Socialism and Capitalism*, a judicious summing up of ideas expressed over the years (concerning particularly the moral directionlessness of capitalism), as if to mark the completion of an extended period of creative development.[1]

The seventeen plays composed between 1928 and 1950 are remarkably vivacious in view of their author's age, 72 to 94. They are even experimental, as if he is testing the boundaries of his dramatic art (Kauffmann, 1986, p. 23). Shaw never quite lost that gaiety of mind which Margery Morgan rightly considered to be his salient characteristic as a writer. But the late work is suffused nevertheless by an unfocused extravagance of style and idea, as Shaw himself realised: 'Old age is telling on me. My bolt is shot as far as any definite target is concerned. . . . I shoot into the air more and more extravagantly, without any premeditation whatsoever' (Ervine, 1956, p. 555). He had been saying 'my bolt is shot' as far back as 1912, but now in the 1930s he had some reason to say so. The 'unruly imagination' (*CL* IV 283) remained, but each play came to seem less and less 'a necessary one' (*CL* IV 507).

The scripts of the late plays contain far fewer authorial comments, signalling a loss of that pervading light irony which helped to establish or enhance the pointedness of earlier confrontations. And with less pointed confrontations, the incongruity between outrageous statement and bland tone, on which much Shavian wit relies, becomes rather silly. Epifania the millionairess bursts into her solicitor's office and instructs him matter-of-factly to will her wealth to her despised husband because money will go to his head and ruin him. The solicitor in turn readily complies with her request for suicide tablets because he knows from experience that his angry clients do not actually take them. Facile surprises, less pressure on language and scene, a slacker tension.

The most successful late plays, in my view, are those subtitled fable, sketch or skit – or at least conceived in that spirit. 'Village Wooing' is a quite successful though slight skit, presenting a male and female figure, A and Z, in three snapshot-like scenes over a period of time. *On the Rocks, Geneva* and *In Good King Charles's Golden Days* effectively exploit the artificial device of bringing into the same place spokesmen for dramatically divergent political and philosophical views. The last of the three is especially charming (despite its name-dropping – Galileo, Hobbes, Dryden, and so on, along with the central figures of Newton, Fox, Kneller and Charles II) because of its frank delight in art and science as forms of play, its putting aside of the big social and political questions that Shaw in old age could not address with much patience and discrimination.

I think the best single lines or characterisations in the late plays are implicitly self-confrontational in that we can see Shaw turning with a certain zest against attitudes in which he has recognisably invested some feeling. I select three. One is from *On the Rocks*. During the Boer War and later Shaw had taken a certain pride in the Empire, despite his barbs against his adopted country. But now, in this play of 1933, his sympathetic Prime Minister foresees the Empire's demise in a comically abrupt insight, commenting on his Foreign Secretary's carelessly expressed irritation in the presence of Sir Jafna Pandranath: 'That one word nigger will cost us India' (*B* 6: 714). A second example is the portrait of Bombardone (Mussolini) in *Geneva* (1938), the mockery of whose romantic megalomania is half-beguiled: 'I am here because it is my will to be here. My will is part of the world's will. A large part, as it happens' (*B* 7: 117). And a third is the portrait of Isaac Newton in *Good King Charles*, in which Shaw has captured the peculiar combination in a certain type of genius like his own (and a little like Peter Shaffer's Mozart) of mental brilliance and emotional regressiveness.

The intensity of conviction that enabled Shaw to become in his lifetime something of a religious force (as he himself said Ibsen had been – see *RS* 3) involved the underpresence of doubt or scepticism more than is commonly believed. But it is just this sense of underpresence that one misses in much of the later work. Both his optimism and his pessimism acquire the appearance of an automatic reflex: 'we must either embrace Creative Evolution or fall into the bottomless pit'. On the one hand, Shaw expresses a far too uncritical confidence in dictatorship. On the other, he finds mere despair in Shakespeare, Swift, *Middlemarch* and even *Ghosts* (*B* 5: 702). The attempts at wit too often discover how shallow is the soil from which this later despair springs: 'I have solved practically all the pressing questions of our time: but . . . they go on being propounded . . . as if I had never existed' (*P&P* 235). But this is to stress Shaw's temperament only and neglect his capacity for self-critical judgement. In a spirit of reasonableness, he declined to contribute to a volume about Freud on the grounds of being 'not qualified' (*CL* IV 418); admitted that he could not 'place Yeats objectively enough to attempt an appreciation of him' (*CL* IV 577); and, for all his confident and freely offered opinions on public questions, reflected in 1945 that the atomic bomb has produced a situation which is beyond the political capacity of any leader (*CL* IV 757).

The most substantial plays after *Saint Joan* were the first to have been written, *The Apple Cart* and *Too True to Be Good*. They readily illustrate Shaw's late treatment of the heroic and the disillusioned will, showing his regrettable tendency to separate an idealising fantasy from the sceptical resistance that made possible the genuine comic sublime. I will comment briefly on these two plays and, through them, on a few other aspects of the late work that best illuminate my approach to the canon.

In a rather preening preface to *The Apple Cart* Shaw announced:

I had written a comedy in which a King defeats an attempt by his popularly elected Prime Minister to deprive him of the right to influence public opinion through the press and platform: in short, to reduce him to a cipher. The King's reply is that rather than be a cipher he will abandon his throne and take his obviously very rosy chance of becoming a popularly elected Prime Minister himself. To those who believe that our system of votes for everybody produces parliaments which represent the people it should seem that this solution of the difficulty is completely democratic, and that the Prime Minister must at once accept it joyfully as such. He knows better. The change would rally the anti-democratic royalist vote against him, and impose on him a rival in the person of the only public man whose ability he has to fear. The comedic paradox of the situation is that the King wins, not by exercising his royal authority, but by threatening to resign it and go to the democratic poll. (*B* 6: 249)

This is concise but disingenuous paraphrase, particularly as regards the force of the comedic paradox in the situation dramatised. King Magnus and Prime Minister Proteus are supposedly on an equal footing, but, as their names suggest, this is not really the case. Although Proteus is given credit for some intelligence, Magnus has the advantage of reputation, experience (much valued by Shaw, though it is gained in this case by way of an inheritance) and charisma. He is presented with far more personal charm. Of course, the play does not want to defend monarchy as an institution, but it is contemptuous of the democratic process and complacent about the advantages of strong leadership. Any pretence of an authentic dramatic debate is dispelled when Magnus dogmatises without a trace of Shavian irony: 'I stand for . . . conscience and virtue, for the eternal against the expedient; for the evolutionary appetite against the day's gluttony' (p. 326).

Contempt and complacency underlie respectively the two major stresses of Shaw's late political thinking: (a) the people cannot govern themselves; (b) a better means of testing the capacity for leadership is needed, and leaders whose efficiency is proven can only be impeded by parliaments and elections. Shaw's exculpatory opinions of Mussolini, Hitler and Stalin, continuing to the end of his life, follow from these convictions.

In 1933 he announced sanguinely, 'The extirpation of the Jew as such figured for a few mad moments in the program of the Nazi party in Germany' (*B* 6: 577). In 1935, as the evidence mounted, he tried to 'urge upon Herr Hitler that his Antisemitism . . . must be pathological' (*B* 6: 869). Even in 1945 when the death camps were revealed to the world, Shaw rationalised that the confused guards meant well but had to deal with overcrowding in the least inhumane way. Hitler and Mussolini, now dead, were 'poor devils' (*B* 7: 30, 36). These snippets epitomise pretty well the phases of Shaw's response to the notorious anti-Semitism of these dictators: he tried to discount it as a deplorable but transient madness; to separate it as a pathology that should not obscure the advantages of efficient leadership; and finally to shake his head over the impossibilism of their ambitions. Stalin, the grim tyrant who played his cards close to the vest, he continued to admire without reserve, as did others in the West. But Hitler and Mussolini were operatic (as the play *Geneva* appreciates), and were treated by Shaw not unlike stage villains, to be applauded for their colour and bravado.

Almost the harshest thing he ever found to say about Hitler was that 'throwing Einstein' ['a much greater man than any mere politician'] to the Antisemite wolves was an appalling breach of cultural faith' (*B* 6: 866). This disconcerting remark at least helps us see that Shaw's interest in political power was always fundamentally an interest in intellectual and creative power. But breach of faith? O Comic Muse, where hast thou fled? Keenly sensitive to cruelty perpetrated in the name of good intentions, Shaw could not really understand deliberate cruelty. Indeed, envy and revenge can hardly be counted in the vocabulary of his affective responses. It was as if he had passed untouched through the Oedipal phase of childhood development, and found a way to fuse the narcissistic conflicts of infancy with the formation of an ego-ideal in boyhood and adolescence. Not unlike one of Swift's Houyhnhnms, Shaw was capable of benevolence and indignation but scarcely of love and hate.

The psychological premises of his moral vision do not change in his late period: we protect ourselves with ideals from recognising our fear of change and improvement; more harm is done from good than from evil intentions. But their restatement now seems tired. 'Our natural dispositions may be good; but we have been badly brought up, and are full of anti-social personal ambitions and snobberies' (*B* 6: 273). Again, 'It is our good men we need to get rid of, our bad ones being politically negligible' (*B* 7: 175).

The stark actuality of totalitarianism proved to be too much for the comic imagination to cope with. In terms provided by Beckett's novel *Watt*, Shaw's laughter was almost always directed at error, seldom at cruelty, and never at the universe itself. We sorely miss an active sense of irony in some of late Shaw, without which his idealism can become indistinguishable rhetorically from that of a Sunday morning sermon: 'There is the eternal war between those who are in the world for what they can get out of it and those who are in the world to make it a better place for everybody to live in' (*B* 6: 712). Belief here (in *On the Rocks*) is no longer something to play with, as it had been in *Man and Superman* and *Major Barbara*. The dramatist and the dialectician have degenerated into the doctrinaire.

The issue of political execution, for example, had come up in the earlier work, but was handled with irony. Caesar shuddered at the 'wise severity' that served him as a rationalisation for the execution of Vercingetorix. Shotover's determination to kill fellows like Mangan is shown to be extreme and is met by objections. But in *The Simpleton of the Unexpected Isles*, an Angel of Death comes on Judgment Day to weed out the human garden of worthless lives, and, although there is a certain whimsy in this conception, there is too much easy satisfaction in evaporating all but two members of the Stock Exchange and all but fourteen of the House of Commons. The preface would distinguish evaluative from merely punitive judgement, but the force of the distinction is lost in the dramatisation.

The ability of a dictator in a totalitarian regime to get things done efficiently so appealed to the ageing writer that it stimulated him to an effort of moral justification. Mussolini and Stalin were the two most responsible statesmen in Europe because they had no hold on their place except their efficiency (*B* 6: 425). Shaw seemed confident that, if a ruler could command only as long as he is efficient, there could be no tyranny (*B* 6: 876). As late as 1949 he suggested offering the Nobel Peace Prize to Stalin on the grounds that no parliament could have accomplished what he accomplished in the same time. We sorely miss, when the great dictators are under discussion, Peter Keegan's passionate attack on Broadbent's 'foolish dream of efficiency'.

Yet it is precisely in regard to this issue of efficiency that Shaw makes the most notable effort in his late work to pass judgement on the self he has put before us. Joan and Epifania are each called a 'born boss', and, though fascinating, are also 'impossible'. In *Saint Joan* this judgement is effectively rendered from inside the play. In *The Millionairess*, Eppy is opposed more weakly, but outside it, in the preface and remarks to biographers (Pearson, 1942, p. 394), she is judged more harshly. And his last, unfinished work features a character actually called Bossborn. But to appreciate more fully the ironic weight of that final judgement, we should return to the substantial *Too True To Be Good* and observe how late Shaw handled the theme of the disillusioned will.

If *The Apple Cart* simplifies reality by not giving us enough opposition to one idealised leader, *Too True* creates an opposite problem. An assortment of spiritual cripples, too readily invoking a bottomless abyss, are spun talkatively about in what Morgan (1972) aptly calls 'a joyless, frenetic farce' (p. 233). Nethercot (1954) discerningly remarks, 'turning characters upside down as Shaw has done is not quite the same thing as turning them inside out as he says he has done' (p. 49). The reversals are not only abrupt but deficient in motivation. A hypochondriac patient at once becomes a robust adventuress. A clergyman, who is the son of an atheist, has become a burglar. Private Meek, in spite of his name and deferential manner, is the omnicompetent figure of a daydream. (Although based on the extraordinary T. E. Lawrence, at that time a friend of the Shaws, the character seems more to resemble the role played by Clifton Webb in the Mr Belvedere films.) A seemingly military-minded colonel turns out to care only about his painting. A sergeant is preoccupied with the dire admonitions of *The Pilgrim's Progress*. The patient's repressive mother, at the bash of an umbrella, is transformed into a rebel and quester.

Moreover, distinctions among the attitudes of the characters (with the exception of Meek) are hard to keep in mind. They all fret about a crumbling universe somehow associated with the idea of unending sex appeal, and several jump toward and away from sexual adventure with equal alacrity. There are quick contrasts between Sweetie's 'lower centres' and the Patient's 'higher centres', between Aubrey's need for religious dogma and his father's for scientific dogma, between the Colonel's interest in escaping to nature and the Sergeant's in escaping from the wrath to come. But they fail to generate much dialectical excitement. Shaw's preacher admits too ingenuously that he likes best to debate spiritual things, not only because they call his gifts into play but because 'I greatly dislike being contradicted' (B 6: 471).

The play enjoys a measure of critical favour, perhaps because like *Heartbreak House* it attempts to dramatise a comprehensive wasteland. The connection it makes between social and sexual disillusionment is at least energetic enough to transcend the coyness that mars the interlude of *The Apple Cart* where, unrelated to the main action, Magnus is pleased by the 'strangely innocent' quality of his romance with Orinthia, and scampers off to his wife for tea with 'hopeless tenderness'. But the theme of despair in *Too True* achieves focus and force only in the last speeches, the Elder's and Aubrey's. There, perhaps more than at any other point in the canon, Shaw's normally overriding will to meaning is exposed as at bottom a will to rhetoric. Aubrey must preach even though he admits he has nothing to say. The company depart one by one as in the epilogue to *Joan*, and the mist gathers round, so that he is increasingly reduced to mere voice, his only defence against loneliness. There is, to be sure, a compulsory optimism in the playwright's appended endorsement of the Patient because of her 'cheerful conviction that the lost dogs always find their own way home' (p. 528), but it is the fragility of that supposedly cheerful conviction that is most apparent.

'The real sorrow of great men', Shaw wrote, apropos of Frank Harris's book on Shakespeare, is not personal heartbreak but 'the political and moral conduct of [their] contemporaries' (*B* 4: 302–3). There is no reason to think that this and other similar statements are at all insincere. But disillusionment as he actually dramatises it in his best texts is shown to be an inextricable mixture of social and individual disappointment. Desire in his great men and women is an absolutising force, exposed as incomplete by the extremity of its own movement. In *The Apple Cart* the heroicised will is rather too complacent and contemptuous to bring out this implication. In *Too True To Be Good* the disillusioned will only begins to find concentrated expression at the end. Whether, in fact, any late play achieves much concentration of effect is doubtful, but the ones most interestingly illustrative of this dialectic of desire are *The Millionairess* and the sketchier 'Why She Would Not'.

The superhuman strength of Epifania Ognisanti di Parerga consists of a 'genius for making money' (*B* 6: 915), for overhauling inefficient businesses and organising the productive capacities of others. But *The Millionairess* does not imagine very well the resistances to its cyclonic heroine. We hear a little about a Polly Seedystockings who is said to have a genius for making people happy in contrast to Eppy's genius for making money. We learn with hardly any pathos that, in her drastic overhauling of a restaurant, Eppy has thrown away the old employees along with the old crockery. The solicitor who supposedly mediates between her will and the law, and the Egyptian doctor who diagnoses her 'disease' ('enormous self-confidence, reckless audacity, insane egotism'), are both too fascinated or infatuated to put up any real resistance. Thus her strength seems more lunatic than inspired. Shaw himself in a letter described the dialogue as 'raving lunacy from beginning to end' (Ervine, 1956, p. 555).

But there is something original in the conception of Eppy. We have discovered a polarised relation throughout Shaw's work between images of great wealth and of sensual power, between capitalistic and sexual luxury. *Heartbreak House* associates them better than any other play, but negatively. Only in *The Millionairess* is there a significant effort to associate the two positively.

Commenting on this association, Margery Morgan (1972) achieves the keenest psychological insight of her fine book:

The power in Eppy has burnt up the ambiguousness that clung to Ann Whitefield, or to Candida, as a vessel of the Life Force. In the line of Shaw's woman characters, she is the ultimate successor to Julia Craven of *The Philanderer*, not now condemned and rejected, but purified and apotheosized. . . . [Eppy] seems to unite what fascinated him in capitalism, the perpetual object of his attack, with the abounding energy that informs and characterizes his own creative work.   (pp. 326–7)

We have earlier discerned that Shaw was covertly fascinated by capitalism, 'the perpetual object of his attack'. John Tanner's self-avowed membership in the Idle Rich Class and Andrew Undershaft's immoral traffic in munitions were dialectically useful devices that by no means concealed the vibrant charm of these millionaires as millionaires. Morgan locates the basis of that positive fascination in the idea of productive power, and accordingly links Shaw's feelings about money (and the strong woman) with his own writerly creativity. His texts cannot ever be described as preoccupied with the problem and process of their own composition, but there is at least an approximation of this self-reflexive interest, so valued today, in *The Millionairess* and in the last pages of *Too True To Be Good*. There, a will to meaning is equally a will to rhetoric. 'A writer of my sort', Shaw wrote elsewhere (this is the one reference I have been unable to track down), 'must keep in training like an athlete. How else can he wrestle with God as Jacob did with the angel?'

Making use of Morgan's linkages, we can add that the exuberance of Shaw's creativity acquires dynamic significance in light of what we have already learned about his ambivalence toward the strong woman and toward wealth. If his idealisation of the female other is an alternative form of self-idealisation and if, as Dervin (1975) plausibly suggests, his wish to rid the world of the poor expressed an unconscious wish 'to get rid of his own poor . . . feelings about himself' (p. 74) – an inference that receives support when we read his late confessional essay, 'Shame and Wounded Snobbery: a Secret Kept for 80 Years' (*SSS* 339–52) – then we can see that to produce in the way that Shaw knew best how to produce would become for him a matter of utmost importance, the re-enforcement of a psychological defence always in need of re-enforcement.

One would not wish to forget in pursuing such a line of inquiry that the privileging of production over consumption was a conspicuous theme among such pre-Shavian nineteenth-century moralists as Morris, Ruskin and Carlyle. Nor should one forget that a literary text reflects mature judgement along with regressive psychodynamics. Shaw himself overtly resists his Eppy, in the Preface on Bosses. We are told there that the rule of born bosses, like the rule of plutocrats, is not at all desirable socially. 'It creates a sort of Gresham's law by which the baser human currency drives out the nobler coinage' (*B* 6: 853). But, by the end of the preface, he is more than a little charmed again by the idea of a natural authority like his heroine's and implies that he wrote his play to give imaginative extension to this attractive idea.

The play itself, showing less resistance to Eppy, cannot be exempted from the charge of farce. But the most important form of judgement that it passes upon her has yet to be spelled out. And that is Eppy's very inability to quench her rage for efficiency, to find a sufficient container for her energy. Her story ends – must end, it seems – equivocally. Having levelled everything in her path, she seeks at last some containment in the prospect of marriage to the Egyptian doctor who appreciates her magnetism. But Shaw was evidently not satisfied with this ending and devised an alternative that might, he said, be more fitting in communist rather than capitalist countries. In the merely stated alternative ending, the heroine's individual executive power is said to be harnessed to the collective executive power of the state.

Neither ending is quite supported by the play because its most sublime speech stresses the limitlessness of Eppy's desire, overshadowing both containments:

> EPPY. I will not have my life dragged down to planes of vulgarity on which I cannot breathe. I will live in utter loneliness and keep myself sacred until I find the right man – the man who can stand with me on the utmost heights and not lose his head – the mate created for me in heaven. He must be somewhere.   (960)

Better than any other single speech in the canon, even the vaticism of Mrs George or the sublime pathos of Joan in her play's epilogue, this illustrates the third version of the Shavian sublime to which I have attached Bloom's phrase 'visionary skepticism' and Lacan's phrase 'dialectic of desire'. There can be no fit mate because there can be no completed attainment of the ideal state of self, no return to the symbiotic fusion that preceded the irreversible development into separateness. As far as conscious memory goes, we are always already alone, and in D. H. Lawrence's phrase, 'calling, calling for the complement'.

Both Eppy's speech and the similar cries in the wilderness at the end of *Too True* are capable of being also interpreted in the context of their author's relation to an audience. Shaw must have sensed in the 1930s that, despite his great fame, the world was slipping away from him or he from it. 'I shoot into the air more and more extravagantly.' This is not only a matter of diminished years in prospect but also of finding that one's audience has largely grown up under different influences and is attracted to newer styles. Even for the writer who remains active and responsive to the world about him, longevity may have this unpleasant surprise in store.

The doomed struggle to have it both ways – to be utterly self-sufficient yet not separated from the other – was still being played out in Shaw's ninety-fourth year, a fact that testifies at least to his stubborn sincerity as an imaginative writer. 'Why She Would Not' is little more than a sketch, and hardly merits a performance, but it expresses this fundamental ambivalence with such directness that it repays a moment's consideration.

Bossborn rescues Serafina from a robber in the woods and asks, for his reward, only a humble job, though with freedom of movement, in her father's timber business. Two years later he has weeded out the inefficient and is *de facto* master, dictating that the old house Serafina is very fond of be knocked down because it is not fit to live in. He prevails, but when he revisits her in an ultra-modern house, she tells him that she will not marry him, resisting the pressure of his will. He protests, and the debate climaxes in this exchange:

> BOSSBORN.   I coerce nobody. I only point the way.
> SERAFINA.   Yes: your way, not our way.
> BOSSBORN.   Neither my way nor yours. The way of the world.
>   Some people call it God's way . . .   (*B* 7: 677)

The born boss claims to serve an impersonal, higher will, but cannot please his angel. His very triumph is rejected as bossiness, yet what else can he do?

In light of 'Why She Would Not', we may reconstruct what might be called a countermyth of the Shavian hero. He feels unloved and unlovable. So he will do without love, deny the need for love. Better, he will become his own parent and seek a perfected self-sufficiency, though the incompleteness of the ideal will now and again become apparent. This imaginative ambivalence evidently reflects Shaw's own divided feelings: on the one hand he admitted the bitter memory of his childhood; on the other, he characteristically denied feelings of separateness and incompleteness.

The history of the Shavian sublime is neatly framed by a contrast between Bossborn's exchange with Serafina and Vivie Warren's final confrontation with her mother, many years earlier, which incorporates the same biblical allusion. In *Mrs Warren's Profession*, God's retort to Job is echoed by the character who stands for a superior energy of will; in 'Why She Would Not' the character who resists such will shares in the allusion. True, Bossborn insists with some authorial endorsement that Serafina's judgement is merely mundane, but he does not prevail (a fact underlined by the title) and he is in truth prejudged by his very name.

Dervin (1975) is suggestive in remarking on the absence of a late manner in Shaw, comparable to that in Shakespeare or Ibsen (pp. 279 ff.). Despite the more schematic form of the late plays, there is little in their tone or mood to be compared to *The Tempest* or *When We Dead Awaken*. Advancing years made them more brittle but not more accepting.

Something perpetually boyish persists in Shaw. He continued to the end of his life to welcome new technology, even when, as in the case of the cinema, it might well have appeared as a threat to his very large investment in the art of the stage. 'The films . . . are still in their infancy. [Eventually] every corner of the country in which a picture house can live will witness performances compared to which this one of Arms and the Man will seem a mere sketch' (*ST* 213). (But he could also be less sanguine about the possibilities of film: see *CL* iv 334 and 401.) In other ways, too, Shaw refused the old man's game of finding the present lacking by comparison with the past. In his last musical notice, written at the age of ninety-four, he observed that the singers of the past are not better than those of the present, only more idealised (*SM* 3: 767).

His zest for the future was, of course, not based altogether on an enthusiasm for the present. In large part it derived paradoxically from a profound attachment to pre-modern ideas, to eighteenth-

and nineteenth-century myths of progress. Unlike many modernists, he never located the source of malaise in history or in nature. The generative moment for his imagination would remain the birth of moral passion as described in the first act of *Man and Superman*, not in the discovery of a loss.

Beatrice Webb's epithet for her friend and fellow Fabian – 'a sprite' – continues to stick. For all of his pragmatism, shrewdness and sanity, which help to give bite both to his eloquence and his comedy, Shaw's extraordinary character retained a fundamental innocence. Whether the mood of the moment was optimistic or pessimistic or both at once, his voice seldom modulated into the key of wisdom.[2]

But even Shaw was not quite exempt from the burden of the human situation. In old age he too had to learn to die, to make his peace. We find the surest literary evidence of this in the more relaxed, less bravura tone of his non-dramatic work: in, for example, the foreword to a new edition of *Our Theatres in the Nineties*, admitting the excesses of his former attacks on Shakespeare (*OTN* I vii); in the gracefully as well as shrewdly balanced appraisal of *Great Expectations*, for which he wrote an introduction (*LC* 49 ff.); in his appreciation of the multitudinous *non-geniuses* without whose help the fine arts could not have remained a living tradition (*SM* 3: 717). Above all, we find it in the disinterested curiosity about the phenomenon of his character and career as reflected in his autobiographical writing: in the prefaces to collected or re-issued or previously unpublished work; in the several late pieces that eke out the *Sixteen Self Sketches* published in 1949; and in various letters and remarks to friends and biographers.

His career in retrospect seemed amazing to him, as in a more remote way it does to us – the high achievement built upon the desolating yet strangely self-nourishing childhood. It is a source of pride and pathos at once, and calls for a tone that registers both without either self-congratulation or self-pity:

> In the ordinary connotation of the word I am the least ambitious of men. . . . I am so poor a hand at pushing and struggling and so little interested in their rewards, that I have risen by sheer gravitation, too industrious by acquired habit to stop working (I work as my father drank), and too lazy and timid by nature to lay hold of half the opportunities or a tenth of the money that a conventionally ambitious man would have grasped strenuously.

I never thought of myself as destined to become what is called a great man: indeed I was diffident to the most distressing degree; and I was ridiculously credulous to the claims of others to superior knowledge and authority. But one day in the office, I had a shock. One of the apprentices, by name C. J. Smythe, older than I and more a man of the world, remarked that every young chap thought he was going to be a great man. On a really modest youth this commonplace would have had no effect. It gave me so perceptible a jar that I suddenly became aware that I had always taken it as a matter of course. The incident passed without leaving any preoccupation with it to hamper; and I remained as diffident as ever because I was still as incompetent as ever. But I doubt whether I ever recovered my first former complete innocence of subconscious intention to devote myself to the class of work that only a few men excel in and to accept the responsibilities that attach to its dignity.   (C 1: xxxvii)

Shaw looks back with wonder at the youth he was, the odd mixture of impotence and potential power, and finds a tone of self-reference that is neither modest nor immodest, different from the theatrical, self-dramatising tone he adopted earlier.

Another preface is especially remarkable for the vividly objective, malice-free view of his mother. If it seems almost inhumanly fair at first, it gradually attains a genuine and complex poignancy. The passage seems to discover her inadequacy even as it continues to appreciate her:

She was not at all soured by all this [her husband's failures]. She never made scenes, never complained, never nagged, never punished nor retaliated nor lost her self-control nor her superiority to spite and tantrums and tempers. She was neither weak nor submissive, but as she never revenged, so she never forgave. There were no quarrels and consequently no reconciliations. You did a wrong; and you were classed by her as a person who did such wrongs, and tolerated indulgently up to a point. But if at last you drove her to break with you, the breach was permanent: you did not get back again. Among my *Maxims for Revolutionists* there is 'Beware of the man who does not return your blow.' From my mother I had learned that the wrath on which the sun goes down is negligible compared to the clear vision and criticism that is neither created by anger nor ended with it.

Under all circumstances it says a great deal for my mother's humanity that she did not hate her children. She did not hate anybody, nor love anybody. The specific maternal passion awoke in her a little for my younger sister, who died at 20; but it did not move her until she lost her, nor then noticeably.

(*SSS* 28–9)

Poignancy was not Shaw's strong suit but he was capable of it. The passage above makes still more moving his letter on his ninety-third birthday to St John Ervine, in which he recalls from early childhood, as a primary experience, his father carrying him when he became tired, and comments: 'I am again unable to walk far. I am as I was under the portico; and there is nobody now to carry me' (Ervine, 1956, p. 37).[3]

Since he lived so long, Shaw experienced the death of many friends, and he left us a number of moving tributes. He was always a fine eulogist. Praise came as naturally to him as irony, and it was usually touched with tenderness, the one affectionate emotion somehow salvaged from childhood and the prohibition against the expression of sentiment. If, like his mother, he neither hated nor loved, unlike his mother he had a wide circle of friends whom he appears to have enjoyed. One has the overall impression that, for all his peculiarities, he made a success of his personal life as well as a brilliant career.

Conclusion

It is fair to describe Bernard Shaw as a didactic writer, not only in the broad sense that he constantly promoted a moral vision but also in the more specific sense that he sought by his writing to change our minds and therefore our conduct concerning both our private and public lives. Indeed, the very distinction between private and public, between personal and political, is one that the whole drift of his work seeks to break down. Essentially his vision internalises the premises of Socialism, exposing with wit and eloquence the 'hopelessly private' person's neglect of a communal imperative, of the necessary drama of unselfing.

Because of this movement of internalisation and because of the dramatic interest he makes of it, Shaw deserves to be called also a kind of poet. His fascination with political, social, economic and religious ideas was always highly coloured by individual temperament. To be sure, Shaw was a poet of a certain kind – projective rather than introjective, eloquent rather than suggestive, dialectical rather than nuanced. But almost always the dramatic conflicts and even the arguments that he created expressed intra-psychic as well as external conflicts, and in the less combative, more relaxed mood of old age he was ready to acknowledge as much: 'I have had no heroic adventures. Things have not happened to me: on the contrary, it is I who have happened to them; and all my happenings have taken the form of books and plays. . . . The best autobiographies are confessions; but if a man is a deep writer all his works are confessions' (*SSS* 18–19).

When Shaw as dramatic poet disappoints us, it is not because he is too external but too shallow. His art depends on the repudiation of one emotion in order to release another, but the repudiation can be too decisive. If fresh energy is released, we have that under-the-surface tension between head and heart, between scepticism and idealisation, that I have called the comic sublime. When this tension slackens, we may surmise that Shaw has not been able to engage the repressed material before re-establishing his characteristic defences.

The cold and loveless childhood was bound, after all, to take its toll. To be 'always on the heroic plane imaginatively', even allowing

193

for some exaggeration, is to be insufficiently burdened by the weight of experience. It means reacting too quickly against one's fears. Emily Dickinson admired Hawthorne because he 'appalls – entices'. One could say that Shaw often entices but never appals. Despite Shotover's call for 'deeper darkness', there is not enough darkness in his vision. Cruelty and greed are repeatedly his targets, but he tends to condemn them before he has imagined them well enough. Attracted to the idea of salvation, Shaw frequently invokes the antithetical idea of damnation, but his hell is sometimes too mild, at least for contemporary taste.

But if Shaw has lost some of his appeal, it is only fair to remind contemporary readers that the iconoclasm of one age is not the same as that of another. Shaw wrote with some pride: 'My mission is not to deal with obvious horrors but to open the eyes of normal and respectable men to evils which are escaping their consideration' (*B* 3: 528). His literary strength is bound up with this conviction, but it can seem a half-disabling one in our age of suspicion in which an ethic of survival has largely replaced an ethic of social progress. Shaw's art seeks to discover and expose our latent Utopianism. Many later de-idealisers have of course been sceptical of latent Utopianism itself; it is more difficult for us to imagine moral nobility in either personal or political terms. But we can feel our way back, imaginatively, from the late twentieth to the late nineteenth century, placing Shaw in his age rather than belittling his achievement.

What fascinates me in the art of Shaw is the infusion of a mythology of self into a description of a recognisable world. When I call Shaw a poet, as he called himself until the end of his life (see *CL* IV 798), I am thinking particularly of this peculiar amalgam of the not-self, that which stands over against our desires and is often called the real, and those imaginative claims on the world that assert our sense of how things should be in the face always of how they are. Like a poet, Shaw was sometimes able to unify these forces, finely called by Yeats reality and justice.

Great dramatic art, Shaw wrote in *Our Theatres in the Nineties*, is 'a revelation of ourselves to our own consciousness' (*OTN* II 145). The remark, clearly deriving from a Romantic tradition, shortsightedly ignores the fact, so richly developed in modern criticism, that such revelation can only occur when the writer diligently discovers and modifies the conventions of the art he practises. The paradox is that the experience of self can only be expressed through language, which is a cultural inheritance. But the point remains a strong one, and applies to his critics as well as to Shaw himself. We discover our own selves through the effectively communicated experience – the mythology – of other selves. And we keep the work of earlier writers alive when we can translate their sensibility and idiom into our own.

Notes

Notes to the Introduction

1. 'I had read much poetry; but only one poet was sacred to me: Shelley' (C 1: xvii). The phrase 'visionary scepticism' applied to Shelley is Harold Bloom's (*Modern Critical Views: Percy Bysshe Shelley*, ed. with Introd. by Harold Bloom (New York: Chelsea, 1985) pp. 7–8).
2. Several books have helped me particularly in formulating a view of authorial character as a textual presence. They are, in order of publication: Richard J. Onorato, *The Character of the Poet: Wordsworth in 'The Prelude'* (Princeton, NJ: Princeton University Press, 1971); David Lynch, *Yeats: The Poetics of the Self* (Chicago, Ill.: University of Chicago Press, 1979); Coppélia Kahn, *Man's Estate: Masculine Identity in Shakespeare* (Berkeley, Calif.: California University Press, 1980); and Richard P. Wheeler, *Shakespeare's Development and the Problem Comedies: Turn and Counter-Turn* (Berkeley, Calif.: California University Press, 1981).
3. Four psychobiographic studies should be mentioned here: Erik H. Erikson, 'Biographic: G.B.S. (70) on George Bernard Shaw (20), reprinted in *G. B. Shaw: A Collection of Critical Essays*, ed. R. J. Kaufman (Englewood Cliffs, NJ: Prentice-Hall, 1965) pp. 19–25; Daniel Dervin, *Bernard Shaw: A Psychological Study* (Lewisburg, Penn.: Bucknell University Press, 1975); Arnold Silver, *Bernard Shaw: The Darker Side* (Stanford, Calif.: Stanford University Press, 1982); and Norman Holland, *The I* (New Haven, Conn.: Yale University Press, 1985) pp. 56–67, 77–8. Erikson's brief piece concerns Shaw's way of resolving his youthful identity crisis by internalising with a difference some aspects of parental behaviour. Dervin's book-length study, though somewhat reductive as criticism, is full of interesting suggestions concerning the relation of the life to the work. Silver is interested in the way a few works, notably *Pygmalion*, seek to gain a revenge against the women in Shaw's life. And Norman Holland, in a dozen pages of his impressive book, discusses Shaw's identity theme ('To find or to be a purposeful and fulfilling opposite'), emphasising, as I shall, the idea of self-sufficiency.

   To these psychobiographical studies must now be added Michael Holroyd's psychologically acute biography, the first volume of which (*Bernard Shaw: 1856–1898: The Search for Love*) appeared while this book was in the process of publication. Although Holroyd endorses the, to me, dubious but in any case unprovable theory that Vandeleur Lee was Shaw's biological father, he writes perceptively of Shaw's attachment to his mother, of his interest in Chichester Bell, his admiration for William Morris as the antitype of Oscar Wilde, of his motive for modifying Marx via Jevons and Darwin via Lamarck, of his prose style, of his mental need for optimism offsetting an emotional instinct that tended to despair, and of the psychological roots of his dramatic plots. But in discussing the plays, Holroyd (1988) sometimes yields to the biographer's tendency to reduce artistic implication to a matter of personal psychology. For example, he writes: 'It is because [Candida as] the Virgin Mother outlaws sex that she is Shaw's ideal. Candida reduces all men to children by emotional castration. In providing other explanations Shaw . . . idealizes' (p. 317). Such a view prevents us from seeing that the outlawed sex also enables Marchbanks to *preserve* the image of Candida, as the poet-to-be falls on his knees to accept the role of her knight. What Holroyd calls idealising can also be called a creative use of a personal problem.

Notes to Chapter 1: The Comic Sublime

1. Hynes (1972) erases a distinction I would preserve between a polemical and an instrumental use of language. But I agree with him that Shaw, unlike Shakespeare or Molière, was great not specifically in his plays but 'in the multitudinousness of his imagination . . . realized . . . in the amplitude of his work' (p. 23).
2. Shaw thus could not accept Tolstoy's reason for condemning capital punishment – nobody's hands are clean enough to perform the execution. (Shaw may have come across this opinion while reading *Fruits of Culture* (or *Fruits of Enlightenment*), a work that influenced his own *Heartbreak House*.) That is to assume an innate depravity. Since Shaw prided himself on his pragmatism, however, he had to concede, more in earnest than in jest, that those 'few' who could not be improved by the strengthening of their will in conjunction with better social arrangements should be executed as humanely as possible.
3. Keith May (1985) comments: 'The difference between Ibsen and Shaw is that to the former the individual is destroyed by an unregenerate society and that is his glory, while to the latter, the individual, destroyed or not, is society's only hope' (p. 198).
4. Kant is here discussing a 'dynamical sublime', an active heightening of mental power which he distinguishes from a 'mathematical sublime', descriptive of the mind's more passive response to immeasurability, its dissolve in cognitive bafflement not unlike a mystical ascesis. There is no correspondence to this latter mode of transcendence in Shaw. It is similar to the kind studied by Rosalie Colie (1964) in regard to seventeenth-century poetry (pp. 145–70). Probably the best study of its romantic version is Thomas Weiskel's (1976).
5. Shelley was less often invoked in this way, perhaps because Shaw imagined him as at ease in the ethereal regions so that he scarcely needed to spur his language thither. Mozart was also cited as an instance of this sort of natural sublimity: 'In the ardent regions where all the rest are excited and vehement, Mozart alone is completely self-possessed' (*SM* 2: 856–7).
6. A good example in the non-dramatic work of this rooted ambivalence

to the strong woman is the following paragraph:

> You do not waste 'homage' on the female Efficient Person; you
> regard her, favorably or unfavorably, much as you regard the male
> of the Efficient species, except that you have a certain special fear
> of her, based on her freedom from that sickliness of conscience, so
> much deprecated by Ibsen, which makes the male the prey of unreal
> scruples; and you have at times to defend yourself against her, or,
> when she is an ally, to assume her fitness for active service of the
> roughest kinds, in a way which horrifies the chivalrous gentlemen
> of your acquaintance who will not suffer the winds of heaven to
> breathe on a woman's face too harshly lest they should disable her
> in her mission of sewing on buttons.   (*SM* 3: 208)

  Although the passage concludes with an effectively controlled irony,
  it wavers uncertainly, to the point of awkward syntax, between the
  strong woman's point of view and that of her victim.

7. Although Shaw admired maturity, he sometimes admitted, especially
   to women, that 'I have never yet been able to feel grown up' (*CL* II
   731), that 'I shall be 56 on the 26th of this month; and I have not yet
   grown up' (Dent, 1952, p. 25). Several of his characters (Praed in *Mrs
   Warren's Profession*, Sonny in *Getting Married*, Higgins in *Pygmalion*)
   express a similar sentiment.

8. 'Still After the Doll's House: a Sequel to Walter Besant's Sequel to
   Henrik Ibsen's Play' (*C* 6: 123–37). Shaw imagines Nora as having
   become the leader of an advanced set, returning and realising in
   discussion with Krogstad that 'the man must walk out of the doll's
   house as well as the woman'. In later years Shaw liked to refer to
   Candida as a reply to *A Doll's House*, showing the man as the doll
   (*ThC* 43 and *CL* IV 657; see also *CL* I 611–12).

9. Martin Price (1983) comments in the same keen spirit on the Circumlo-
   cution Office in *Little Dorrit*: 'Dickens presents it with a mixture of
   outrage and delight. His "indignant steam" becomes at last a tribute
   to the cool enormity of the bureaucratic performance' (p. 127).

10. Probably, as Elsie Adams (1971) has shown, Shaw was in reaction to
    the religion of art that he discovered, and partly shared, in the London
    drawing rooms of the 1870s and 1880s. But he was sensitive all his
    life to the corruptive as well as the inspirational power of art. Nor
    was it only in popular art that he found a morality that flattered and
    pandered to snobbery. Traces of this morality were present for
    him even in such meritorious writers as Thackeray and Trollope.
    Significantly, when Shaw in *The Perfect Wagnerite* is absorbed in an
    explication of what he thinks of as the highest art, the word 'didactic'
    becomes pejorative (*SM* 3: 477).

11. A sense of fairness to Pinero and Jones requires one to cite Leon
    Hugo's (1971) reminder that, a decade before Shaw emerged as a
    playwright, 'they infused their drama with a moral purposiveness
    which the old theatre had lacked' (p. 69).

12. In this respect, of course, Shaw is no different than many artists who

play down the deliberative aspect of artistic creation (sometimes in the teeth of manuscript evidence), either because they cannot or will not acknowledge it. On one occasion at least, he was pleasantly wry about the matter, remarking that 'The only play which I planned and plotted was *Captain Brassbound's Conversion*, which was neither the better nor the worse for the ceremony.' See 'Dramatists Self-Revealed: a Questionnaire' (British Library MS 50709).

13. The whole question of Lee, which I have slighted, is fully discussed in B. C. Rosset, *Shaw of Dublin: The Formative Years* (University Park, Pa.: Pennsylvania State University Press, 1964).

14. Harold Bloom (1987) comments intriguingly: ' "He who is willing to do the work gives birth to his own father," Kierkegaard wrote, and Nietzsche mused: "If one hasn't had a good father, then it is necessary to invent one." Shaw . . . had suffered an inadequate father and certainly he was willing to do the work. Like his own Major Barbara, he wished to have a God who would owe everything to G. B. S.' (p. 2).

Notes to Chapter 2: Emergence of the Comic Sublime

1. Trefusis himself explains the name as 'a compound of the words smile and eyelash'. Probably this is disingenuous, and the name is meant to fuse smile with lash in the sense of 'to strike'.

2. These notes, consisting of thirteen pages dated 14 January 1888, were prepared for a meeting of the Blackheath Essay and Debating Society. The manuscript is at the Humanities Research Center in Austin, Texas.

3. R. W. Ellis (ed.), *Bernard Shaw and Karl Marx: A Symposium, 1884–1889* (New York: Random House, 1930).

4. In a particularly enthusiastic moment of his youth, Shaw composed but did not publish a piece about the day when the arts themselves will be superseded, not in futuristic time like *Back to Methuselah* but in a foreseeable historical moment: 'The day will come when society will so completely satisfy spiritual needs of potential artists that they will not recognize the arts as needs [and instead will enjoy] a healthy Philistinism' (unpublished manuscript dated 13 June 1880, in Humanities Research Center, Austin, Texas). This idea (versions of which may be found in Yeats and Lawrence) was discussed among the Socialists whom Shaw knew, but, for the most part, even in the 1880s, his attacks on art are attempts to distinguish what is sentimental and retrograde in existing art from what is robust and progressive. Marx, in other words, helped Shaw apply a double perspective to the moment.

5. Proto-dramatic elements in the novels themselves are discussed in Stanley Weintraub, 'The Embryo Playwright: Bernard Shaw's Early Novels', *University of Texas Studies in Literature and Language*, vol. I (1959) pp. 327–55.

6. Eric Bentley has observed that 'the ending of *A Doll's House* is the

model for a great deal in Shaw: having the strength to slam the door' (Turco, 1986, p. 15).

7. Ervine (1956) notes the derivation of the character from the Casby-Pancks relation in *Little Dorrit* (p. 245).

8. The MS copy is in the Berg Collection, New York Public Library.

9. But Shaw's proud belief that the challenge to conventional morality is what accounted for the censorship of the play (*B* 1: 233–64) probably cannot be sustained. Charles Berst (1973) has pointed out that the censor had only objected to the suggestion of incest (p. 6), and this, as we shall see, is handled by Shaw with considerably less artistic confidence than the confrontations of mother and daughter.

10. Arthur Ganz (1980), finding the resolution of the play unrealistic, asks why Vivie couldn't maintain relations with such a woman as her mother and still retain her self-respect (pp. 60–1). This sort of objection doesn't allow the poet in Shaw to emerge very well. His heroine's withdrawal is a symbolic repudiation of a social structure, which, it is understood, she herself cannot literally escape. Shaw is realistic enough to suggest the cost, in solitude, of Vivie's gesture, but he would undermine its symbolic value if he had spelled out her future.

11. 'Oh, how can you remind me of it – how can you bear to think of it? Never that again – never whilst we live: it is all tainted, horrible: Goodbye' (British Library Additional MS 50598).

Notes to Chapter 3: Development of the Comic Sublime

1. The Shelley model was suggested by Oliver Elton's review, quoted in Henderson (1911) p. 346. Shaw himself mentioned De Quincey (Bentley, 1960, p. xxiii).

2. Frequently asked for clarification of this passage, Shaw could become very emphatic in contrasting the 'greasy fool's paradise' of domesticity to the true joy of the poet (*CL* II 415). Perhaps he sensed that he had allowed Candida too much fascination. On at least one occasion, however – a talk to a group of Rugby students in 1920 – he was attractively undogmatic about the whole matter: 'It is only my way of looking at it; everybody who buys the book may fit it with an ending to suit his own taste' (Berst, 1973, p. xvi).

3. On the unusual degree of sexual imagery in the play (particularly in act 3), see the remarks of Bentley (1967), Berst (1973), Morgan (1972) and Silver (1982). (For remarks on the surprising amount of submerged sexual imagery in other works by Shaw, see Ina Rae Hark (1986), Sally Peters (1986) and Rodelle Weintraub (1986). To these I would only add that the Oedipal aspect of the confrontation between the rivals is both pointed and curiously unaggressive. Marchbanks asks Morell, 'How did you get past the flaming sword that stopped me?' Then he suggests that they both give up Candida, and finally he hands her over to Parson James with love because his rival has filled the heart of the woman he himself loves.

4. See my 'Two Anti-Puritan Puritans: Bernard Shaw and D. H.

Lawrence', *Yale Review*, vol. LVI, no. 1 (Autumn 1966) pp. 76–90.

5. The manuscript indicates that Shaw changed her description of her son from someone who 'defied his maker' to someone 'who went with smugglers and gypsies' (British Library Additional MS 50606 B). One guesses that a lighter tone was thought suitable, but the change does risk cuteness.

6. Edward McNulty remarked that there was more of the boyhood friend he remembered in this role than in any other created by Shaw (British Library MS 50709). I suspect he was alluding particularly to the combination of highmindedness and boyish high spirits.

Notes to Chapter 4: The Big Three

1. The evidence for a Don Juan play was in his mind as early as 1884, evidenced by the abortive effort, 'Un Petit Drame', published in volume 7 of Dan Laurence's Bodley Head edition of the *Collected Plays with their Prefaces* (London: Max Reinhardt, 1970–4).

2. It may not be irrelevant to note that I trace the germinating moment of the present book to Ellis Raab's production of the whole play at the Phoenix Theater in New York City during the mid-1960s.

3. Cf. Shaw's own description of the difference: 'In *A Doll's House* and *Candida* you have action producing discussion, in *The Doctor's Dilemma* you have discussion producing action and that action being finally discussed. In other plays you have discussion all over the shop' (quoted in Dukore, 1973, p. 36).

4. The play was written at the request of Yeats for the Abbey Theatre, and was withdrawn at least partly because Yeats found it uncongenial, though doubtless there was some truth in the excuse that it was difficult to mount at the Abbey.

5. It is at least of symptomatic interest that a short play composed in an interim period of a few days ('How He Lied to Her Husband', written between 13 and 16 August 1904, the composition of *John Bull's Other Island* extending from 17 June to 23 August) should dramatise a deflated sublime in a frankly sexual frame of reference. The poetic lover of a married woman named Aurora Bompas, feeling himself dragged down to a prosaic level, pleads for help 'to find the way back to the heights' (*B* 2: 1041). The husband is disappointed that the lover no longer courts his wife with poems so *he* can think of her romantically too, and offers to have the lover's poems published and displayed. Appearance, then, is equated with the romantic name Aurora and reality with the deflationary Bompas.

Notes to Chapter 5: Compromise and Negation of the Comic Sublime

1. But Louis Crompton (1971) stresses the neatness of the parallels between the dilemmas created by medical monomania and amatory infatuation (p. 140). Wisenthal (1974), adding another twist, writes

that 'the main dilemma of the play . . . is . . . the choice that *we* must make between Dubedat and the doctors' (p. 114).

2. It is worth noting, however, that Shaw traced the origin of his inspiration to an actual incident in which he heard physicians describe as 'no good' the character of someone being considered for the treatment devised by his friend, Sir Almroth Wright. Although their opinion did not apparently influence the medical decision that was made, the very juxtaposition of moral and medical judgements gave the dramatist his idea (*B* 3: 442–3).

3. In a 1915 programme note to this play, Shaw celebrates Dickens's 'delightful gift of burlesquing a character to the very verge of hilarious insanity without ever losing his grip on reality; so that though nobody ever heard a human being say the things that Dickens's characters say or saw them do the things they do, everybody recognizes in them familiar persons, made more real than reality and more vivid than life' (*B* 3: 441).

4. An undated holograph carbon in the Humanities Research Center at Austin questions the critics' inference that, because the play shows a young artist dying under the treatment of six doctors, the artist is the hero and the doctors the villains: 'On the contrary, it is the artist who is the villain of the piece; and the doctors are all upright and kind men.'

5. Eric Bentley comments, apropos of the fifth act, that the audience, unlike the critic, never quite gets the point, that Ridgeon's corruptness is too subtle to come across in performance (Turco, 1986, pp. 13–15).

6. The censor, be it noted, objected to this play's description of God as 'sly' and 'mean'. That is, he saw *no* irony where I would consider the irony too pat. The preface's indignation at the censor for not tolerating heresy thus has a weak basis. To appreciate this, we have only to compare it to the more thoughtful eloquence Shaw brings to the subject in the preface to *Saint Joan*.

7. This is a position that Shaw continued to hold and even take pride in, despite the keener insight of *Pygmalion*. In a later letter he asserts: 'Long before Freud I held that Nature had introduced an element of antipathy into kinship as a defence against incest (*CL* iv 392).

8. This ending, revised in 1939, read rather differently in the Standard Edition of 1930:

> LIZA [*disdainfully*]. Buy them yourself. [*She sweeps out*]
> MRS HIGGINS. I'm afraid youve spoilt that girl, Henry. But never mind, dear: I'll buy you the tie and gloves.
> HIGGINS [*sunnily*]. Oh, dont bother. She'll buy them right enough. Goodbye.
>> *They kiss. Mrs Higgins runs out. Higgins, left alone, rattles his cash in his pocket; chuckles; and disports himself in a highly self-satisfied manner.* (C 14: 289)

The revised ending makes more pointed the mutual rejection of the antagonist.

Notes to Chapter 6: Baffled Apocalypse

1. Crompton (1971) points out also the link between Hector's multiple roles and those of Sergius Saranoff in *Arms and the Man* (p. 159). Certainly, the extraordinary Cunninghame Graham stands behind both, as Crompton demonstrates, but Sergius is not quite a prophetic presence, the aspect of the role I am stressing here.
2. Part of the difficulty with Mangan's role seems to result from the late insertion of Ellie's mystic marriage with Shotover. Nicholas Grene (1984) comments that this scene is 'almost completely unintegrated with the dramatic action, and it made necessary a re-ordering of the scenes around it [Mangan's revelation that he had no money and the scene in which he offers to undress himself] which disrupted their continuity' (p. 119). I agree that the continuity of the Mangan scenes is affected, but I think the symbolic value of the mystic marriage offsets this by clarifying the conception of the heroic in the play.
3. Crompton (1971) suggests that Hesione is 'of the race of Kundry, Circe, and Astarte', and reminds us that 'her appearance and manner are those of Mrs Patrick Campbell' (p. 158).
4. A. M. Gibbs in his *Shaw* (1969, p. 73) skilfully relates this final scene to a pattern of light and dark imagery in the play (involving Shotover's black wife, Ellie's fondness for Othello, Hesione's hair, and so on). His comments seek to make a case for the outright apocalyptic force of the play.
5. Ervine (1956) implies that Eve's repugnance reflects the author's own (pp. 383–4). But the play itself is more complex, combining fastidiousness *with* fascination. And in fact Shaw's letter to Ervine, now published in full (*CL* IV 96), is more complex, stressing Eve's 'pre-sexual innocence' and the consequent appropriateness of her 'wry face when it is explained to her that Nature, in a fit of economy, has combined a merely excretory function with a creatively ejaculatory one'.
6. For Shaw, the importance assigned to chance was the most repugnant aspect of Darwin's theory, but many other religious thinkers have found it so too and have tried to argue that there is a some built-in tendency toward improvement of the species. If Shaw is to be distinguished from this line of speculation, it is perhaps in his effort to stay close to the Darwinian point (argued in recent times by the biologist Jacques Monod) that 'the genetic material is constant [and] can change only through mutation' (Ernst Mayr, *Scientific American*, September 1978, p. 50).
7. It is likely that the idea of the Ancients' power to kill at a glance was suggested by Bulwer-Lytton's *Vril in the Coming Race* (Henderson, 1932, p. 530). But the fascination of the idea for Shaw solicits psychological explanation, and calls to mind the glosses on the Medusa myth by Freud and Ferenczi who proposed that the Medusa's serpentine hair symbolised the mother's genitalia, the sight of which arouses in the male child a fear of castration. A student of Shaw will probably be reminded in this connection of a striking autobiographical passage:

> I well remember, when I was a small boy, receiving perhaps a greater shock than I have ever received since. I had been brought up in a world in which woman, the angel, presented to me the appearance of a spreading mountain, a sort of Primrose Hill. On the peak there was perched a small, pinched upper part, and on top of that a human head. That, to me, at the period of life when one is young and receiving indelible impressions, was a woman. One day, when I was perhaps five years of age, a lady paid us a visit, a very handsome lady who was always in advance of fashion. Crinolines were going out; and she had discarded hers. I, an innocent unprepared child, walked bang into a room and suddenly saw, for the first time, a woman not shaped like Primrose Hill, but with a narrow shirt which evidently wrapped a pair of human legs. I have never recovered from the shock, and never shall. (*P&P* 173)

The passage is perhaps too artful to be taken at face value as a confession, but in the spirit of Freud and Ferenczi, one is tempted to say that the shock Shaw speaks of has been 'displaced upward' so that the eyes acquire lethal power. For further comment, see my 'Literature and Repression: the Case of Shavian Drama' (1980).
8. These are almost the precise words that Shaw used to describe his own mother and her relation to her three children (*SSS* 29).

Notes to Chapter 7: The Summing Up

1. A similar objection to the rationalism of her response to Baudricourt was raised some time ago by J. van Kan, *Saint Joan: Fifty Years After, 1923–24/1973–74*, ed. Stanley Weintraub (University Park, Pa.: Pennsylvania State University Press, 1973) p. 50.
2. Shaw himself appreciated this compromise in a peculiarly wry statement that might strike someone not used to his manner as either too vain or too modest: '*Saint Joan* is magnificent . . . I am certainly a wonderful man; but then historical plays hardly count: the material is readymade' (Weintraub, 1986, p. 233). In truth, Shaw is more bemused by the paradox than self-regarding.
3. Shaw was quite aware that 'there is a voluptuous side to religious ecstasy and a religious side to voluptuous ecstasy' (Chappelow, 1969, p. 646).

Notes to Chapter 8: Relaxation of the Comic Sublime

1. The artfulness and cogency of the *Guide* are nicely appreciated by A. M. Gibbs in *The Art and Mind of Shaw* (1983) pp. 191–4.
2. Bentley comments that Shaw 'wished to be a wise man but was not' (Turco, 1986, p. 25).
3. There is also a remarkable passage in Stephen Winsten's *Days with Bernard Shaw* (1949, p. 69) that belatedly expresses his appreciation for

his father (who took some interest in his writing) and resentment toward his mother (who never did). It is worth noting too that his last full-length play, *Buoyant Billions* (1949), begins with an unusually affectionate scene between a father and a son. But it cannot really be said that these feelings are active in forming the images and attitudes of his principal writings.

Works Cited

See the List of Abbreviations (pp. vii–viii) for the publication details for works by Shaw.

Adams, Elsie B. (1971), *Bernard Shaw and the Aesthetes* (Columbus, Ohio: Ohio State University Press).

Albright, Daniel (1984), 'All the King's Men', review of *The Land and Literature of England*, by Robert M. Adams, in *New York Review of Books*, 15 March, p. 32.

Archer, William (1923), *The Old Drama and the New: An Essay in Revaluation* (Boston, Mass.: Small).

Bakhtin, Mikhail (1984), *Rabelais and His World*, trans. Helene Iswolsky (Bloomington, Ind.: Indiana University Press) pp. 34–5.

Beerbohm, Max (1930), *Around Theatres*, 2 vols (New York: Alfred A. Knopf) vol. 2, pp. 570–1.

Bentley, Eric (1947), *Bernard Shaw* (Norfolk, Conn.: New Directions).

—— (1960), Foreword, *Plays by George Bernard Shaw* (New York: Signet NAL).

—— (1967), *The Life of Drama* (New York: Atheneum).

—— (1986), 'Shaw 40 Years Later', interview with Alfred Turco Jr, in *Shaw: The Neglected Plays*, ed. Alfred Turco, Jr (University Park, Pa.: Pennsylvania State University Press) pp. 7–29.

Berst, Charles (1973), *Bernard Shaw and the Art of Drama* (Urbana, Ill.: University of Illinois Press).

Bloom, Harold (1976), *Poetry and Repression: Revisionism from Blake to Stevens* (New Haven, Conn.: Yale University Press).

—— (1985), *Modern Critical Views: Percy Bysshe Shelley*, edited with an Introduction by Harold Bloom (New York: Chelsea).

—— (1987), *Modern Critical Views: George Bernard Shaw*, edited with an Introduction by Harold Bloom (New York: Chelsea).

Boxhill, Roger (1969), *Shaw and the Doctors* (New York: Basic).

Burke, Edmund (1968), *A Philosophical Enquiry into the Origin of Our Ideas of the Sublime and Beautiful*, ed. James T. Boulton (Notre Dame, Ind.: University of Notre Dame Press).

Chappelow, Allan (1969), *Shaw – 'the Chucker Out': A Biographical Exposition and Critique* (London: Allen and Unwin).

Chesterton, Gilbert Keith (1909), *George Bernard Shaw* (New York: Hill, reprinted 1956).

Colie, Rosalie L. (1964), 'The Rhetoric of Transcendence', *Philological Quarterly*, vol. XLIII (1964) pp. 145–70.

Crane, Hart (1958), *The Complete Poems of Hart Crane*, ed. Waldo Frank (Garden City, NY: Doubleday).

Crompton, Louis (1971), *Shaw the Dramatist: A Study of the Intellectual Backgrounds of the Major Plays* (London: Allen and Unwin).

Dent, Alan (ed.) (1952), *Bernard Shaw and Mrs Patrick Campbell: Their Correspondence* (London: Gollancz).

Dervin, Daniel (1975), *Bernard Shaw: A Psychological Study* (Lewisburg, Pa.: Bucknell University Press).

Dietrich, R. F. (1969), *Portrait of the Artist as a Young Superman: A Study of Shaw's Novels* (Gainesville, Fla: University of Florida Press).

Drew, Elizabeth (1949), *T. S. Eliot: The Design of His Poetry* (New York: Scribner's).

Dukore, Bernard F. (1973), *Bernard Shaw, Playwright: Aspects of Shavian Drama* (Columbia, Mo.: University of Missouri Press).

Ellis, R. W. (ed.) (1930), *Bernard and Karl Marx: A Symposium, 1884–1889* (New York: Random House).

Erikson, Erik H. (1965), 'Biographic: G. B. S. (70) on George Bernard Shaw (20)' in R. J. Kaufman (ed.), *G. B. Shaw: A Collection of Critical Essays* (Englewood Cliffs, N.J.: Prentice-Hall) pp. 19–25.

Ervine, St John (1956), *Bernard Shaw: His Life, Work and Friends* (London: Constable).

Felperin, Howard (1986), *Beyond Deconstruction: The Uses and Abuses of Literary Theory* (New York: Oxford University Press).

Forster, E. M. (1938), *Two Cheers for Democracy* (reprinted New York: Harvest, 1951).

Freud, Sigmund (1957), *Standard Edition of the Complete Psychological Works*, 24 vols (London: Hogarth).

Frye, Northrop (1970), *The Stubborn Structure: Essays on Criticism and Society* (Ithaca, N.Y.: Cornell University Press).

Furbank, P. N. (1968), Introduction to *Martin Chuzzlewit* by Charles Dickens (New York: Penguin) pp. 11–27.

Ganz, Arthur (1980), *Realms of the Self: Variations on a Theme in Modern Drama* (New York: New York University Press).

Gibbs, A. M. (1969), *Shaw*, in A. Norman Jeffares and R. L. C. Lorimer (eds), Writers and Critics series (Edinburgh: Oliver and Boyd).

—— (1983), *The Art and Mind of Shaw: Essays in Criticism* (London: Macmillan).

Gordon, David J. (1966), 'Two Anti-Puritan Puritans: Bernard Shaw and D. H. Lawrence', *Yale Review*, vol. LVI, no. 1 (Autumn) pp. 76–90.

—— (1980), 'Literature and Repression: the Case of Shavian Drama' in Joseph H. Smith (ed.), *The Literary Freud: Mechanisms of Defense and the Poetic Will* (Psychiatry and the Humanities, vol. 4) (New Haven, Conn.: Yale University Press).

Grene, Nicholas (1984), *Bernard Shaw: A Critical View* (New York: St Martin's Press).

Hark, Ina Rae (1986), 'Tomfooling with Melodrama in "Passion, Poison, and Petrifaction"' in Alfred Turco, Jr (ed.), *Shaw: The Neglected Plays* (University Park, Pa.: Pennsylvania State Univeristy Press) pp. 137–50.

Henderson, Archibald (1911), *George Bernard Shaw: His Life and Works* (Cincinnati, Ohio: Stewart).

—— (1932), *Bernard Shaw: Playboy and Prophet* (New York: Appleton).

—— (1956), *George Bernard Shaw: Man of the Century* (New York: Appleton).

Hertz, Neil (1985), *The End of the Line: Essays on Psychoanalysis and the*

Sublime (New York: Columbia University Press).

Holland, Norman N. (1985), *The I* (New Haven, Conn.: Yale University Press).

Holroyd, Michael (1988), *Bernard Shaw: A Biography*, vol. 1: *1856–1898, The Search for Love* (New York: Random House).

Hone, Joseph Maunsell (1962), *W. B. Yeats, 1865–1939*, 2nd edn (New York: St Martin's Press).

Hugo, Leon (1971), *Bernard Shaw: Playwright and Preacher* (London: Methuen).

Hume, David (1966), *A Treatise of Human Nature*, 2 vols (London: Everyman).

Hynes, Samuel (1972), *Edwardian Occasions* (New York: Oxford University Press).

Irvine, William (1949), *The Universe of G. B. S.* (New York: Whittlesey).

Kahn, Coppélia (1980), *Man's Estate: Masculine Identity in Shakespeare* (Berkeley, Calif.: California University Press).

Kant, Immanuel (1982), *The Critique of Judgment*, trans. James Creed Meredith (London: Oxford University Press).

Kauffmann, Stanley (1986), 'On the Unknown Shaw', interview with Jane Ann Crum, in Alfred Turco, Jr (ed.), *Shaw: The Neglected Plays* (University Park, Pa.: Pennsylvania State University Press) pp. 31–44.

Kaye, Julian B. (1958), *Bernard Shaw and the Nineteenth-Century Tradition* (Norman, Okla: University of Oklahoma Press).

Lacan, Jacques (1977), *Ecrits: A Selection*, trans. Alan Sheridan (New York: Norton).

Laplanche, J. and J.-B. Pontalis (1973), *The Language of Psychoanalysis*, trans. Donald Nicholson Smith (New York: Norton).

Lasch, Christopher (1984), *The Minimal Self: Psychic Survival in Troubled Times* (New York: Norton).

Laurence, Dan H. and Martin Quinn (eds) (1985), *Shaw on Dickens* (New York: Ungar).

Lawson, Steve (1977), Program note to production of *Misalliance* (Williamstown, Ma, Summer Theater).

Levin, Harry (1987), *Playboys and Killjoys: An Essay on the Theory and Practice of Comedy* (New York: Oxford University Press).

Lindenberger, Herbert (1984), *Opera: The Extravagant Art* (Ithaca, N.Y.: Cornell University Press).

Lynch, David (1979), *W. B. Yeats: The Poetics of the Self* (Chicago: University of Chicago Press).

MacCarthy, Desmond (1973), 'St Joan: the Theme of the Drama' in Stanley Weintraub (ed.), *Saint Joan: Fifty Years After: 1923/24–1973/74* (Baton Rouge, La: Louisiana University Press) pp. 31–8.

McDowell, Frederick P. W. (1967), 'Politics, Comedy, Character, and Dialectic: the Shavian World of "John Bull's Other Island"', *PMLA*, vol. 82 (December) pp. 542–53.

—— (1986), 'Shaw's "Higher Comedy" Par-Excellence: "You Never Can Tell"', in Alfred Turco, Jr (ed.), *Shaw: The Neglected Plays* (University Park, Pa: Pennsylvania State University Press).

Mahler, Margaret M. (1974), 'On the First Three Subphases of the

Separation–Individuation Process', *Psychoanalysis and Contemporary Science*, vol. 3, pp. 295–306.

Martz, Louis (1973), 'The Saint as Tragic Hero', in Stanley Weintraub (ed.), *Saint Joan: Fifty Years After: 1923/24–1973/74* (Baton Rouge, La: Louisiana University Press), pp. 144–65.

May, Keith (1985), *Shaw and Ibsen* (New York: St Martin's Press).

Mayr, Ernst (1978), 'Evolution', *Scientific American*, vol. 239, pp. 46–55.

Meisel, Martin (1963), *Shaw and the Nineteenth-Century Theater* (Princeton, N.J.: Princeton University Press).

Morgan, Margery M. (1972), *The Shavian Playground: An Exploration of the Art of George Bernard Shaw* (London: Methuen).

Murray, Gilbert (1951), 'A Few Memories', *Drama: The Quarterly Theatre Review* (GBS issue) vol. 20, pp. 7–9.

Nethercot, Arthur H. (1954), *Men and Supermen: The Shavian Portrait Gallery* (Cambridge, Mass.: Harvard University Press).

Northam, John (1965), 'Ibsen's Search for the Hero' in Rolf Fjelde (ed.), *Ibsen: A Collection of Critical Essays* (Englewood Cliffs, N.J.: Prentice-Hall).

Ohmann, Richard M. (1962), *Shaw: The Style and the Man* (Middletown, Conn.: Wesleyan University Press).

Onorato, Richard J. (1971), *The Character of the Poet: Wordsworth in 'The Prelude'* (Princeton, N.J.: Princeton University Press).

Paulson, Ronald (1984), 'Discussion: Versions of a Human Sublime', *New Literary History. The Sublime and the Beautiful: Reconsiderations*, vol. xvi, pp. 427–37.

Pearson, Hesketh (1942), *G. B. S.: A Full Length Portrait* (New York: Harper and Row).

—— (1950), *G.B.S.: A Postscript* (New York: Harper and Row).

Peters, Sally (1986), 'Shaw's Double Dethroned: "The Dark Lady of the Sonnets", "Cymbeline Refinished", and "Shakes versus Shav"', in Alfred Turco, Jr (ed.), *Shaw: The Neglected Plays* (University Park, Pa: Pennsylvania State University Press) pp. 301–16.

Price, Martin (1969), 'The Sublime Poem: Pictures and Powers', *Yale Review*, vol. 59, pp. 195–213.

—— (1983), *Forms of Life: Character and Moral Imagination in the Novel* (New Haven, Conn.: Yale University Press).

Rattray, Robert F. (1951), *Bernard Shaw: A Chronicle* (London: Leagrave).

Rosenberg, Edgar (1978), 'The Shaw/Dickens File: 1885–1950: Two Checklists', *The Shaw Review*, vol. xx, pp. 148–70; vol. xxi, pp. 2–19.

Rosset, B. C. (1964), *Shaw of Dublin: The Formative Years* (University Park, Pa: Pennsylvania State University Press).

Sachs, Hanns (1942), *The Creative Unconscious: Studies in the Psychoanalysis of Art* (reprinted Cambridge, Mass.: Sci-Art, 1951).

Schiller, Friedrich (1965), *On the Aesthetic Education of Man, in a Series of Letters*, trans. Reginald Snell (New York: Ungar).

—— (1966), *Naïve and Sentimental Poetry, and On the Sublime: Two Essays*, trans. Julius A. Elias (New York: Ungar).

Scholes, Robert (1982), 'Structuralism: Around and Beyond', *Yale Review*, vol. 72, no. 1 (Autumn) pp. 105–8.

Shapiro, Gary (1985), 'From the Sublime to the Political: Some Historical Notes', *New Literary History*, vol. xvi, pp. 213–35.

Silver, Arnold (1982), *Bernard Shaw: The Darker Side* (Stanford, Calif.: Stanford University Press).

Skura, Meredith Anne (1981), *The Literary Use of the Psychoanalytic Process* (New Haven, Conn.: Yale University Press).

Spender, Stephen (1953), 'The Riddle of Shaw', in Louis Kronenberger (ed.), *George Bernard Shaw: A Critical Survey* (Cleveland, Ohio: World) pp. 236–9.

Stamm, Julian L. (1965), 'Shaw's Man and Superman: His Struggle for Sublimation', *American Imago*, vol. 22, pp. 250–4.

Stanton, Stephen B. (ed.) (1962), *A Casebook on Candida* (New York: Crowell).

Stoppel, Hans (1973), 'Shaw and Sainthood', in Stanley Weintraub (ed.), *Saint Joan: Fifty Years After, 1923/24–1973/74* (Baton Rouge, La: Louisiana University Press) pp. 166–84.

Swinnerton, Frank (1950), *The Georgian Literary Scene*, 6th edn (New York: Farrar).

Turco, Alfred, Jr (1976), *Shaw's Moral Vision: The Self and Salvation* (Ithaca, N.Y.: Cornell University Press).

—— (ed.) (1986), *Shaw: The Neglected Plays. The Annual of Bernard Shaw Studies*, vol. 7 (University Park, Pa: Pennsylvania State University Press).

Twitchell, James B. (1983), *Romantic Horizons: Aspects of the Sublime in English Poetry and Painting, 1770–1850* (Columbia, Mo.: University of Missouri Press).

Ussher, Arland (1953), *Three Great Irishmen: Shaw, Yeats, Joyce* (New York: Devin-Adair).

Valency, Maurice (1973), *The Cart and the Trumpet: The Plays of George Bernard Shaw* (Oxford: Oxford University Press).

Van Kan, J. (1973), 'Bernard Shaw's Saint Joan: An Historical Point of View', in Stanley Weintraub (ed.), *Saint Joan: Fifty Years After, 1923/24–1973/74* (Baton Rouge, La: Louisiana State University Press) pp. 44–53.

Weintraub, Rodelle (1986), 'Johnny's Dream: "Misalliance"', in Alfred Turco, Jr (ed.), *Shaw: The Neglected Plays* (University Park, Pa: Pennsylvania State University Press) pp. 171–85.

Weintraub, Stanley (1959), 'The Embryo Playwright: Bernard Shaw's Early Novels', *University of Texas Studies in Literature and Language*, vol. i, pp. 327–55.

—— (ed.) (1969–70), *Shaw: An Autobiography*, 2 vols (New York: Weybright).

—— (1971), *Journey to Heartbreak: The Crucible Years of Bernard Shaw 1914–1918* (New York: Weybright).

—— (ed.) (1973), *Saint Joan: Fifty Years After, 1923/24–1973/74* (Baton Rouge, La: Louisiana State University Press).

—— (ed.) (1986), *Bernard Shaw: The Diaries, 1885–1897*, 2 vols (University Park, Pa: Pennsylvania State University Press).

Weiskel, Thomas (1976), *The Romantic Sublime: Studies in the Structure and Psychology of Transcendence* (Baltimore, Md: Johns Hopkins University Press).

Wells, Herbert George (1934), *Experiment in Autobiography: Discoveries and*

Conclusions of a Very Ordinary Brain (since 1886) (London: Gollancz).
Wheeler, Richard P. (1981), *Shakespeare's Development and the Problem Comedies: Turn and Counter-Turn* (Berkeley, Calif.: California University Press).
Whitaker, Thomas R. (1983), *Tom Stoppard* (New York: Grove).
Williams, Raymond (1969), *Drama from Ibsen to Brecht*, rev. edn (New York: Oxford University Press).
Winsten, Stephen (1949), *Days with Bernard Shaw* (London: Vanguard).
Wisenthal, J. L. (1974), *The Marriage of Contraries: Bernard Shaw's Middle Plays* (Cambridge, Mass.: Harvard University Press).
—— (1979), *Shaw and Ibsen: Bernard Shaw's 'The Quintessence of Ibsenism' and Related Writings* (Toronto: University of Toronto Press).
Wright, Elizabeth (1984), *Psychoanalytic Criticism: Theory in Practice* (London: Methuen).
Zimbardo, Rose (ed.) (1970), *Twentieth-Century Interpretations of 'Major Barbara': A Collection of Critical Essays* (Englewood Cliffs, N.J.: Prentice-Hall).

Index

212

Christianity, 1, 7, 17, 107, 126, 134, 143–6, 168
see also Jesus Christ
Coleridge, Samuel T., 7, 25
Colie, Rosalie, 197
comedy, 4, 6, 7, 35, 39, 40–1, 43, 44, 51, 56, 61, 81, 115, 176
as resistance to the sublime, 5, 38–9, 42–3, 56, 84, 91, 107, 129, 180
see also Shaw on comedy
commedia dell'arte, 83
Common Sense about the War, 153
Conrad, Joseph, 104
Cotterill, Erica, 131
Court Theatre, 111
Crane, Hart, 32
Creative Evolution, 1, 32, 56, 164-70, 179
Crompton, Louis, 101, 112, 160, 201, 203
Cunninghame Graham, R. B., 203

Dante, 77
Darwin, Charles, 53, 167–8, 196, 203
Darwinism, 17, 95, 134–5, 156, 167, 203
Dear Dorothea, My, 68–9
Deconstruction, 11, 168
democracy, see Shaw on democracy
Dent, Alan, 37, 83, 148, 198
De Quincey, Thomas, 92, 200
Derrida, Jacques, 29
Dervin, Daniel, 56, 60, 62, 186, 189, 196
Des Grieux (*Manon Lescaut*), 75
Devil's Disciple, The, 6, 12, 24, 27, 33, 38, 42–3, 91, 92, 96, 97–104, 105, 113, 118
Devonport, Lord, 160
dialectic of desire, 62, 137, 172, 185, 187
Diaries of George Bernard Shaw, The, 77
Dickens, Charles, 5, 8, 27, 31, 39, 43–4, 77, 79, 80, 99, 132, 190, 198, 200, 202
Dickinson, Emily, 194

dictatorship, see Shaw on dictators
didacticism, see propaganda; Shaw as didactic writer
Dietrich, R. F., 72
Doctor's Dilemma, The, 9, 18, 44, 131–5, 201
Donat, Robert, 100
Dostoevski, Fyodor, 109
drama of ideas, 3, 47, 59–60, 112
dramatic form, see genre
dramatic poet, see Shaw as dramatic poet
Drew, Elizabeth, 20
Dukore, Bernard F., 201

Economic Basis of Socialism, The, 19–20
ego boundaries, see under psychoanalysis
ego ideal, see under psychoanalysis
Einstein, Albert, 182
Eliot, George, 77, 180
Eliot, T. S., 20, 146
The Waste Land compared to *Heartbreak House*, 155, 163
Ellis, R. W., 199
Elton, Oliver, 200
English, the, see Shaw on the English
Enlightenment, the, 26, 54, 189–90
Erikson, Erik, 196
Ervine, St John, 52, 56, 67, 82, 178, 185, 192, 199, 203

Fabian Essays in Socialism, 19–20, 78
Fabian Society, 76, 109, 135, 146
Fanny's First Play, 9, 22, 131, 142–3
farce, 39, 40–2, 89, 90, 104, 147, 176
Farr, Florence, 41
'Fascinating Foundling, The', 141
Felperin, Howard, 168
Ferenczi, Sandor, 203–4
fictional v. dramatic form, see genre
Fielding, Henry, 24, 75
Filon, Auguste, 83
Forbes-Robertson, Sir Johnston, 111
Forster, E. M., 130
Frank, Joseph, 129

Shaw, George Bernard – *continued*
  on incest, 17, 58, 60, 87–8, 140–
    2, 147–8, 200
  on marriage, 21, 37–8, 55, 70, 110,
    113–14, 118, 129, 137–8, 145
  and his mother (Lucinda
    Elizabeth Gurly Shaw), 21,
    32–3, 56, 57–8, 60, 69, 93,
    111, 141, 152, 191–2, 204
  on natural virtue (*v.* innate
    depravity), 2–3, 23, 105, 131–
    2, 197
  on romance, 7, 21, 22, 37, 73–4,
    84, 87, 118, 136, 147–51, 201
  as romantic, 10, 12, 22, 36–7, 89–
    91, 147, 194–5
  on self-improvement, 17–18, 19,
    23, 39, 58, 69, 105, 113, 115,
    140, 145
  and self-sufficiency, 8, 21, 22, 30,
    33, 62, 163, 171, 196
  and his wife (Charlotte Shaw),
    32, 38, 56, 60, 109, 110–11
  on the Will, 2, 4, 13, 31–2, 53–4,
    61, 161, 185
  works, *see under titles of individual
    works*
Shelley, Percy Bysshe, 1, 7, 8, 23,
    40, 44, 46, 68, 70, 79, 92, 113,
    196, 197, 200
Sheridan, Richard Brinsley, 23–4,
    83
Shewing-Up of Blanco Posnet, The, 47,
    96, 138–9, 145, 171, 202
Silver, Arnold, 152, 196, 200
Simpleton of the Unexpected Isles, The,
    74, 183
Sixteen Self Sketches, 190
Skura, Meredith, 11
Slochower, 61
social Darwinism, *see* Darwinism
Socialism, *see also* Fabian Society, 2,
    17, 18, 19, 35, 80, 92, 135, 145,
    146, 168, 171, 193
Socrates, 171
Sophocles (*Oedipus Rex*), 58
Spender, Stephen, 54
Stalin, Josef, 181, 183
Stamm, Julian, 28

Stanton, Stephen, 94
'Still After the Doll's House', 198
Stoppel, Hans, 172
sublimation, *see under*
  psychoanalysis
sublime, the
  history of, 4, 24–6
  nature of, 4–5, 7–8, 24, 29, 96
  versions of, in Shaw, 5–8, 26–7,
    34, 61–2, 170–2, 176–7, 187–
    8
'Superman, The, or Don Juan's
  great grandson's grandson',
  110
Sweet, Henry, 148
Swift, Jonathan, 55, 180, 182
  Gulliver's Travels, 164, 166–7
Swinnerton, Frank, 49

Tales from Shakespeare, 69
Terry, Ellen, 19–30, 34, 54, 60, 62,
    94, 111
Thackeray, William M., 77, 198
Thorndike, Sybil, 173
Three Plays for Puritans, 95, 100
Titian, 94
Tolstoy, Leo, 138–9, 156, 197
Too True to Be Good, 180, 183–5, 186,
    188
tragedy, 3, 32, 35, 45–6, 62, 131–2,
    176
tragi-comedy, *see* comedy
transvaluation of values, 28, 34, 36–
    7, 39
Tree, Sir Herbert Beerbohm, 146
Trollope, Anthony, 198
Turco, Alfred, Jr, 1, 23, 40, 83, 176,
    199, 202
Twain, Mark, 138
Twitchell, James B., 25

'Un Petit Drame', 201
Unfinished Novel, An, 75–6
Unsocial Socialist, An, 36, 74–5, 80
Ussher, Arland, 54

Valency, Maurice, 89, 93, 134, 142,
    147, 162
van Kan, J., 204